HTML 3.2
MANUAL OF STYLE

HTML 3.2 MANUAL OF STYLE

Larry Aronson and Joseph Lowery

Ziff-Davis Press
an imprint of Macmillan Computer Publishing USA
Emeryville, California

Publisher	Joe Wikert
Associate Publisher	Juliet Langley
Acquisitions Editor	Juliana Aldous
Development and Copy Editor	Deborah Craig
Technical Reviewer	Walter Whitting
Production Editor	Ami Knox
Proofreader	Jeff Barash
Cover Illustration and Design	Regan Honda
Book Design	Gary Suen
Page Layout	M. D. Barrera
Indexer	Tom McBroom

Ziff-Davis Press, ZD Press, and the Ziff-Davis Press logo are trademarks or registered trademarks of, and are licensed to Macmillan Computer Publishing USA by Ziff-Davis Publishing Company, New York, New York.

Ziff-Davis Press imprint books are produced on a Macintosh computer system with the following applications: FrameMaker®, Microsoft® Word, QuarkXPress®, Adobe Illustrator®, Adobe Photoshop®, Adobe Streamline™, MacLink®Plus, Aldus® FreeHand™, Collage Plus™.

Ziff-Davis Press, an imprint of
Macmillan Computer Publishing USA
5903 Christie Avenue
Emeryville, CA 94608

ISBN 1-56276-529-9

Manufactured in the United States of America
10 9 8 7 6 5 4 3 2 1

Contents at a Glance

TABLE OF CONTENTS

ACKNOWLEDGMENTS

I'd like to thank all the people who helped me write this book. Clay Shirky, who originally got me involved in this project, has my eternal gratitude. ZD Press's Suzanne Anthony, who guided the book through production; and Nicole Clausing and Madhu Prasher, who edited the manuscript, get a big thank you for their hard efforts and for being so wonderful to work with. I'd also like to thank the people who gave permission to display their works in the examples section and the many others who provided feedback and advice. A very special thank you hug goes to my best friend, Lynne Thigpen, for all her help and encouragement. Finally, I'd like to acknowledge my deep debt of gratitude to the many people who continually sustain the Web by writing documentation and software tools and by participating in the World Wide Web and HTML discussion groups.

—L.A.

I greatly appreciate the continuing advocacy offered by Adler & Robin Books through their agents, Lisa Swayne, Patty Benford, and Laura Belt. This opportunity has meant a lot to me and I'd like to thank Juliana Aldous for the chance. A special bi-coastal hug goes to Deborah Craig for her extremely valuable advice and superb editing skills. A tip-of-the-techno-hat goes to Walt (Skip) Whiting for his timely tech editing. I'd also like to thank my good friends: Stephen Jacobs for all his late-night calls of assistance and encouragement; and Ray Deter and Dennis Zentek who, to a very real extent, made my contribution to this book possible. Finally, a very special thank you must go to my wife, Debra, and daughter, Margot, for their love and never-ending support.

—J.L.

INTRODUCTION

During the past several years a revolution has been happening over the world's communication networks. It's called the World Wide Web, and its growth has been nothing less than phenomenal. Of course, no revolution comes out of nowhere, and so it is with the World Wide Web. Developments—both technological and social—have prepared the way for the emergence of the Web. Computers, once used only by those who could master the arcane mysteries of programming languages, are now part of the everyday world of business people, artists, and school children. The Internet, a set of protocols that permitted universities to exchange data, has now become the hottest trend of the nineties. The World Wide Web ties the two together, breaking the physical barriers of cyberspace to establish the foundation of a global electronic village.

The World Wide Web provides a means of accessing the resources of the Internet without requiring that you know how those resources are transmitted and stored. The Web's graphic user interface expands the potential of the Internet and empowers both technical and nontechnical people alike with a simple, low-cost method of providing information, opinions, and art to a worldwide audience of millions. This book is about harnessing that power. It is an instructional guide to HTML 3.2, the current version of the Hypertext Markup Language that is the lingua franca of the Web. In this volume lie the means by which you can join the revolution—to be not just a passive consumer of information, but a publisher.

This book is primarily for those who are already exploring the Web with programs such as Microsoft Internet Explorer and Netscape Navigator, and who now wish to put their own information out there for others to use. Don't fret if you're not there yet. Web browsers are available for most computer platforms and, in most cases, are free to try. Getting an Internet connection used to be rather difficult. Now, however, on the same bookshelf where this book can be found, you will find all-in-one kits that will get you connected to the Internet and have you surfing the Web in a matter of hours.

HTML is very easy to learn. You do not need any prior experience with programming languages. A familiarity with any modern word processing program will suffice. Because the World Wide Web encompasses most of the other protocols of the Internet, some knowledge of basic Internet procedures, such as e-mail, FTP, gopher, and newsgroups will be helpful. Such knowledge, however, is not required to understand how the Web works and how to publish information on it.

This is a book in the middle. The first edition was written just before HTML2 was finalized. Today, HTML has reached version 3.2 and is preparing for the next leap. The Web itself has moved from an academic to a commercial focus. Some of the topics covered here are illustrated using products that were still in beta testing, which means that some features may change when they are finalized and released. This book will get you started in Web publishing; the rest of your education will come online.

This book consists of ten chapters and three appendices: Chapter 1 provides an introduction to HTML, the basic concepts of hypertext and hypermedia, the World Wide Web, and the Internet. Chapters 2 and 3 explain the structure and syntax of the language and cover the details of the various elements. Chapter 4 provides a discussion of proper HTML style and shows how to avoid common mistakes. The focus in Chapter 5 is on planning a Web site from conception through design. Chapter 6 covers advanced design techniques and Chapter 7 provides an overview of what can be done to make your HTML pages interactive. Chapter 8 takes a look at the next generation of HTML—much of it available today. Chapter 9 is a tutorial-style walk through of several typical Web applications. Chapter 10 presents a collection of World Wide Web pages and the complete HTML source that generates each example page. Appendix A contains a quick reference to HTML, and Appendix B contains a quick reference on Cascading Style Sheets (an important addition to HTML covered in Chapter 8). Finally, Appendix C is a helpful resource guide.

We welcome your comments, suggestions, and criticism. Please visit the Web site for the book at www.mcp.com/zdpress/features/5299/. There you'll find loads of examples, lots of links and some surprises as well. Thanks, and enjoy.

—Larry Aronson

—Joseph Lowery

New York City

The World of HTML

HTML, the Internet, and the World Wide Web

Characteristics of HTML

HTML Style

HTML is the language of the World Wide Web, the most exciting new way of communicating electronically. Although you've probably heard the terms "World Wide Web," "Internet," and "HTML," you may not know exactly what they mean. The Internet is a system of interconnected computers created to allow the sharing of information and ideas. The World Wide Web (also known as the Web or WWW) is an extension of the Internet that allows text and color graphics to be displayed simultaneously on what are known as Web pages. HTML stands for Hypertext Markup Language, which is shorthand for a relatively easy to understand set of codes that you add to regular text files to create Web pages.

If, for example, I wanted to emphasize the word "exciting" in the first sentence of the previous paragraph in HTML, it would look like this:
HTML is the language of the World Wide Web, the most <STRONG>exciting</STRONG> new way of communicating electronically.

When you looked at this sentence on a Web page it would look like this:
HTML is the language of the World Wide Web, the most **exciting** new way of communicating electronically.

HTML is simple, yet powerful. This chapter will introduce you to the world of HTML—its past, present, and future—familiarize you with some of the jargon, and lay out some guiding principals to keep in mind as you delve into the world of HTML.

HTML, THE INTERNET, AND THE WORLD WIDE WEB

As of early 1997, over 40 million people had connections to the Web that allowed them to electronically visit one of the hundreds of thousands of existing Web sites. (Approximately 18,000 Web sites are added daily!) Educational institutions, governments, industry, and individuals around the world have helped to transform the Web into the fastest growing community on the planet.

HTML has made the phenomenal growth of the Web possible for three primary reasons. First, by design, HTML is universally accessible across all computer platforms—from the most powerful university UNIX system to the highly popular Windows and Macintosh personal computers. Second, HTML is easy to use; instead of having to enter a complex series of arcane computer instructions, you just use a series of "tags" to mark up the text (like the <STRONG> and </STRONG> tags in the earlier example), making it comparatively simple to create Web pages. HTML's accessibility has added to the Web's popularity and encouraged the emergence of tens of thousands of personal Web pages. Finally, HTML enables you to create links from one Web site to another. (These links are often called "hypertext" links. For more on just what hypertext is, check out the section "Hypertext and Hypermedia" later in this chapter.) When you click on one of these links—which could be either a phrase or a picture—you can easily jump to other Web locations, and tap into a vast, growing interlinked and interactive knowledge base.

A Web page can include far more than formatted text and images. Today's HTML allows for sound, music, animation, video, and much more. A collection of Web pages is known as a Web site. A Web site is typically structured around a home page with links to other pages or documents both in and outside of the Web site. A home page is generally the first page you see when you visit a site and functions as a kind of central information booth. Creating a home page is easy. You write it in HTML.

To make your life even easier, there are many home pages with information about HTML and the World Wide Web. HTML is a language under construction. The continuing development of HTML is conducted on the Web in an open process. (See Appendix C for more information.) New tools and techniques appear frequently and are quickly spread throughout the community of Web authors.

A CONCISE HISTORY OF THE INTERNET, THE WEB, AND HTML

Is the World Wide Web the same thing as the Internet? Well, yes and no. The Internet is physically much bigger than the Web, but just about everything on the Internet can be accessed by a link from a Web page. In a way, the Web is the Internet seen from a different point of view—one not tied down to the physical hardware.

The Internet started in the late 1960s as a U.S. Department of Defense project called ARPANET. The design called for a network without hierarchy or center; each computer on the Internet is the equal of any other. The first on-ramp on the information highway was enabled at UCLA in September 1969 and by year's end, three additional host computers were connected. The Internet was launched. At the same time, the important tradition of using the network itself to research building and bettering the network was born. This tradition continues with the wide-open discussion of evolving HTML standards as well as the availability of tools and examples.

More and more institutions joined their networks to the Internet in the 1970s and people started using it for their own purposes, like exchanging e-mail and hosting science fiction discussion groups. In these early years, the Internet was an exclusively text-based medium, primarily used to distribute linear documents, such as research papers, created with a complex document formatting language known as SGML (Standard Generalized Markup Language). In 1989, scientists led by Tim Berners-Lee at CERN, the European laboratory for particle physics in Switzerland, developed a simplified version of SGML, a hypertext-based protocol called HTML. HTML made possible the interconnectivity that distinguishes the modern Web.

HOW THE WEB WORKS

To get on the Web, from your home computer, you start up a program called a "browser." A browser is an interpreter that acts as an intermediary between your computer and the Internet computers with which you are communicating. The language that browsers understand is HTML. Browsers on the market include those from Netscape (Navigator), Microsoft (Internet Explorer—often labeled "The Internet" on Windows 95 desktops), and Sun Systems (HotJava). There are also numerous browsers available on the Internet itself, either for free (called freeware) or for a small direct contribution to the programmer (known as shareware). Figures 1.1 and 1.2 show the current incarnations of Netscape's and Microsoft's browsers. For more detailed information on browsers, see the section "The HTML-Browser Connection" later in this chapter.

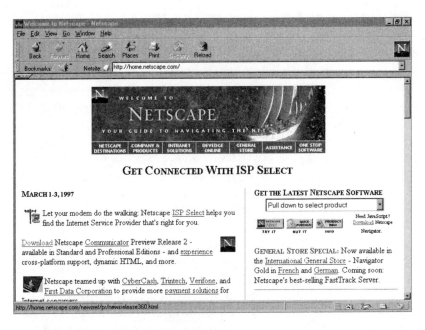

Figure 1.1: Netscape's Navigator 4.0 interface

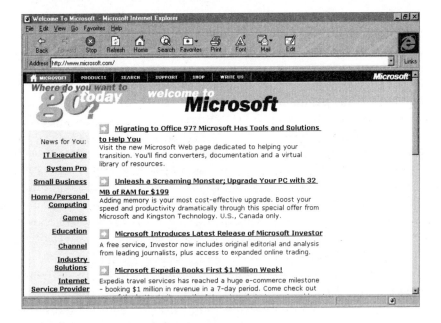

Figure 1.2: Microsoft's Internet Explorer interface

Your browser calls your Internet Service Provider's computer (your ISP) via your computer's modem. An ISP is your connection to the Internet and the Web—the on-ramp to the Information Superhighway, if you will. General information services such as America Online and CompuServe can connect you to the Internet, as can independent ISPs. The software provided makes the connection fairly straightforward. Once the two computers have established a link—after a series of high-pitched dial tones usually audible over your modem's speaker—your browser sends a request consisting of the address of the browser's home page. This home page is the one that your browser defaults to every time it initializes; you can usually modify this through the browser's preferences. Each page has a unique address on the Web called a URL (Uniform Resource Locator), which can look something like www.somecompany.com. The address your browser sends is the home page's URL.

Your ISP attempts to locate this address and, if successful, forwards your request to the computer at that address. That computer, in turn, sends the Web page at this address in HTML format back to your computer through the ISP. The browser then interprets the HTML code and reconstructs the page on your screen, according to your preferences. Figure 1.3 details this process.

In this situation, your computer is also known as the *client* and the computer from which you draw the information is the *server*. The client-server relationship is a cornerstone of the Web. Certain HTML commands are said to be either client-side or server-side, depending on which computer they originate from. Server-side commands generally fall into the more advanced interactive techniques of HTML, which are covered in Chapter 7.

INTRANETS—THE INTERNAL WEB

One of the fastest growing areas for HTML use is not on the Internet at all, but rather on intranets. An Intranet is a private network that uses HTML, servers, and browsers to share information. This term evolved as more and more companies began to apply the principles and tools of the World Wide Web to their internal networks. Because the same basic client-server technology is used in both situations, the extension is quite natural and extremely powerful.

Intranets often connect to the Internet through what are known as "firewalls." A firewall is a combination of hardware and software that allows people to browse the Web from within the company, but protects the internal network from unauthorized outside visitors. Firewalls and Internet security are examined in Chapter 5.

Intranets are used throughout large and not-so-large organizations to promote corporate unity, streamline in-house communications, and enhance

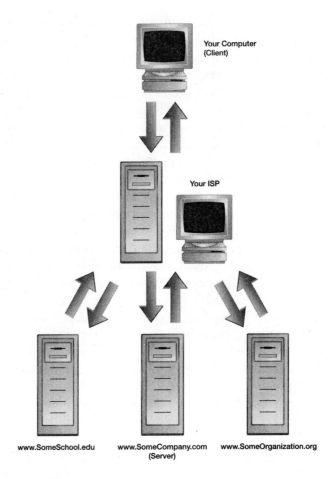

Figure 1.3: How the Web works

profitability. Because every desktop in an intranet has a uniform, easy-to-master interface that can access a combination of company documents, departmental policy literature, and even current inventory and sales figures, every intranet-empowered employee is better informed at a much lower cost.

One of the challenges confronting Web designers is that not all browsers are created equal: One browser can have a different set of features and restrictions than another. For this reason, you generally have more freedom when designing Web pages for an intranet because you know the capabilities of all the browsers that will be accessing the system and don't need to program to the lowest common denominator.

In addition, the multimedia possibilities on intranets can be greater than those on the Web at large. With the increased bandwidth—that is, the network capacity—of an enclosed system, intranets make possible processes such as real-time video webcasting or teleconferencing with full video and audio telephone communications, which would be too slow on the Internet. Integrating these hot technologies while keeping an eye on bandwidth requirements is a challenge you can master using HTML.

Characteristics of HTML

HTML is not a programming language and an HTML document is not a computer program. It's a lot simpler than that. A computer program is a series of procedures and instructions applied, typically, to external data. An HTML document, however, *is* the data. The definition of HTML specifies the grammar and syntax of markup tags that, when inserted into the data, instruct browsers—computer programs that read HTML documents—how to present the document.

Technically, HTML is defined as a Standard Generalized Markup Language (SGML) Document Type Definition (DTD). An HTML document is said to be an *instance* of an SGML document.

SGML originated as GML (General Markup Language) at IBM in the late 1960s as an attempt to solve some of the problems of transporting documents across different computer systems. The term *markup* comes from the publishing industry. SGML is generalized, meaning that instead of specifying exactly how to present a document, it describes document types, along with markup languages to format and present instances of each type. GML became SGML when it was accepted as a standard by the International Standards Organization (ISO) in Geneva, Switzerland (reference number ISO 8879:1986).

An SGML document has three parts. The first describes the character set and, most importantly, which characters are used to differentiate the text from the markup tags. The second part declares the document type and which markup tags are accepted as legal. The third part is called the *document instance* and contains the actual text and the markup tags. The three parts need not be in the same physical file, which is a good thing because it allows you to forget about SGML and deal only with HTML. All HTML browsers assume the same information for the SGML character-set and document-type declarations, so you only have to work with simple text files.

In traditional publishing, the author supplies content in the form of a manuscript that an editor marks up with instructions for the printer specifying the layout and typography of the work. The printer, following the markup, typesets the pages and reproduces copies for distribution. With the Web and HTML, you are both the author and the editor, and your work is a set of files on a Web server. A single marked-up version of each page is "visited" by your readers, not distributed to them. The page is typeset by each reader's browser with layout and typography appropriate to the browser's computer environment and the reader's preferences.

The base character set of an HTML document is Latin-1 (ISO 8859/1). It's an 8-bit alphabet with characters for most American and European languages. Plain old ASCII (ISO 646) is a 7-bit subset of Latin-1. There is no obligation to use anything but the 128 standard ASCII characters in an HTML document. In fact, sticking to straight ASCII is encouraged as it allows an HTML document to be edited by any text editor on any computer system and be transported over any network by even the most rudimentary of e-mail and data transport systems. To make this possible, HTML includes character entities for most of the commonly used non-ASCII Latin-1 characters. (A character entity is a special code that, when translated by a browser, displays the intended special character.) These character entities begin with the ampersand character (&), followed by either the name or number of the character, followed by a semicolon. For example, the named character entity for a small *è* (with a grave accent) is è the same *è* can be represented using a numeric code (&232;). You'll learn more about character entities in the next chapter, and there is a complete table of character entities in Appendix A.

HTML markup tags are delimited by the angle brackets, < and >. They appear either alone, like the tag <BR>, to indicate a line break in the text, or as a pair of starting and ending tags that modify the content contained. <B>Attention!</B>, for example, is an instruction to present the text string **Attention!** in bold. There are tags for formatting text, tags for specifying hypertext links, tags for including sound and picture elements, and tags for defining input fields for interactive pages.

That's all there is to Hypertext Markup Language: character entities and markup tags. However, this system of entities and tags is evolving. There are currently several standardization levels of HTML:

▶ Level 1 is the level mandatory for all WWW browsers. It is essentially what was accepted by the first browsers (level 0), plus images.

▶ Level 2 includes all the elements of level 1, plus tags for defining user input fields.

▶ A transitional level initially known as HTML 3.0 was never finalized. Several tags that were proposed for this version are not supported.

▶ Level 3, now known as HTML 3.2, is being finalized. It includes markup tags for objects such as tables, figures, and mathematical equations. This level has widespread support through the commercial browsers from Netscape and Microsoft.

The next two chapters describe the basic HTML language, including most HTML 3.2 features. Almost all of the development work on HTML is done on the Internet in the form of discussion groups, which post proposed changes and issue requests for comments. You can always find the complete HTML specifications on the Web with the overseeing body the W3 Consortium (www.w3.org); Figure 1.4 shows a page from their site. The Web is also the place to look for the most up-to-date HTML and SGML documentation, most of it in hypertext. Appendix C includes a list of Web addresses for many of these documents.

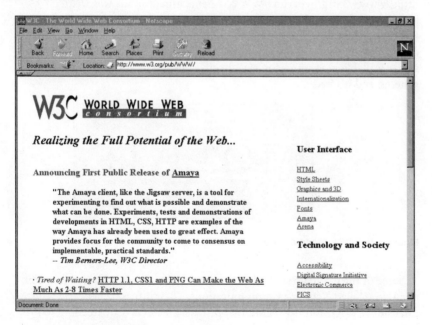

Figure 1.4: The World Wide Web Consortium

HYPERTEXT AND HYPERMEDIA

Hypertext is text that is not constrained to be linear. In reading this book, for example, you may skip some chapters and make occasional trips to the appendices. Still, it is, as presented to you, a linear sequence of pages. In contrast, hypertext organizes information as an interconnected web of linked text. Different readers can follow different paths through the work; readers can choose, among all the links the authors provided, those associations most relevant to their immediate needs.

Hypermedia refers to hypertext applications that contain things other than text objects. Hypermedia applications encompass images, video, sound, and more. The Hypertext Markup Language contains markup tags for specifying links to multimedia objects. How these objects are displayed is left up to the

Mosaic, whose logo appears in Figure 1.5, was the first graphical browser for the Web. There are now many. An up-to-date list of browsers and related software is usually available from a link on the Web home page, http://www.w3.org/hypertext/WWW/Clients.html. Mosaic was written by graduate students at the National Center for Supercomputing Activities (NCSA) at the University of Illinois in Urbana, home of the HAL 9000. Many other browsers are built on Mosaic technology licensed from the U. of I. Mosaic is available in versions for Macintosh, Windows, and UNIX/X-Windows systems, and it's free.

Figure 1.5: NCSA Mosaic logo

Some of the graduate students who created Mosaic left to form a new company, now called Netscape Communications. Their browser, Netscape Navigator, features extensions to HTML that provide greater artistic freedom to the Web author. It has become the most popular browser, by far. Like Mosaic, it comes in versions for Macintosh, Windows, and UNIX/X-Windows systems.

browser, but generally, images are expanded as illustrations or figures within the text, while sound and video are presented in their own windows with stop and play controls.

Links from an HTML hypertext page appear as highlighted text, usually blue and underlined. The text itself is called the *anchor* of the link and can be embedded in other HTML elements, like lists and tables. Images can be anchors as well as text. Small images can be used as clickable icons. This is useful for creating navigational controls that appear on a series of Web pages. Images can also have defined subareas, each an anchor linking to somewhere else. Such images are called *imagemaps* and are quite handy for organizing spatially related data.

The wonderful thing about hypertext is that it adds an extra dimension of structure to the content of your work. With hypertext, you can highlight alternative relationships in the text besides the linear ordering of sections, chapters, and subchapters found in the table of contents. The size of a hypertext work is limited only by the physical storage space available. Because the World Wide Web is on and of the Internet, this means that terabytes (trillions of bytes) of data are organized and given structure by the Web. Because the Web is growing faster than any one person could possibly keep up with, your experience is that of "surfing" through an unbounded information space.

You activate HTML hypertext links by clicking on highlighted text or an image. The link may be to a point in the text on the same page, to a new Web page, or to some other object or resource on the network. An HTML page can be many physical pages long, corresponding to a chapter in a book or a section of a manual; however, the width is variable—the browser presenting the page word-wraps the text and positions the images to fit the width of the display window.

Unlike other hypermedia, where every user has their own copy, HTML documents exist in a client-server environment where one copy serves all. The clients are the readers' browsers. The servers are programs running on remote computers that provide the Web pages requested by the browsers. Because media like paper don't have to be physically reproduced and distributed each time information is added or changed, Web pages can be updated quickly at low cost.

For an HTML application to be "on the Web" means that the HTML files and other documents that make up the application must reside in a directory that is accessible to a server. Note that this does not mean there must be a link from some existing Web page to your document for your document to be part of the Web. There is a URL for practically every file and resource on the Internet.

There are even URL formats for resources involving protocols other than hypertext; protocols determine how the information transferred will be interpreted. The most popular protocols include

▶ **Hypertext Transfer Protocol (HTTP)** The basic protocol for Web communication. Most URLs have "http://" at the beginning.

▶ **File Transfer Protocol (FTP)** As the name suggests, this protocol is used for moving files (both text and binary) back and forth across the Internet.

▶ **Gopher** A text-only protocol for transferring a system of menus and documents.

▶ **Network News Transfer Protocol (NNTP)** A protocol used to share messages among Usenet newsgroups, specific topic discussion groups that anyone can join.

▶ **Wide Area Information Servers (WAIS)** A database protocol with a built-in search engine.

The concepts of hypertext and hypermedia have been around for a while; Ted Nelson is given credit for coining the terms in 1965. One of the first practical hypermedia applications was the Aspen Movie Map done at MIT in 1978. It used videodisc and touch-screen technology. Filevision from Telos, released in 1984, gave hypermedia databases to early Macintosh users. In 1987, Apple introduced Hypercard, written by Bill Atkinson, which incorporated many hypermedia concepts. Windows users take advantage of a hypertext-based help system. The development of CD-ROM drives for personal computers made the commercial development and marketing of multimedia applications a reality. And in 1989, Tim Berners-Lee and Robert Cailliau submitted a proposal to their colleagues at CERN for a client-server-based hypermedia system, and the World Wide Web was born.

HTML hypermedia applications are similar in many ways to Macintosh Hypercard applications; enough so that it's possible to mimic simple Hypercard applications in HTML and vice versa. Both systems take the form of a web of linked nodes with one node designated as home—the home stack for Hypercard and the home page for a Web server. The differences, however, are significant, not the least important of which is that Hypercard applications only run on Apple Macintosh computers, whereas HTML applications run on networks connecting a variety of computers.

Because most browsers can load any URL entered by the user, just about any-thing on the Internet is also on the World Wide Web. To get an idea of the ex-plosive expansion of the Web, take a look at Figure 1.6, which shows the growth of the number of servers.

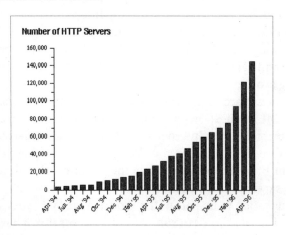

Figure 1.6: Number of HTTP servers (Courtesy Webcrawler)

THE HTML-BROWSER CONNECTION

Although hyped as the cutting edge of technology, Web browsers are really very simple programs based on technology that has been around for a while. They've just achieved their impact by taking advantage of today's sophisticated computer networks and operating systems to do stuff that people want to do better and cheaper.

There are three ways you can browse the Web: in TTY or linemode, through a commercial online service provider, or as an Internet host.

Linemode browsers are level 1 browsers that display text in a single font. Probably the most popular of these is Lynx from the University of Kansas, which works with DEC VT-100s, a common display terminal that's emulated by most telecommunications software. Cursor keys are used instead of a mouse to select and activate links. Most people have abandoned linemode browsers in favor of graphical browsers, which are easier, and more fun, to use.

The big commercial online service providers—such as CompuServe, Amer-ica Online, and Prodigy—provide graphical Web browsing capabilities. They differ in pricing and capability and in what support they extend to authors who wish to publish on the Web. Still, the online services provide the easiest ways to get wired. The third and best way is to have your computer directly connected to the Internet using TCP/IP—the transport protocol of the Internet. You can connect via a local area network that has a gateway to the Internet, or you can connect to an Internet service provider (ISP) with a dial-up or cable modem. This kind of setup is the most complicated technically, but, for heavy use, it is much more economical; many Internet service providers charge flat monthly fees for unlimited connect time. ISPs generally advertise in local computer magazines and most provide software to help you get online; the degree of technical support each service offers can vary, so be sure to ask when shopping around.

Most browsers can access documents locally—in other words, you can implement an HTML application on your own computer or local area network and not be connected to the Internet at all. In fact, this is how most Web pages are built: You store all the files for your Web page on your hard drive, view them using your browser and then, when the files are finished, you upload them to a Web server on the Internet.

For your application to be part of the World Wide Web, your documents must be on the Internet. You can run your own server if you have a direct Internet connection (and your system administrator's approval). There is free server software from CERN, NCSA, and others. Generally, though, it's better to find space on someone else's Web server and rely on their expertise to keep their machine and your Web site available 24 hours a day.

Designers just starting to work with HTML often grumble about its limitations as a page-layout tool. They are right. HTML is not a good page-layout tool; in fact, it's not a page-layout tool at all. HTML is an interactive information system that provides general instructions about how the Web page will be laid out. The browser is what determines how the tags are interpreted—which specific fonts will be used and so on.

EXTENDING HTML

One of the essential characteristics of HTML is its ability to expand beyond its own boundaries and incorporate other languages and processes. Certain codes within your HTML files allow you to communicate with the Web server, provide single-purpose programs for added computing power, and share information with other computers. Currently, HTML uses three different, potentially overlapping methods for increasing its power: CGI scripting, Java applets, and ActiveX controls.

CGI Programming   From the beginning, Web site designers have understood that interactivity is the key to a dynamic interchange between a site and its visitors. The CGI (Common Gateway Interface) standard allows Web developers to communicate with the server to break away from the cycle of static image after static image being passed at the client's request. You can call CGI scripts from within your HTML code. A good example of CGI programming are the many hit counters gracing Web pages: Every time a page is viewed, a CGI program is called that adds one to the current number of hits and displays it in the onscreen counter. You'll learn more about the capabilities of CGI programming in Chapter 7.

Java Applets   In 1995, Sun Microsystems introduced Java, a language designed to add further interactive capabilities to Web pages. One of the most important additions to HTML 3.2 is the APPLET tag, which allows the processing of Java applets. Once invoked, the applet downloads to the user's computer, performs its limited function, and then disappears. Graphics animation, spreadsheet calculation, and database reporting are all possible over the Web with the use of Java, and to a more limited degree, its easier-to-program offshoot, JavaScript. Naturally, HTML lets you include JavaScript code as well as Java.

ActiveX and VBScript   Not to be outdone, Microsoft has revamped its Object Linking and Embedding (OLE) technology and introduced VBScript (derived from Visual Basic) with ActiveX controls to enhance Web interactivity. With OLE, it was commonplace to share data between applications, such as a word processing and a spreadsheet program. The ActiveX controls extend that capability and more to the Internet. HTML, again, extends its capabilities by allowing you to embed VBScript code, although only Internet Explorer currently supports the necessary OBJECT tag.

Browser Compatibility   Although HTML 3.2 lets you use these various extensions, it takes a compatible browser to interpret the added code correctly. For example, only Java-compatible browsers such as Netscape's Navigator (version 2.0 or better) or Sun's HotJava can handle Java and JavaScript properly, but neither can understand VBScript and ActiveX controls without an additional plug-in. Likewise, the current version of Microsoft's Internet Explorer (3.0) handles ActiveX beautifully, but doesn't speak a word of Java. This means that Web developers must know their audience and weigh the incorporation of extended features that are not standard HTML against the limitations of a particular browser. Hopefully, the so-called "browser wars" will bring a convergence of these exciting technologies and enable a healthy standardization of techniques and code.

HTML STYLE

The Web is a wide open frontier of design and application. In part because of HTML's accessibility, there are literally thousands of different kinds of Web pages, ranging from the most basic personal home page to the most elaborate multilayered corporate Web site. Following certain stylistic conventions that reflect the underlying basis of HTML will broaden your audience and your audience appeal.

BELIEVE IN THE UNIVERSALITY OF HTML

Key to HTML is its computer platform independence. In one view, a successful Web page is one that can be viewed with no content and little stylistic loss by a Macintosh, a Windows 95 (or Windows 3.1) system, or a UNIX workstation. As you become increasingly familiar with HTML and its variations, you will begin to understand the range of available options and the trade-offs inherent in the various versions and extensions. Initially, stick close to the authorized version of HTML 3.2. This is a good foundation for Web page programming, and will provide your sites with the widest possible audience.

FORM STILL FOLLOWS FUNCTION

By its very nature, HTML is quite a utilitarian language—the essence of a "what you see is what you get" (WYSIWYG) system. The more that you can keep the primary message of your site in mind, the more coherent your sites will appear to visitors. If you, as a Web page designer, adhere to the philosophy of form follows function, your sites will load faster and be more usable—both features greatly prized on the Web.

LINKS RULE

As if to underscore the importance of connectivity, half the acronym HTML stands for "hypertext." The use of links to connect your Web site to another not only grows the World Wide Web, but also directly benefits your site with increased visibility. Not only should you as a webmaster include links to outside sites wherever appropriate, internal links are just as, if not more, important. Keep in mind that once your Web site has been indexed by a search engine, all your pages become possible entry points. If you want someone who comes in the back door of your site to see the splashy animations on your entry page, you have to provide easy navigational access to it.

LEARN ABOUT HTML ON THE WEB

Where can you find any bit of information about the Web? On the Web, of course! The Web provides an overwhelming wealth of information, including information about itself. The Web is truly self-documenting; there are tools, techniques, and examples for creating Web sites on the Web itself. The Web is especially filled with examples because you can look at the source code for any Web page, either online through your browser or by downloading it. Remember, all HTML files are just text files.

So, there are really two ways to learn about HTML on the Web. First, you can seek out some of the tremendous number of tutorials and guides, many of which are referenced in Appendix C of this book. Second, you can surf the Web frequently, stop when you see a page that makes you say, "I wonder how did they do that?," and then download the page by saving it from your browser. With the help of an ordinary text editor, you can examine the code to figure out all the secrets. The next chapter will outline the HTML language so that you can follow almost any code.

Basic HTML, Part I

OVERVIEW

STRUCTURE TAGS

ANCHORS AND LINKS

INLINE IMAGES

Chapter 2

T his chapter presents the various elements of the HTML language—
the syntax of character entities and markup tags, and how they are interpreted by a browser to display a page. This description corresponds
to the HTML 3.2 standard recognized by the World Wide Web Consortium's
HTML Working Group. Chapter 8 covers some of the more advanced features
that are available through specific browsers, but are not HTML 3.2 standard.
You can count on all commands used in this chapter being recognized by any
browser that is 3.2 compliant.

OVERVIEW

A page on the World Wide Web is composed of a set of files stored on a computer that either is, or is accessible to, a Web server. The exact file location of a
page is known by its URL (Uniform Resource Locator). A Web page has content consisting primarily of text and images. The page's marked up text is in
one file and each individual image is in a separate file. Images are typically referenced by their file names so the same image can be used more than once on
a page or on many different pages. All other multimedia (such as sound,
video, and animations) are accessed through helper applications or plug-ins
that are launched by the browser when the reader clicks on a link. Helper applications launch a separate window to display their results; plug-ins integrate
their output into the browser's window. The documentation or online help for
your browser will list the recommended helper applications appropriate to

your operating system. There are numerous online sources for plug-ins and helper apps. Check Appendix C under Web sites for the latest links.

Authoring Web pages is different in many respects from traditional desktop publishing. For one thing, a page has no fixed size. The reader's browser will word-wrap the text to fit the width of the display window and enable scrolling to accommodate the length. In desktop publishing, you specify fonts, type styles and sizes, and the precise placement of text and images. As a Web author, you have only general control over the typography and layout of your page. However, each advance in HTML gives you more control over design without sacrificing critical platform independence.

What you do when you write a Web page is insert codes called markup tags that describe the parts of the page in a language that's not dependent on the properties of any display device. After all, you don't know what fonts are available on your readers' computers or how their browsers are configured. Once you upload the marked up file to a Web server, you're done. The actual typography and layout of the page is the responsibility of the reader's browser.

The advantages of this approach are obvious. Having one electronic copy of your work that can serve all your readers is more efficient than pushing tons of paper and ink around the world. Pages on the World Wide Web can be updated with new information more quickly and cheaply than paper pages.

The point is that Web pages are dynamic, "living" documents, requiring continuing care and maintenance. Web sites, in particular, have the tendency to grow like weeds. Existing pages are cloned and adapted to new uses continually. Unlike traditional desktop publishing pages, which are finished works rushed out the door to meet a deadline, Web pages are perpetually "under construction." Web sites often mark their "pages in progress" with signs similar to the one shown in Figure 2.1.

Figure 2.1: Courtesy of The Earth School (www.idest.com/earthschool)

PAGE STRUCTURE

A file containing the marked up text of a Web page is called an HTML file. It begins and ends with the tags <HTML> and </HTML>. It is divided into two parts, a head and a body. The head contains general information about the document and the body contains the specific text of the document. Markup tags are used to define and separate the two parts, as in the following minimal HTML file. Figure 2.2 shows what this file will look like in Netscape Navigator.

```
<HTML>
<HEAD>
<TITLE>Minimal HTML Page</TITLE>
</HEAD>
<BODY>
Your text goes here...
</BODY>
</HTML>
```

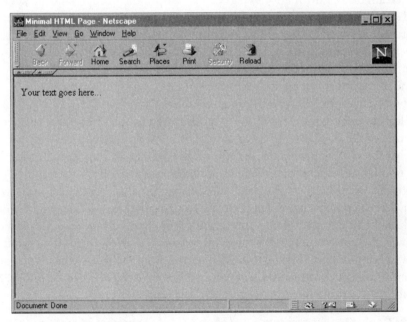

Figure 2.2: A minimal Web page

The primary tags to focus on are <HTML>, <HEAD>, and <BODY>. <HTML> indicates the type of document so that a browser can recognize and process it. The <HEAD> and </HEAD> tags contain the title (enclosed within the <TITLE> and </TITLE> tags) and other information about the document.

<BODY> indicates the start of the main part of the document; </BODY> marks the end. You'll learn about all these tags in detail as this chapter progresses.

It's important to understand that the markup elements <HEAD></HEAD> and <BODY></BODY> divide the page into its two parts, not the carriage returns and line spacing used. If you removed all carriage returns from the preceding example and replaced them with blank spaces, the code would still generate the same page. You are free to use returns, tabs, and white space to improve the readability of your HTML files without affecting the rendering of the page in a Web browser.

Head Elements   In the minimal HTML example, the only information specified in the head of the document is the document's title. For many pages, this is all there is in the document's head.

Certain other informational tags can go within the head, including keyword and style sheet declarations, under the general <META> tag. Some head tags represent advanced features that may not be supported by your Web server; check with your systems administrator or your local webmaster to find out what features are supported by your Web server software. You'll learn about some of the advanced attributes of the <HEAD> tag in Chapter 6.

Every page should have a title—preferably a short one that's meaningful in the larger context of the work. With most browsers, the title appears either as the title of the display window or at the top of that window. Titles are not absolutely required; many text documents on the Web are simply text files, containing no markup elements and having no titles. Most browsers are quite forgiving and will accept the page with or without a title. Increasingly, however, search engines that index your site so that other people can find it will look to the title as a keyword representation of what's on the site. Most browsers will also allow you to omit the head and body tags, although it's a good idea to keep them in. The opening BODY tag, for instance, is where you can specify page background and text colors other than the browser's defaults. See Chapter 6 for more information on how to do this.

Body Content   The real substance of an HTML document is contained within the <BODY> tags. Most of your work of marking up the document takes place here. The BODY section can include any amount of text from a single sentence to several pages' worth of text. It can also contain numbered or bulleted lists, and tables of information with varying numbers of rows and columns.

The body of an HTML page can contain many non-text elements as well. Inline graphics, animated images, sounds, music, video, and links to other areas, pages, Web sites, files, or databases all have their place here.

HTML ELEMENTS

There are only a few general syntax rules to learn in HTML. First, there are two kinds of HTML elements: markup tags and character entities. The minimal HTML page shown earlier contained four markup tags: <HTML>, <HEAD>, <TITLE>, and <BODY>.

Markup Tags   As you've seen, the simplicity of HTML stems from its use of markup tags. Browsers are unforgiving about spelling errors and extra white space within the tags—so if you misspell your tags, you will not get the results you expect.

For example, if you put a space between the opening angle bracket (<) and the code "HTML," like this

```
< HTML>
```

the browser won't recognize your page as one to be interpreted at all and will display all of your code as text. This can happen in the middle of a Web page as well. In the following code, the </HTML> tag was purposely misspelled. Figure 2.3 shows the result as interpreted through a browser.

```
<HTML>
<HEAD>
   <TITLE>Bad Code</TITLE>
</HEAD>
<BODY>
This is what happens when Bad Code happens to Good People.
</BODY>
</HTML
```

Character Entities   A *character entity* is a distinct code that defines a character that cannot normally be entered with a single keystroke. To make it easy for any text editor to produce and read HTML code, these special characters are conveyed by a specific numeric or named code. Although character entities are important for depicting particular characters, most of your HTML coding will involve markup tags.

A character entity begins with an ampersand (&) and is followed by either the name of a predefined entity or a pound sign (#) followed by the decimal number of the character, as defined in the ISO Latin-1 character set, included in Appendix A. A semicolon terminates the character entity. The tilde (~), for

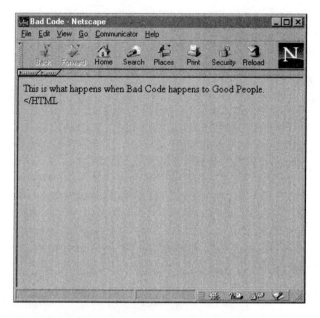

Figure 2.3: The result of bad code

example, can be generated by the sequence ~. Character entities are pre-defined for characters from the ISO Latin-1 alphabet that are not defined in ASCII, and characters that are needed to mark the beginnings and ends of HTML elements. There's a complete list of predefined character entities in Appendix A. Three are particularly useful because they are the entities that you must use if you want to show a character that would ordinarily be taken as the beginning (or end) of a character entity or markup tag:

&lt;	"<"	The left-angle bracket or less-than sign
&gt;	">"	The right-angle bracket or greater-than sign
&amp;	"&"	The ampersand

Also useful are

&quot;	" - "	The double quote mark
	" "	A nonbreaking space
&copy;	"©"	The copyright symbol
&reg;	"®"	The registered mark

There isn't a character entity for the trademark symbol, ™, but because HTML 3.2 now supports superscript via the pair, you can roll your own, like this:

```
<H2>HTML 3.2 Manual of Style<SUP>TM</SUP></H2>
```

which would produce the desired result: **HTML 3.2 Manual of Style**™.

TAG SYNTAX

Every markup tag has a tag ID (or name). Most have modifiers known as attributes. For example, the tag for a horizontal line is <HR>; you can make it a specific width by including the WIDTH attribute and specifying a value, like this:

```
<HR WIDTH=50%>
```

which would draw a horizontal line across half of the browser screen. Markup tags are considered to be either empty or nonempty.

Containers Nonempty tags, known as containers, act upon text enclosed in a pair of starting and ending tags. A starting tag, such as <BODY>, begins with the left angle bracket (<) followed immediately by the tag ID, one or more attributes, if any, separated by spaces, and then the right angle bracket (>) to close the tag. Ending tags are exactly the same except that there is a slash (/) immediately between the opening left angle bracket and the tag ID: </BODY> would close out this section of the page. Ending tags do not contain attributes. Here are some examples of container tags:

```
<TITLE>Don Quixote's Home Page</TITLE>

<I>This should appear in italics</I>

<TT>Fixed width, typewriter font</TT>

<A HREF="catalog.html">our current catalog</A>
```

The last example is an anchor. Anchors are tags that define the nodes of hypertext links. In this example, the browser will highlight the phrase "our current catalog" (usually by making it blue and underlined) to indicate that clicking on it (or selecting it if you're using a nongraphical browser) will link the reader to another page, in this case, the file catalog.html—the value of the HREF (Hypertext REFerence) attribute. (See "Anchors and Links" later in this chapter for more on addressing formats.)

Empty Tags Whereas containers modify content, empty tags insert things into the content. The empty tag stands alone; there's no corresponding ending tag with a slash. Here are some examples of empty tags:

     Line break, following text begins at the left margin.

<HR>   Horizontal rule, draw a line across the page.

The following empty tag specifies that an inline image be inserted. It has one attribute, the SRC attribute, whose value is the name (source) of the file ("corplogo.gif") containing the image:

```
<IMG SRC="corplogo.gif">
```

Putting HTML Tags to Work   Here's a simple example illustrating the use of markup tags and character entities:

```
<HTML>
<HEAD>
<TITLE>Simple HTML Example</TITLE>
</HEAD>
<BODY>
<H1>Level 1 Headings</H1>
<P>Whereas <STRONG>Titles</STRONG> should have some relation to the outside
world, Level 1 Headings should introduce the major sections of the work.</P>
<P>This is a second paragraph of text inserted to show how paragraph tags are
used to separate text and to point out the use of the &lt;STRONG&gt; tag in the
first paragraph.</P>
</BODY>
</HTML>
```

Figure 2.4 shows what this example looks like on a Windows 95 system using Netscape Navigator with the default preferences set.

First, note that the title of the page, "Simple HTML Example," appears in the window's title bar. The body of this example page consists of a level 1 heading marked with the <H1> and </H1> tags, and two paragraphs of text enclosed by paragraph tags, <P> and </P>. You can also see how the browser has ignored the carriage returns placed in the HTML page and word-wrapped the text to fit the width of its window.

In the second paragraph, to get the string <STRONG> to appear without being interpreted as a tag, character entities are used—< for the less-than sign (<), and > for the greater-than sign (>).

Although the HTML text in this example is neatly formatted, it doesn't actually matter where the tags are placed with respect to the page. The following HTML fragments will all produce the exact same heading as Figure 2.4:

```
<H1>Level 1 Headings</H1>
<h1>
Level 1 Headings
</h1>
<H1>Level 1
Headings</h1 >
```

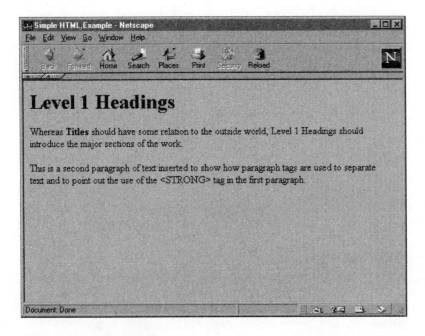

Figure 2.4: Simple HTML example

That's right! Tag elements are not case sensitive. You can freely mix upper-and lowercase letters. Spaces are only allowed after the tag ID and before the closing bracket, though there's little reason to put any there. The string

```
< H1 >What Went Wrong?< /H1 >
```

will not be processed as a heading. The brackets and their contents will be ignored and only the enclosed text, What Went Wrong? (which is *not*, by the way, what WWW stands for!), will appear. Browsers are very tolerant of errors; most are just ignored. If an anchor tag is correct but the link is in error, browsers will return a status message such as "Unable to connect to remote host" or "Unable to access document."

Markup tags usually can be nested—for example, anchors inside of list structures. However, some nestings are not allowed—for instance, anchors inside of other anchors or a heading inside preformatted text. Other nestings are allowed but discouraged—for example, using style tags inside a heading.

You can place comments in an HTML document to annotate your work just as you would with other computer languages. Comments are completely ignored by the browser. An HTML comment starts with the string <!--, can contain any character, and ends with the first occurrence of the string -->. As a general rule, place each comment on a separate line and avoid using any of the special characters, such as <, >, &, or !. Some older browsers may not parse the comment correctly. Comments cannot be nested. A commented version of the previous code might look like this:

```
<HTML>
<HEAD>
<TITLE>Simple HTML Example</TITLE>
</HEAD>
<BODY>
<H1>Level 1 Headings</H1>
<!--Begin Text Here -->
<P>Whereas <STRONG>Titles</STRONG> should have some relation to the outside
world, Level 1 Headings should introduce the major sections of the work.</P>
<P>This is a second paragraph of text inserted to show how paragraph tags are
used to separate text and to point out the use of the &lt;STRONG&gt; tag in the
first paragraph.</P>
<!--End Text Here -->
</BODY>
</HTML>
```

Attributes   You can modify a great many HTML tags by adding *attributes* within the starting tag. Attributes most often take the form ATTRIBUTE="value". For example

```
<BODY BGCOLOR="black">
```

specifies that the background color of the entire document will be black. (You can also use the BGCOLOR attribute with tags other than then <BODY> tag.)

Although it's safe to drop the quotes when the value is a simple number or constant, you should generally enclose the value in double quotes for consistency. Using quotes also prevents errors produced by tags such as <META Name=Shark Business School>, which should be <META Name="Shark Business School"> to convey the full name. If a tag includes more than one attribute, you should separate the attributes by spaces, not commas. Finally, you can specify some attributes just by using their name; for example, BORDER is equivalent to BORDER="yes", which is also the same as BORDER=1.

STRUCTURE TAGS

HTML tags can be divided into two loose classes: those that change the page structure and those that change text styles. Into the structure class go tags for designating headings, paragraphs, lists, and tables. Structure tags always imply paragraph breaks before and after the marked-up text and, thus, create the layout of the page. Style tags affect the typography of the text—font size and styles such as bold or italic—but do not modify the layout. The Anchor tag creates hyperlinks; although it can change the style of the text it is highlighting, it is in a class by itself. The same is true of the Image tag. Both of these tags are discussed later in this chapter.

DOCUMENT STRUCTURAL ELEMENTS

The initial section of an HTML page is concerned with its overall structure: identifying it as an HTML document, noting the version of HTML used to create it, and giving general information about the document such as the title. The upcoming sections describe in detail each of the tags responsible for passing on this information.

The <!DOCTYPE> Element   The growing proliferation of HTML versions and variations has given rise to the <!DOCTYPE> element, which goes at the very beginning of the HTML document. (By the way, if you haven't guessed already, the term "element" is interchangeable with "tag.") <!DOCTYPE> is an empty tag and is referred to as a document type declaration (DTD). It takes this form:

```
<!DOCTYPE HTML PUBLIC "-//W3C//DTD HTML 3.2//EN">
```

This declaration identifies an HTML document as compliant with a specific version of HTML—in this case, with HTML 3.2. Because the <!DOCTYPE> tag is relatively new, omitting it will not stop any browser from recognizing your page as HTML. However, it's good professional practice to include the <!DOCTYPE> element. To check your code efficiently, you must use a program known as a validator, which verifies that your code conforms to a specific version of HTML. To do this, the validator must know which version to check your code against; it does this by looking at the <!DOCTYPE> line. As more and more features and versions are updated, the validator can assure that you are reaching your desired audience and can also alert you to errors in your code that could cause unwanted results when used with a different browser. Be sure to include the exclamation point at the beginning of the <!DOCTYPE> tag.

The <HTML> Tag   The HTML tag encompasses your entire document and signals to the browser the beginning and the end of your page. Under some circumstances, a browser will load in the page if it has an .htm (Windows) or .html (Macintosh) extension and is saved locally—that is, on your own hard drive—even if you omit the <HTML> tag. But, you have no guarantee that any other browser will be able to read your code; for this reason, it's good practice to always start your Web page with the <HTML> tag and end it with </HTML>.

The <HEAD> Tag You declare the overall heading information in the area demarcated by the <HEAD> and </HEAD> tags.

The following elements can be part of the document head:

▸ **TITLE** Defines the document title, which appears at the top of the browser window in the title bar.

▸ **ISINDEX** Used for simple keyword searches, although the META tag is now used more frequently.

▸ **BASE** Defines the base URL and is used to correctly reference relative URLs. (You'll learn about these topics later in this chapter.)

▸ **SCRIPT** An element that is reserved for future use with scripting languages. Currently, both JavaScript and VBScript put their code here.

▸ **STYLE** Another element reserved for future use—this one with style sheets. Internet Explorer uses this element to define their Cascading Style Sheets, which are covered in Chapter 8.

▸ **META** Used to supply overall information such as a description, keywords, program creator, and so on. The META options are described in a moment.

▸ **LINK** Used to label relationships with other documents. This tag is often used to point to related glossaries or indexes, but can also be used to outline the tree-like structure of the Web site and this document's place in the tree.

<TITLE>, <SCRIPT>, and <STYLE> are containers and require both starting and ending tags—</TITLE>, </SCRIPT> and </STYLE>, respectively. The other elements are empty tags.

Like the <HTML> tags, the <HEAD> tags can often be omitted with no ill effects. But it's good HTML programming practice to include them. It will make your code more readable, and will also assure you of future compatibility with newer versions of HTML as they emerge.

As the Web grows, more and more tools are developed to manage this information explosion. Search engines such as Yahoo, AltaVista, WebCrawler, and Excite provide a valuable service with their constantly updated indexes of available Web sites. For them to do their job correctly—and, more importantly, for you to get your site listed the way you wanted it to be listed—you need to use the <META> tag within the <HEAD> section of the document. You would use the <META> tag with the HTTP-EQUIV attribute.

If, for example, you wanted your film noir book review site to list correctly and to be relevant for someone searching for "detective books," you might include the following in your <HEAD> section:

```
<META HTTP-EQUIV="Keywords" Content="Books, Reviews, Fiction, Detective, Film Noir">
<META HTTP-EQUIV="Description" Content="Soft-boiled reviews of hard-boiled books - mostly, dark crime fiction from the 1990's.">
```

You can also use the META tag to redirect the user to another page after a specified time period. This allows you to display a "splash page," which just gives the opening blurb and then, after a short period of time, sends the Web surfer to the main home page. In the following example, the browser will display the current page for 5 seconds and then link to the home page.

```
<HEAD>
<TITLE>Noirville - The Hard-Boiled Site</TITLE>
<META HTTP-EQUIV="Refresh" Content="5; URL=http://www.noirville.com/home.htm">
</HEAD>
```

The <BODY> Tag As noted, the <BODY> tags contain the content of the document. They can also contain a wide range of other elements:

- ▸ Headings, which are primarily used for headlines;
- ▸ Block-level elements that define paragraphs types
- ▸ Text-level elements, which alter the style of the text

Within the <BODY> tag, the main attributes are BACKGROUND, BGCOLOR, TEXT, LINK, VLINK, and ALINK. You use BACKGROUND to set a background image; if the image is not large enough to fill the browser screen it will be repeated, or tiled, until it does. Alternatively, you can use BGCOLOR (background color) to give the entire document a uniform color. BACKGROUND will take precedence over BGCOLOR if you use both. You use the remaining attributes to specify the colors for the normal text and hypertext links. TEXT specifies the color for normal text. LINK specifies the color for unvisited links. VLINK specifies the color for visited links. ALINK specifies the color for links that are being clicked on. Here's an example:

```
<BODY BGCOLOR=white TEXT=black LINK=red VLINK=maroon ALINK=fuchsia>
```

This code will produce a white background with black text and red links that turn fuchsia when clicked and then maroon to indicate they have already been selected.

If you change the background color or image, you should probably choose particular colors for the hyperlinks, to make sure they don't become unreadable. Be sure to check all three states of the link under a new background color or image: normal (LINK), clicked (ALINK), and visited (VLINK).

HEADINGS

Major divisions of a document are introduced and separated by headings. HTML supports six levels of headings, designated by the tag pairs <H1></H1>, <H2></H2>, <H3></H3>, <H4></H4>, <H5></H5>, and <H6></H6>. This is sufficient for most hypertext applications, because much of the structure of a hypertext work is in the web of links. You can generate additional structure by using list and table elements. All heading tags are containers and require a corresponding ending tag.

H1 is the highest level of heading. It is customary to use a level 1 heading as the first element in the body of the home page to serve as the internal title of the page, as opposed to the window title, which you insert with the <TITLE></TITLE> tags. A heading element implies a style change, including a paragraph break before and after the heading, and whatever white space is needed to render a heading of that level. Adding style tags to a heading or inserting paragraph tags to emphasize the heading is neither required nor recommended.

You should use headings in their natural hierarchical order, as in an outline, although it is legal to skip heading levels to follow an H1 with an H3, for example. Here is an HTML page illustrating the six different heading levels:

```
<!DOCTYPE HTML PUBLIC "-//W3C//DTD HTML 3.2//EN">
<HTML>
<HEAD>
<TITLE>Heading Levels</TITLE>
</HEAD>
<BODY>
<H1>Level 1 Heading</H1>
First paragraph of text.
<H2>Level 2 Heading</H2>
Second paragraph of text.
<H3>Level 3 Heading</H3>
Third paragraph of text.
<H4>Level 4 Heading</H4>
Fourth paragraph of text.
<H5>Level 5 Heading</H5>
Fifth paragraph of text.
<H6>Level 6 Heading</H6>
Sixth paragraph of text.
</BODY>
</HTML>
```

Color Names You specify colors in what are referred to as RGB numbers, and write them as either hexadecimal numbers or as one of 16 widely understood color names, as shown in Table 2.1. If you write them in hexadecimal form, enclose them within quotes and start the six-digit number with a pound sign (#): "#008000" is the same as "green".

Table 2.1: Color Names and Hexadecimal Equivalents

Color Name	Hexadecimal RGB Value
Black	"#000000"
Green	"#008000"
Silver	"#C0C0C0"
Lime	"#C0C0C0"
Gray	"#808080"
Olive	"#808000"
White	"#FFFFFF"
Yellow	"#FFFF00"
Maroon	"#800000"
Navy	"#000080"
Red	"#FF0000"
Blue	"#0000FF"
Purple	"#800080"
Teal	"#008080"
Fuchsia	"#FF00FF"
Aqua	"#00FFFF"

Originally, these colors were chosen because they were the standard 16 colors supported with the Windows VGA palette. Although there is a move to extend the color names, nothing has been settled upon yet.

Figure 2.5 shows how these headings will appear.

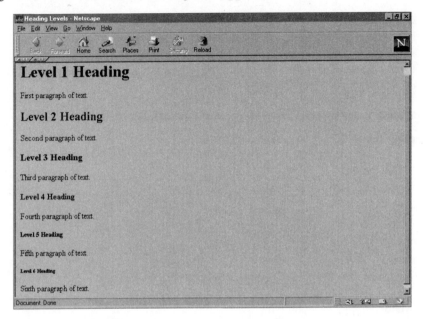

Figure 2.5: Heading example

By default, headings are aligned to the left margin. You can add the ALIGN attribute to the tag to produce other alignments. Figure 2.6, generated by the following HTML, shows how a set of centered headings can create a playbill effect.

```
<!DOCTYPE HTML PUBLIC "-//W3C//DTD HTML 3.2//EN">
<HTML>
<HEAD>
<TITLE>Centered Headings</TITLE>
</HEAD>
<BODY>
<H3 ALIGN=center>HTML Manual of Style</H3>
<H5 ALIGN=center>presents</H5>
<H1 ALIGN=center>A Centered Heading</H1>
<H5 ALIGN=center>For Your Viewing Pleasure</H5>
</BODY>
</HTML>
```

Like tag names, attribute names are not case sensitive. My convention is to use uppercase for tag and attribute names and lowercase for attribute values (except for URLs, which should always be considered case sensitive). You're

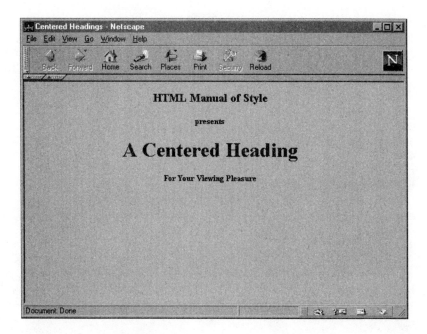

Figure 2.6: Centered headings

free to adopt any other convention, or abandon all convention entirely, although in the long run, a consistent programming style will make your code easier for both you and others to read.

COMMON ATTRIBUTES

ALIGN is one of a set of common attributes that you can use with headings and most of the other structural markup tags described in this chapter.

The ALIGN attribute can have the values, "left" (the default), "center," and "right." Some other browsers recognize the <CENTER></CENTER> tags for positioning page elements. This is a Netscape extension and although it is not included in HTML 3.2, it is recognized by most popular browsers. Note that because the <CENTER></CENTER> tags will add additional paragraph returns to your document under Netscape but not under any other browser, your output will vary needlessly. However, if you stick with the ALIGN="center" attribute you'll get the desired result across browser platforms.

You can use NOWRAP (equivalent to NOWRAP="yes") with most tags to turn off normal text wrapping. Within the text contained by the tags, you must use line breaks (<BR>) to separate the lines. There's also a Netscape extension, the <NOBR></NOBR> tags, that does much the same thing.

The following code shows the use of the various alignment and <BR> tags; the results are shown in Figure 2.7. Notice that the centered text wraps on this relatively small screen so that it fits correctly into the browser window.

```
<HTML>
<HEAD>
<TITLE>Declaration of Independence</TITLE>
</HEAD>
<BODY>
<H1 ALIGN="center">Declaration of Independence</H1>
<H5 ALIGN="right">(Adopted in Congress 4 July 1776)</H5>
<H3 ALIGN="left">The Unanimous Declaration of the Thirteen United States of
America</H3>
<P><H4 ALIGN="center">When, in the course of human events, it becomes necessary
for one people to dissolve the political bonds which have connected them with
another, and to assume among the powers of the earth, the separate and equal
station to which the laws of nature and of nature's God entitle them, <BR>a
decent respect to the opinions of mankind requires that they should declare the
causes which impel them to the separation.</H4></P>
</BODY>
</HTML>
```

You can add the ID attribute to a tag to assign a name to the enclosed content. You can then specify this name as part of an URL, letting you link to specific points within the body of a document. There's more on this in the section on anchors and links later on in this chapter.

You can use the LANG attribute to specify that an alternate language should be applied to the tag's content. This affects hyphenation rules and the choice of ligatures and quotation marks.

You use the CLASS attribute to assign a specific name to the content of the HTML element. Different HTML tag types can share the same class name value; this allows an entire class to be identified by a common label. See Chapter 8 for more about style sheets.

You use the CLEAR attribute in conjunction with content that flows around images and figures. It is an instruction to space down the page, as far as necessary, until the margin is clear before placing the content. The CLEAR attribute can have a value of "left", "right", or "all". This is a very important feature for mixing graphics and text; it's demonstrated under "Inline Graphics" later in this chapter.

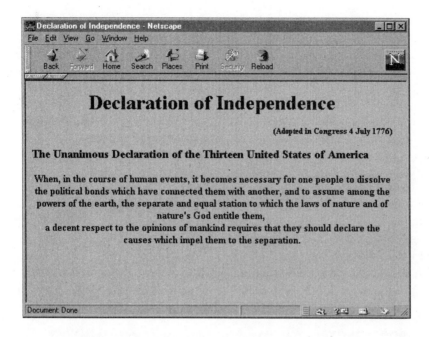

Figure 2.7: Alignment demonstration

BLOCK ELEMENTS

Block elements include both plain text paragraphs and some special-purpose paragraphs, such as external quotes, side notes, and footers. Browsers insert paragraph breaks and extra line spacing before and after all block elements. In the text contained within a block element, all carriage returns, tabs, control characters, and redundant spaces are replaced with single spaces and the text is word-wrapped to fit the browser's display window.

Paragraphs   You create your everyday plain text paragraph with paragraph tags, <P></P>. The first line of the paragraph may or may not appear indented; that's up to the browser. The paragraph is the simplest HTML page element and may contain any of the common attributes mentioned earlier. For example, to center a paragraph of text, you would enter

```
<P ALIGN=center>Just a few words here</P>
```

In HTML2, the paragraph tag was an empty tag, without attributes, that forced text that would normally flow together into two separate paragraphs. In HTML 3.2, the paragraph tag is a container and separates a block of text from other page elements. It's a small but significant change. In HTML2, content is marked up only if it must be treated differently from plain text. In HTML 3.2, all content is marked up. From the language developer's point of view, having plain paragraphs belong to a broader class of objects called block elements makes the HTML cleaner to implement. The HTML2 approach seems the more natural style for pages where most of the content is straight paragraphs of text, but the HTML 3.2 approach is much better when the paragraphs need attributes and are intermixed with other elements. Because most browsers are backwards compatible with pages written for HTML2, both approaches will work; however, HTML editors that do syntax checking may issue a warning or error message on finding an HTML2-style empty paragraph tag.

The <BLOCKQUOTE> Tag   Often some portion of a page's content is quoted material. To visually distinguish such paragraphs, you can use the block quote element, which consists of the tags <BLOCKQUOTE></BLOCKQUOTE>. Any text within the tags is rendered as a paragraph with wider right and left margins than a plain text paragraph. If more than one paragraph is quoted, you can use empty paragraph tags to separate the paragraphs within the block quote rather than using separate <BLOCKQUOTE> tags to enclose each paragraph.

The <ADDRESS> Tag   You can use the address element, <ADDRESS></ADDRESS>, for signatures, addresses, and other authorship information that usually appears at the top or bottom of a page. Address text is typically rendered in italic and may be indented or right justified. No more than a single paragraph of text should be in an address block. Use line break tags, <BR>, if you want to lay out the address content as separate lines of information.

The following code employs both the <BLOCKQUOTE> and <ADDRESS> tags, as illustrated in Figure 2.8.

```
<!DOCTYPE HTML PUBLIC "-//W3C//DTD HTML 3.2//EN">
<HTML>
<HEAD>
   <TITLE>Blockquote and Address</TITLE>
</HEAD>
<BODY>

<H1>Blockquote and Address</H1>

<P>Charles,</P>

<P>I like the new ending much better than the old, especially the final
paragraph, which I copy herewith:</P>

<BLOCKQUOTE>I took her hand in mine, and we went out of the ruined place;
```

```
and as the morning mists had risen long ago when I first left the forge,
so the evening mists were rising now, and in all the broad expanse of tranquil
light they showed to me, I saw no shadow of another parting from her.</BLOCKQUOTE>

<P>But, really Charles, couldn't you have made it two sentences?</P>

<HR>

<ADDRESS>C.H. Townsend<BR>
London, 1861</ADDRESS>

</BODY>
</HTML>
```

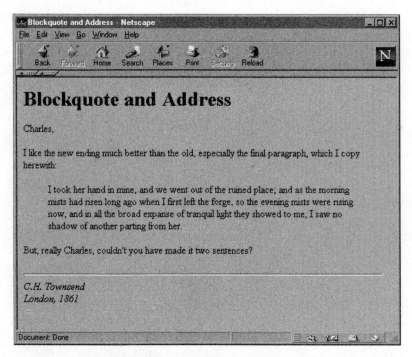

Figure 2.8: Blockquote and address example

Preformatted Text   The preformatted text block element is sort of an anti-paragraph. Any text between the starting and ending tags, <PRE></PRE>, will be left essentially as is—well, almost, anyway. Preformatted text is rendered in a monospaced font, and all line breaks and redundant spaces are retained. This makes it ideal for text that is formatted with columns such as numeric tables or any text where spacing must be preserved. Horizontal tabs are recognized and expanded as if there are tab stops every eight characters across the page.

Three other elements depict your text with a fixed-width font: <LISTING>, <XMP>, and <PLAINTEXT>. You can use the <LISTING> tag to depict condensed monospaced fonts, formatted for 132 characters per line. <XMP>, short for "Example," also results in a monospaced font, but formats the font for 80 characters per line. <PLAINTEXT> is not fully implemented on any current browser version and should be avoided; it renders any HTML tags that appear after it as, you guessed it, plain text. Figure 2.9 illustrates the difference between the <PRE>, <LISTING>, and <XMP> tags.

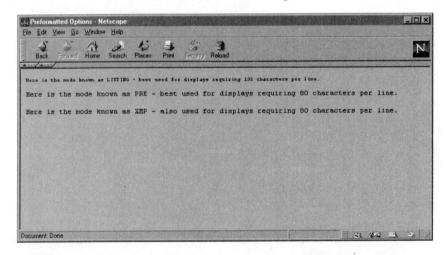

Figure 2.9: Preformatted text examples

Like other block elements, preformatted text implies a paragraph break before and after the defining tags. Within the preformatted block, you shouldn't use any other structure tags. Style tags are appropriate, as are anchor and image tags. Here's a simple example of preformatted text:

```
<HTML>
<HEAD>
<TITLE>Preformatted Text example</TITLE>
</HEAD>

<BODY>
<H2>Puzzle</H2>
<PRE>
```

```
                       |\   /
     Here's one way to   o o o
         connect all 9.  |  X
     dots using only 4   o o o
        straight lines:  |/   \
                         o-o-o-
</PRE>
</BODY>
</HTML>
```

This will create the display shown in Figure 2.10.

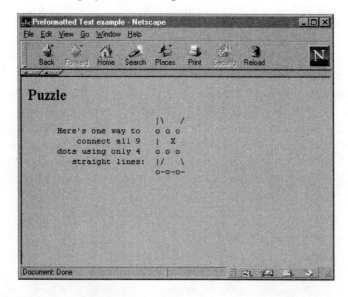

Figure 2.10: A preformatted puzzle

The preformatted tag has one optional attribute, WIDTH, which tells the browser the maximum line length that can be expected within the preformatted text. With this information, the browser can adjust the margins or font size to accommodate the text. You should use values of either 40, 80, or 132 for best results. Here's an example:

```
<PRE WIDTH=80>This is preformatted text.</PRE>
```

This allows you to use one tag, <PRE>, consistently without switching to any of the other variations of preformatted text like <LISTING>. Contrary to what you might assume, the command <PRE WIDTH=40> will not make the font larger than <PRE WIDTH=80>. Rather, the WIDTH attribute lets the browser know the maximum number of characters expected across the width of the screen.

LINE BREAKS

When all you need to do is end the current line and begin the next one at the margin, use the line break tag, <BR>. It is an empty tag, differing from the paragraph tag in that it does not insert any extra white space. You can think of it as inserting a newline character into the text. You should use line break tags where you need more than one line in a heading or list item.

HORIZONTAL RULES

HTML provides a horizontal rule element for visually organizing headings and paragraphs into larger units. The horizontal rule tag, <HR> (an empty tag), instructs the reader's browser to insert a paragraph break into the content with a horizontal line separating the paragraphs. It's a nice feature, because the browser will adjust the line to fit the width of the display window.

HTML 3.2 recognizes additional attributes to the <HR> tag. The SIZE attribute specifies the height or thickness of the rule in pixels and the WIDTH attribute specifies its width; you can specify an exact pixel width or a percentage of the browser display window. If you don't use either attribute, the default is a line 3 pixels high that stretches the width of the screen. When you specify a WIDTH attribute, ALIGN is meaningful. For example:

```
<HR SIZE=10 WIDTH=50% ALIGN=center>
```

specifies a horizontal rule ten pixels tall, aligned in the center of the window, occupying exactly half of the display width.

The default horizontal rule is shaded and has an engraved look. You can specify a solid bar by using the NOSHADE attribute with the <HR> tag. (Many Web sites use multicolored, patterned, or even animated rules—these are actually images used as separators instead of the <HR> element.)

Note the use of two different rules to set off the text in the following example; these rules differ in both size and relative width. Figure 2.11 shows the HTML output.

```
<HTML>
<HEAD>
<TITLE>Paragraphs, Line Breaks and Dorothy Parker</TITLE>
</HEAD>
<BODY>
<H1 Align="center">Pearls from Parker, Dorothy...</H1>
<HR Width=50% Align="center">
<HR Width=75% Size=3 Align="center"><H3>On learning that Calvin Coolidge was dead
```

```
she remarked, &quot;How could they tell?&quot;</H3>
<H3>&quot;Brevity is the soul of lingerie.&quot;</H3>
<H3>&quot;Are you Dorothy Parker?&quot; a guest at a party inquired.
<BR>&quot;Yes, do you mind?&quot;</H3>
<H3>For her own epitaph: &quot;Excuse my dust.&quot;</H3>
<HR Width=75% Size=3 Align="center">
<HR Width=50% Align="center">
</BODY>
</HTML>
```

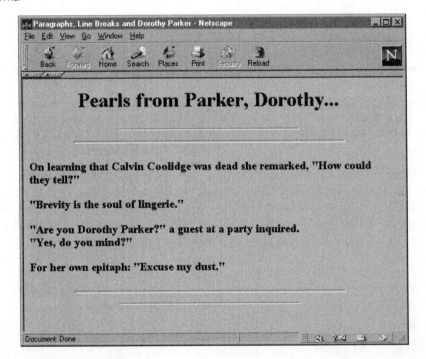

Figure 2.11: Horizontal rules

ANCHORS AND LINKS

The hyperlink is the essence of the Internet and what makes the Web web-like. Perhaps because of its central importance in HTML, the link tag is known as the Anchor. Designated by <A>, the anchor tag allows any word, image, or object to link to any other word, image, or object available on the Web. Naturally, the anchor tag also allows you to create links to anywhere on the currently open document—such as an bibliographical endnote—or any page on your particular Web site.

The hyperlink tag is one of the simplest to use, with the fewest attributes and features, but it is by far the most powerful. The syntax is exact and unforgiving: If you do not use it correctly, you'll know it immediately because your link will not work. Usually, a forgotten closing quotation mark or ending tag is the culprit.

THE ANCHOR TAG (<A>)

Anchors are the parts of the page that, when clicked on, take the reader somewhere else. Anchors are what link Web pages together; they and are often referred to as just that, links. There are two ways you can recognize a link on a page: It is typically underlined and appears in blue on your screen (the usual default color of the link). In addition, your cursor usually turns into a pointing hand when it passes over the link. At this point, your browser displays what Internet address that particular link goes to at the bottom of the screen.

The HREF Attribute   The anchor tag has one prime attribute, HREF, which stands for "Hypertext Reference." The element is usually written

```
<A HREF="some_url">Go to some URL</A>
```

The value of the HREF attribute is a Uniform Resource Locator, or URL. This is what is commonly known as the Web address. When both the start and the destination of the link are within the same document, the value of the HREF attribute is a name preceded by a pound sign. For example:

```
Addresses of <A HREF="#sources">additional sources</A>
can be found at the end of this chapter.
   *
   *
<P NAME="sources">Finally, some more sources of information.</P>
```

Clicking on the phrase "additional sources" tells the browser to jump to the named section somewhere else in the document.

The NAME Attribute   In the preceding example, the NAME attribute in the paragraph tag is used to identify the HREF link destination. If you use the NAME attribute in the same place in the document, but with the anchor link, like this,

```
<A NAME="Sources">Additional Sources</A><P>Your new paragraph here.. </P>
```

the jump will still occur and "Additional Sources" will be the new destination. This method allows you to hyperlink within your own document for swift navigation. Often, in extremely long pages, the top line in a document will use a NAME attribute so you can create a link to the top of the page.

URL Syntax   The URL format permits you to address almost any resource on the Internet, whether that resource is an HTML file on a Web server or some other Internet resource, such as a gopher server or a Usenet newsgroup. The URL has several parts, not all of which are required for the URL to be valid. In order of appearance, they specify the

- ▸ Method to be used to access the resource
- ▸ Name of the server providing the resource
- ▸ Port number to be used on the server
- ▸ Directory path to the resource
- ▸ Filename of the resource
- ▸ Named element in the HTML document

These parts are separated by various delimiters and the whole URL is enclosed within quotes, as follows:

```
"method://server:port/path/file#anchor"
```

The port number is sort of like the telephone extension number of the server. Most URLs do not include a port number because most servers use the defaults.

RELATIVE AND ABSOLUTE ADDRESSING

To link to another HTML document in the same directory as the current one, you just need the filename; all the missing information is taken from the current document. This is called *relative URL addressing* and it should be used in creating any links to documents within the Web site. The following example provides a link to a file spot_info.html:

```
His cat is named <A HREF="spot_info.html">Spot</A>.
```

Relative addressing gives your hypertext work portability, because, as long as the files stay together in the same logical directory, none of the relative links need to be respecified when the collection is moved from one server to another. To link to a specific anchor in the destination page, follow the filename with a pound sign and the name of the anchor, like this:

```
<A HREF="spot_info.html#habits">Spot</A>
```

Suppose that the file is in a subdirectory of the directory of the current file, say, one named pets. You would write a link to the preceding file like this:

```
<A HREF="pets/spot_info.html">Spot</A>
```

It makes no difference how directory paths and filenames are actually constructed in the operating system under which the server is running—whether backslashes separate directories, as in Windows, or square brackets are used, as in VMS. URL syntax uses slashes for all these forms. The server is responsible for converting the request to the actual form used to reference the file.

If the file is on a different server than that of the current file, you must specify the access method and the domain name of the server, separated by double slashes. Here's an example:

```
<A HREF="http://www.enterprise.ufp.mil/officers/data/spot_info.html">Spot</A>
```

This is called *absolute URL addressing*. The only assumption made is that the Web server, www.enterprise.ufp.mil, is running on port 80, which is the default port for World Wide Web servers. If this is not the case—say, www.enterprise.ufp.mil is on port 1080—you must specify the port as follows:

```
<A HREF="http://enterprise.ufp.mil:1080/officers/data/spot_info.html">Spot</A>
```

As you can see, URLs can be quite lengthy.

Other resources on the Internet besides HTML documents can be linked from an HTML document. The general philosophy is, if it's out there, you can construct a URL to point to it. There are specific methods for ftp, gopher, news, and WAIS servers, and for accessing Telnet sessions. Browsers will take different actions depending on the type of resource accessed.

Here are some examples of Internet URLs:

```
ftp://ftp.uu.net/doc/literary/obi/World.Factbook
gopher://gopher.micro.umn.edu/
telnet://compuserve.com/
news:alt.cows.moo
```

A gopher is assumed to be on the default gopher port, port 70. If the gopher uses another port, you must specify this port by following the server name with a colon and the number. If a URL for a gopher or ftp resource ends in a specific filename, that file is downloaded to the reader's computer. If the URL points to a directory, the browser displays the directory in a standard format with links for subdirectories and files. You can add a TITLE attribute to an anchor tag to provide a title for this display window.

The format for accessing Usenet newsgroups, as you can see, is different from the format for accessing other Internet resources in that it does not specify a news (NNTP) server. The server name is set somewhere else, typically somewhere in the browser's preferences dialog. The idea is that, theoretically, all NNTP servers have the same content, so the server choice should be left up to the reader.

INLINE IMAGES

An image or two will go a long way toward making your Web page more attractive. The images on your home page will give information to the reader that cannot be gleaned from the text; a simple line graph is more informative than a table of numbers. Images also play an important function as page design elements.

To include an inline image in your page, use <IMG>, which is an empty tag. No paragraph breaks or other white space around the image is implied. If you don't specify the text flow around the image, the image is inserted into the text like a single odd-sized character. Unlike an image in a page layout program, which can be anchored to a specific spot on the page, an inline image on a Web page is part of the text in which it is embedded. Anywhere that you can place a character of text, you can put an inline image.

BASIC IMAGE TAG ATTRIBUTES

The image tag has three important attributes:

- ▸ **SRC** The source attribute is mandatory. Its value is the URL of the file containing the image to be embedded. Specify the URL as you do for the HREF attribute of the anchor tag.

- ▸ **ALIGN** For an inline image, use one of three values—"top", "middle", or "bottom"—to define how the image should be aligned with the adjacent text and other HTML elements.

- ▸ **ALT** The ALT attribute is used to specify a text string that can be displayed if the image is not available or the reader has chosen not to load images.

Here's an example of a page with two small, inline images; the second image is the anchor of a link:

```
<HEAD>
<TITLE>Image Example</TITLE>
</HEAD>
<BODY>
<H1>Inline Images</H1>
<P><IMG SRC="Mosaic.GIF"> Mosaic was the first graphical browser capable of
displaying in-line images.</P>
<P>Need <A HREF="http://www.ncsa.uiuc.edu/Mosaic/QuickStart.html">
<IMG SRC="More.GIF" ALT=" more " ALIGN=middle> information</A>?</P>
</BODY>
```

Figure 2.12 shows how this would be displayed.

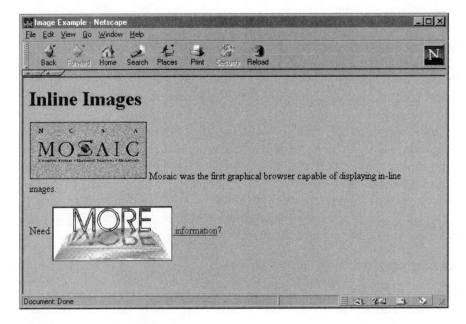

Figure 2.12: An inline image example

In the preceding example, both images are decorative; the page would function just as well without them. A browser that could not display the image would substitute the word "more," specified as the value of the ALT attribute, as the anchor of the line. Note that the example has spaces before and after the image tag. They are used here because the browser regards inline images as odd-sized characters in the text, and, in word-wrapping the paragraphs, we want the inline images to behave as one-letter words rather than be attached to adjacent text.

ADVANCED <IMG> ATTRIBUTES

One of the most potent tools in the webmaster's toolbox is the ability to resize and highlight the graphics used on the page. The HEIGHT and WIDTH attributes of the <IMG> tag let you use the same image in different sizes—repeating a smaller version of the opening splash screen logo at the bottom of a page, for example. Here's how they and the other attributes for the IMG tag work:

▶ **WIDTH** Determines the width of the image in pixels. When given together with the height, it allows browsers to set aside page space for the image before the image data has arrived over the network, resulting a box outline representing an image before the image is fully loaded.

- ▶ **HEIGHT** Defines the height of the image in pixels.

- ▶ **BORDER** When the <IMG> element appears as part of a hypertext link, the browser generally draws a colored border (typically blue) around the image. You can use the BORDER attribute to set the width of this border in pixels. If you don't want a border, you can use BORDER=0 to completely eliminate it.

- ▶ **HSPACE** Enables you to provide white space to the immediate left and right of the image. HSPACE sets the width of this white space in pixels. By default, HSPACE is a small nonzero number.

- ▶ **VSPACE** Enables you to provide white space above and below the image. VSPACE sets the height of this white space in pixels. By default, VSPACE is a small nonzero number.

- ▶ **USEMAP** Identifies the code for a client-side image map defined with the MAP element. Imagemaps are covered in Chapter 6.

- ▶ **ISMAP** The server-side equivalent of USEMAP. When clicked on, causes the location to be passed to the server. An early solution to the imagemap problem, this mechanism causes problems for text-only and speech-based user agents. Whenever possible, use the MAP element instead.

IMAGE FILE FORMATS

Although there are, conservatively, a zillion different graphic file formats used in computing today, only a small handful of file types are generally recognizable across the board. The main two are the GIF and the JPEG.

GIF Files: Illustrations GIF, which stands for Graphics Interchange Format and is pronounced with a hard "G," was developed by CompuServe for the exchange of pictures across computer platforms. GIFs are said to be 8 bits wide, meaning that they can hold up to 256 colors per image. Because this equals a standard SVGA screen, GIFs are the perfect lowest common denominator graphics format for illustrations, line drawings, and cartoons. Using the appropriate graphics tool, you can save GIFs in as few as two colors. The lower the number of colors, the smaller the file size, which correspondingly increases the page loading speed.

GIFs come in two varieties. The older, GIF87a, has been for the most part replaced by the newer version, GIF89a, which offers significant enhancements.

GIF89a allows you to specify a transparent region, allowing the otherwise rectangular picture to appear to be any shape you want and to float on the background if you like. Also, this latest version of the GIF format allows the picture to be interlaced; if the interlace is enabled for a picture it will appear first in a blocky outline and then gradually become more defined as the browser loads it. In addition, the GIF89a format enables animations to occur. You'll learn about animations in Chapter 6.

JPEG Files: Photographs   While GIFs are used primarily for illustrations, photographs, with their much higher demand for color, are generally used on the Web in the JPEG format. JPEG was developed by the Joint Photographic Experts Group to display up to 24 bits per pixel or over 16 million colors. JPEGs, which use either the .JPEG or .JPG extension, are compressed according to a variable algorithm. When the graphics are saved or converted to JPEG format, you can specify the degree of compression—the higher the compression, the smaller the file. However, after a certain point the increased compression can adversely affect the image. Moreover, when the browser reads a JPEG image, it must decompress the file. This decompression represents a performance hit and can slow down the loading of your Web page; you must balance the size, quality, and download time of the image.

PNG Files: The Next Generation   GIF ran into a spot of trouble in the early 90s: UniSys and CompuServe, the developers of the format, decided that it was a copywritable entity and should be protected. Therefore all graphics in GIF format potentially owed a royalty to Unisys. After the uproar reached an undeniable peak, CompuServe indicated that they would never enforce the copyright to such an extent; however, they retained the right. In response, a freely distributable format was proposed: Portable Network Graphics or PNG (pronounced "ping"). The PNG format was designed by the World Wide Web Consortium to provide a new, well-compressed standard for bitmapped image files. All of the important GIF features have been retained, including 8-bit (256 color) images, progressive display, transparency, and complete hardware and platform independence.

Although the initial motivation for developing PNG was to replace GIF, the design provides some useful new features not available in GIF, including

- ▶ Truecolor images of up to 48 bits per pixel
- ▶ Grayscale images of up to 16 bits per pixel
- ▶ Full alpha channel (general transparency masks)

- ▶ Image gamma information, which supports automatic display of images with correct brightness/contrast, regardless of the machines used to originate and display the image

- ▶ Reliable, straightforward detection of file corruption

- ▶ Faster initial presentation in progressive display mode

What's the downside? All new formats take time to take hold and proliferate, so you won't find the PNG format as widely supported as GIF or JPEG. Currently, both Netscape and Microsoft are promising support for the PNG format, although neither is committed to placing it in the IMG tag, but rather their EMBED or OBJECT tags that are used for Java and ActiveX controls. Time, and perhaps competition, will tell what happens with PNG.

There is, of course, a lot more to putting images on a Web page. In Chapter 6 you'll find discussions of text flow around images and figures, imagemaps with clickable areas, and some of the tricks you can do with image loading and placement.

Basic HTML, Part II

Text Styles

Lists

Tables

Chapter 3

This chapter completes the examination of HTML fundamentals by describing how to format your text. You'll discover the difference between logical and physical styles, including which is better and why. Then, you'll explore the lists in HTML, learning how to generate bulleted and numbered lists. Finally, you'll work with tables, a key element in modern Web page design.

TEXT STYLES

Style tags change the typography of contained text. Style tags can be nested within other style tags much as you would apply type styles in a word processing program. However, HTML styles are abstract or logical constructs, whereas the styles used in word processing programs are explicit. Text styles can be either "logical" or "physical." Logical styles are contextual—that is, related to their meaning. <STRONG>, a logical style tag, emphasizes the text it surrounds. Physical text styles are taken from modern typography—for example, <U> underlines the text it contains. Logical styles are relative and physical styles are absolute.

LOGICAL STYLES

Logical styles are an underlying concept in HTML; their purpose is to make it easier for various browsers on various computer systems to interpret the same code. By making the text styles relative—saying, in effect, this text should be emphasized more than the text surrounding it, or this text should be treated as a citation as opposed to the rest of the text—logical styles sidestep the stumbling block of exact translation on a per platform basis.

Most markup tags can occur within style tags, although you should generally avoid the use of structural elements inside of a style. In other words, it is better to start your style tags after you've begun the paragraph or blockquote rather than before: <P><STRONG>...</STRONG></P> is better than <STRONG><P>...</P></STRONG>.

Here are the most common logical style tags from HTML 3.2:

▸ **<EM></EM>** Emphasis, usually rendered in italic or underlined to bring out the text slightly from the background text

▸ **<STRONG></STRONG>** Strong emphasis, usually rendered in boldface. Must be rendered differently from emphasis

▸ **<CITE></CITE>** Citation, for titles and references within the text, typically rendered in italic

▸ **<TT></TT>** Typewriter Text, a monospaced font (every character has the same width) such as Courier is used

Figure 3.1 shows the result of using the preceding text in a definition list.

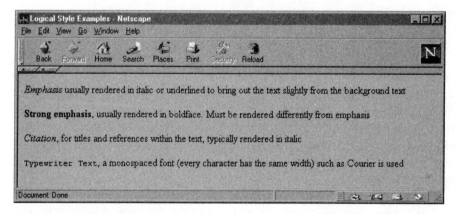

Figure 3.1: Logical styles in effect

Following are most of the other style tags recognized by the majority of browsers. Different browsers will render these styles differently, and many browsers will not render each style in a way distinct from all other styles.

▸ **<BIG></BIG>** Designates that a font somewhat larger than the current size should be used

- ▸ **<DFN></DFN>** Defining instance, used to mark the introduction of a new term
- ▸ **<S></S>** or **<STRIKE></STRIKE>** Strikethrough text, as in legal documents
- ▸ **<SMALL></SMALL>** Indicates that a font somewhat smaller than the current size should be used
- ▸ **** Subscript, the text is lowered and may be rendered with a smaller font size than normal
- ▸ **** Superscript, the text is raised and may be rendered with a smaller font size than normal

For manuals, computer system documentation, and user's guides:

- ▸ **<CODE></CODE>** Coding, for samples of computer programming, usually rendered in a monospaced font
- ▸ **<KBD></KBD>** Keyboard, a sequence of characters to be typed in, exactly, by the user
- ▸ **<SAMP></SAMP>** Sample, a sequence of literal characters
- ▸ **<VAR></VAR>** Variable, in instructional text, the name of a value to be supplied by the user

PHYSICAL STYLES

HTML does include physical, or explicit, styles, specifically the tag pairs <B></B>, <I></I>, and <U></U>, for, respectively, bold, italic, and underlined text. You can use these tags when you need to have exact control—for example, when one part of the text must refer to other parts (such as "Optional rules are specified in italics"). However, you should use the logical style tags wherever possible to provide greater consistency among documents from different sources.

HTML 3.2 now recognizes a special style tag, <FONT>, which you use with the SIZE and COLOR attribute. The SIZE attribute can have a positive or negative value from 1 to 7 specifying that the enclosed text be rendered in a font size larger or smaller than the size currently in effect. This is an easy way to fake a small caps font. For example:

```
<FONT SIZE=+3>K</FONT>OOL TRIC<FONT SIZE=+3>K</FONT>
```

makes the beginning and ending letters, the "K," larger than the interior letters because the "SIZE=+3" attributes is turned on.

FONT can also have a COLOR attribute that uses either a hexadecimal triplet or one of the named colors (see the section "Color Names" in Chapter 2 for a list of the recognizable colors and their hexadecimal equivalents). One browser, Internet Explorer, has added a FACE attribute that lets you specify a particular typeface to be used, if it's available. However, because this practice infringes significantly on the platform-independent nature of HTML, you should avoid it for the time being. The World Wide Web Consortium is leaning toward endorsing the more general Cascading Style Sheets (covered in Chapter 7), rather than single tag attributes like FACE, to give more layout control.

One area where you might be safer using the physical styles is within an intranet. Because an intranet is more of a "closed system," you are more likely to know which browser your site visitors are using, and can avoid any incompatibilities you might encounter on the wide-open Web. There are two "gotchas" here. First, different departments might employ different computers or even different browsers. Second, one of the current trends is to open up a selected portion of a company's intranet for public access; make sure your browser-specific material is not in this open area.

And, finally, there's one other Netscape-only tag that should be used sparingly, if at all: the <BLINK></BLINK> element.

LISTS

A *list* is a structured paragraph containing a sequence of list items. HTML provides three kinds of lists: ordered, unordered, and definition lists.

ORDERED AND UNORDERED LISTS

Ordered lists have numbered items; unordered lists have bulleted items. Ordered lists use the <OL></OL> tags to enclose and mark the entire list structure; unordered lists use <UL></UL> tags. Each item on either of these two lists is enclosed within list item tags, <LI></LI>. When rendered by the browser, list items are usually indented in from the left margin a little bit.

Lists can be nested, making them ideal for implementing outlines and tables of contents. Other than nesting, however, you should not use any other tags in an ordered or unordered list item that imply paragraph breaks, such as headings, horizontal rules, tables, or forms; images and links are just fine. Here's an example using ordered and unordered lists:

```
<HTML>
<HEAD>
```

```
<TITLE>Examples of Lists</TITLE>
</HEAD>
<BODY>
<H1 ALIGN="center">HTML Book</H1>
<HR>
<!-- USE HEADINGS FOR MAJOR SECTIONS -->
<H2>Table of Contents</H2>
<H3>Chapters</H3>
<OL>
   <LI>Introduction</LI>
   <LI>The Language</LI>
   <! - USE BULLETS FOR THIS LEVEL - >
   <UL>
      <LI>Syntax</LI>
      <LI>Formatting</LI>
   </UL>
   <LI>Writing Documents</LI>
</OL>
<HR>
</BODY>
</HTML>
```

Figure 3.2 shows how this example looks.

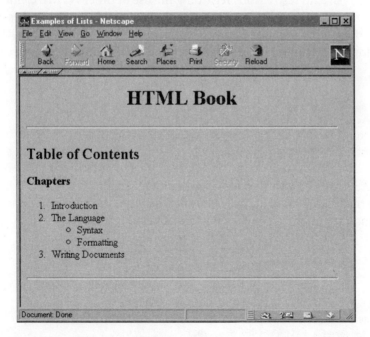

Figure 3.2: Ordered and unordered lists

The indentations used in the preceding code are only there to make the HTML easier to read; in no way do they affect how a browser formats the text. Note that the nested unordered list appears between two ordered list items, not inside an item. In other words, it would be incorrect to write

```
<LI>
<UL>
<LI>Syntax</LI>
<LI>Formatting</LI>
</UL>
</LI>
```

DEFINITION LISTS

Definition lists have, as each item of the list, a pair of objects called the definition term and definition description. The definition term is enclosed within the <DT></DT> tags and is aligned to the left margin. The definition description is enclosed within the <DD></DD> tags and is indented from the left margin. The entire definition list is enclosed within the tags <DL> and </DL>. No number or bullets are added.

Definition lists are very powerful. Unlike ordered and unordered lists, definition lists have no restrictions regarding the use of other HTML elements within either the defining term or description part. This is what makes them so powerful. Here's a simple example of a definition list. (Remember, <DT> stands for definition term and <DD> stands for definition description.)

```
<H2>Cast of Characters</H2>
<DL>
<DT>Orsino</DT><DD>Duke of Illyria.</DD>
<DT>Sebastian</DT><DD>Brother to Viola.</DD>
<DT>Antonio</DT><DD>A sea captain, friend to Sebastian.</DD>
<DT>Fabian</DT><DD>A pop star of the early 'sixties.</DD>
</DL>
```

Figure 3.3 shows how this example looks on the screen.

Note that there's no white space inserted between the term and description. A common technique is to make the term a heading, that is,

```
<DL>
<DT><H3>Bucky Balls</H3></DT>
<DD>Technically, Buckminster Fullerene, a family of all carbon
molecules named after the great designer-architect-engineer,
Buckminster Fuller. The most stable member, C60, is a
hollow sphere with the same architecture as the geodesic structures
Fuller pioneered a half century ago.</DD>
<DT><H3>Penrose Tiling</H3></DT>
```

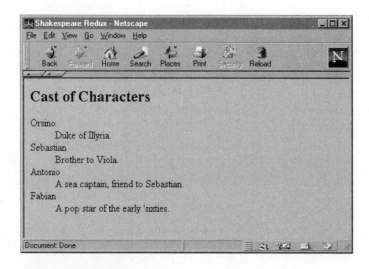

Figure 3.3: Simple definition list

```
<DD>A method of tiling a plane thought impossible until discovered by
Dr. Roger Penrose. Combining two differently shaped rhomboids,
the tiling has five-fold symmetry, yet <EM>the pattern is not
periodic!</EM>. A mathematical curiosity until it was found in
some natural minerals with rather strange properties.</DD>
</DL>
```

As you can in Figure 3.4, this technique visually emphasizes each list item.

OTHER LIST ELEMENTS

In HTML2, the list item tag was empty, so you are likely to find many pages on the World Wide Web where list items are missing the closing </LI> tag in the HTML source. They still work. Also, in the HTML 2.0 specification, two additional kinds of lists used the list item tag: the menu list, with the <MENU></MENU> tags, and the directory list, with the <DIR></DIR> tags. The menu list was intended for lists of short items, rendered more compactly than <UL>, and the directory list was for lists of very short elements, such as filenames, rendered in multiple columns. Both these lists are functionally replaced in HTML 3.2 by new attributes to the ordered and unordered lists tags, as discussed in a moment. Therefore, although <MENU></MENU> and <DIR></DIR> are still supported, they are no longer recommended to authors.

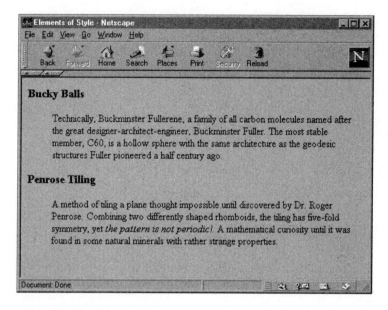

Figure 3.4: Definition list with headings

LIST ATTRIBUTES

HTML 3.2 added two attributes to the ordered and unordered lists elements, TYPE and START. For ordered lists, the TYPE attribute can take the following values:

TYPE="1"   Normal numeric numbering; the default

TYPE="A"   Uppercase letters; A, B, C, D, ...

TYPE="a"   Lowercase letters; a, b, c, d, ...

TYPE="I"   Uppercase Roman numerals; I, II, III, IV, ...

TYPE="i"   Lowercase Roman numerals; i, ii, iii, iv, ...

For unordered lists, Netscape lets the TYPE attribute take the values "circle", "square", or "disc" to indicate the type of bullet to be used. Figure 3.5 illustrates use of the TYPE attribute for both ordered and unordered lists.

The value of the START attribute is a number indicating which value list numbering should start with. The START attribute is ignored in unordered lists.

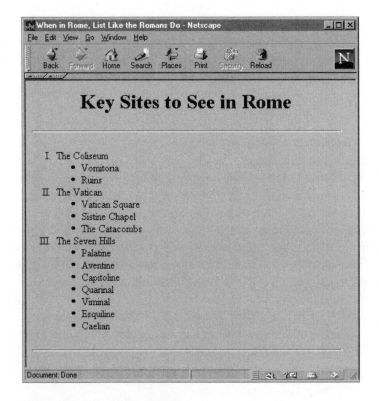

Figure 3.5: TYPE attribute demonstration

TABLES

Often you'll need to present information in a more structured fashion than that provided by lists. Tables allow you to display information organized into rows and columns. Tables are an HTML 3.2 feature that Netscape Navigator implemented originally. Before there were tables, you had to use the preformatted text element using tabs to align columns of data. This is still an acceptable way to present simple tables, especially tables of numeric data where the fixed-width font imposed by the <PRE></PRE> tags doesn't look so bad. You can directly include spreadsheet data, exported in tab-delimited format, in a Web page in this manner. The latest version of Excel also features an excellent HTML export Wizard that outputs spreadsheet data either into a new or existing Web page.

For more complex requirements, it's better to use the table element. Tables are defined as a series of rows each containing a series of cells. This model allows cells to span multiple rows or columns. The rows can be grouped into a table head and one or more table body sections. Certain tags are used with a <TABLE></TABLE> tag pair to specify which type of table element follows; these are known collectively as table subelements.

BASIC TABLE SUBELEMENTS

Table cells come in two varieties: header cells and data cells. By default, data cell content is rendered in normal left-justified text, while header cell content is rendered in boldfaced text and centered. A table cell can contain any other HTML elements—lists, images, headings—and even other tables.

A table begins and ends with the <TABLE></TABLE> tags. Table rows are defined by <TR></TR>, header cells by <TH></TH>, and data cells by <TD></TD>. A table must have at least one row and one cell. An optional table subelement, <CAPTION></CAPTION>, supplies—you guessed it—a caption for the table. The caption is centered above the table by default, but you can use the ALIGN attribute to specify that it appear on the left, right, top, or bottom. Figure 3.6 shows the simple three-row by three-column table generated by the following HTML:

```
<TABLE>
<CAPTION>Total Table Items</CAPTION>
<TR><TH></TH> <TH>Lunch</TH> <TH>Dinner</TH></TR>
<TR><TH>Kitchen</TH> <TD>23</TD> <TD>30</TD></TR>
<TR><TH>Dining Room</TH> <TD>31</TD> <TD>45</TD></TR>
</TABLE>
```

TABLE ATTRIBUTES

Netscape Navigator implemented tables about half a year before the HTML 3.2 specification for tables was set. Fortunately, many of the table attributes implemented by Netscape have been adopted into the HTML 3.2 specification. The complete set of table attributes and subelements is robust and lets you create many different styles of tables. Let's start with Netscape's extensions, as they provide one method of control of the table layout, and progress from there to the more powerful methods provided by HTML 3.2.

The ALIGN attribute is supported in the table tag and the subelements <TR>, <TH>, and <TD> with the standard values of "left", "center", and "right". Tables normally occupy the full width of the browser's display window. You should use the ALIGN attribute in the <TABLE> tag in conjunction with the WIDTH attribute to control the placement of the table with respect to the

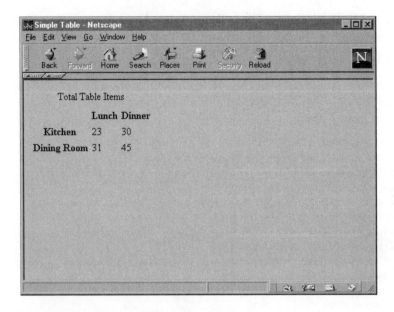

Figure 3.6: A simple table

display, for example, <TABLE ALIGN="center" WIDTH=50%>. When specified in the <CAPTION> tag, ALIGN is either top (the default) or bottom, and
controls whether the caption appears above or below the table.

ALIGN, specified with the other table elements, controls the placement of
the contents within table cells. The allowed values are: "left", "center", and
"right". Alignment specified at the table cell level has precedence over row
alignment, which has precedence over table body or head alignment. Con-
versely, alignment is inherited from the head/body level if not specified at the
row level and cell alignment is inherited from the row level if not specified at
the cell level.

The VALIGN attribute is similar to ALIGN. It controls the vertical positioning of table cell contents and can have the values "top", "middle", or "bottom".
The default is "middle". Obviously, the more complex the content of a data
cell, the more careful you should be about using ALIGN and VALIGN.

The <TABLE> tag can have these additional attributes; the value, represented by *n* in each case, is a whole number of screen pixels:

▶ BORDER=*n*   The table is displayed in a rectangle with *n*-pixel weight
   lines defining table cell walls. The default is BORDER=0.

▶ CELLPADDING=n The table is rendered with n pixels space between the contents of the table's cells and the walls of the cells.

▶ CELLSPACING=n The table is rendered with cell walls n pixels thick.

At the data cell level, Netscape's table implementation provided the attributes ROWSPAN and COLSPAN for a little more control. Figure 3.7 shows how they can be used.

```
<TABLE CELLPADDING=5 BORDER=2>
<CAPTION ALIGN="bottom">The Inner Planets</CAPTION>
<TR><TH ROWSPAN=2></TH>
 <TH COLSPAN=2>Distance from Sun</TH>
 <TH ROWSPAN=2>Year<BR>Length</TH>
 <TH ROWSPAN=2>Day<BR>length</TH> </TR>
<TR><!-- spanned cell -->
 <TH>kilometers</TH><TH>AUs</TH>
 <!-- 2 spanned cells --> </TR>
<TR><TH>Mercury</TH>
 <TD>57,900,000</TD> <TD>.38</TD> <TD>88 days</TD> <TD>59 days</TD></TR>
<TR><TH>Venus</TH>
 <TD>108,200,000</TD> <TD>.72</TD> <TD>225 days</TD> <TD>243 days</TD></TR>
<TR><TH>Earth</TH>
 <TD>149,600,000</TD> <TD>1.0</TD> <TD>365 days</TD> <TD>24 hrs</TD></TR>
<TR><TH>Mars</TH>
 <TD>227,900,000</TD> <TD>1.5</TD> <TD>687 days</TD> <TD>24.6 hrs</TD></TR>
</TABLE>
```

SPECIALIZED TABLE SUBELEMENTS

A great many table subelements that were included in the HTML 3.0 specifications did not get carried over into HTML 3.2. These included

▶ The <THEAD></THEAD>, <TFOOT></TFOOT> and <TBODY></TBODY> tag pairs, which permitted the application of alignment and class attribute values to subsections of the table. This would allow browsers to scroll the data portion of a long table without moving the header and the footer rows, much like the Freeze Pane option in spreadsheets.

▶ The empty <COL> tag provided a convenient means of applying attributes to one or more columns of the table. There should be one <COL> tag for each table column. Also, a <COLS> tag informed the browser in one statement how many columns to expect in the upcoming table, allowing much faster loading times without having to read in the entire table structure.

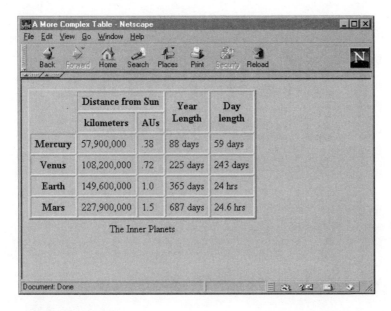

Figure 3.7: A complex table

▸ The <RULES> attribute gave far more complex control over the inner and outer borders on a per cell basis, as opposed to the all-encompassing <BORDER> command, which turns on borders of a specific width for the entire table.

To date, only Microsoft Internet Explorer supports these table extensions—and many more, including the ability to include background pictures and individual cell colors. Although they aren't available to all browsers, these features, which are covered in greater detail in Chapter 8, offer the intranet webmaster a tremendous amount of flexibility.

Writing HTML Documents

GENERAL HTML DESIGN PRINCIPLES

GOOD CODING STYLE

I f you've gone through the previous chapter you should now know
enough to start gathering together your content (text and images) and
marking it up into Web pages. Web site development is always done locally. You can create HTML files with a wide variety of software, from simple
text editors to sophisticated HTML authoring environments. You open and
check the files with your favorite browser. It's an iterative process, rechecking
and making corrections until you get it right, and then uploading directories
and files from your desktop or portable PC to a Web server.

You can put information on the World Wide Web very quickly. In a day or
two, you can get up the core of a Web site that will establish a solid presence for
you or your organization on the Web. However, it's just as easy to create a sloppy
hypertext work as it is to create a neat one. This chapter discusses the principles
of writing good Web pages and points out some common mistakes to avoid.

The art and practice of Web publishing is rapidly growing and changing.
New technologies and techniques are introduced and spread quickly. Although
you can write a simple home page in a few hours, you can continually update
it: Web pages are living documents that grow and change as you do. This is
one reason that it can be so important to observe a few principles of good design. Constructing a personal home page, in particular, is an act of creative ex-
pression in a brand new medium. It is like setting up your booth in cyberspace
to provide information, goods, and services, and to define who you are to the
Global Electronic Village.

GENERAL HTML DESIGN PRINCIPLES

Another reason good design is so important with Web applications is that you have no control over the context from which people will establish links to pages in your Web site. Think of your Web site as a house in cyberspace; the door is always open. Each HTML page is a room in this house. Most people will enter via your home page—the front door. A good home page welcomes its visitors and lets them know where they are and what interesting resources are inside. The browsers' navigation controls let readers exit the way they came in; still, it's nice when the home page provides suggestions and links to other places to visit in cyberspace.

Not everybody will enter your Web site through its home page. Some people will come in through the windows of other rooms in your cyberspace house. There are a number of automated programs that continually explore the Web. These programs—variously called robots, spiders, worms, or Webwalkers— link from one Web server to another, building databases of titles, headings, and URLs as they go. There are many Web sites from which you can search these databases (check the "Internet Search" item under Netscape Navigator's Directory menu). For example, you could search for all Web pages that have the word "fractal" in their titles and the result would be a dynamically gener- ated page of links. Such links are independent of the structure intended by the authors of those pages. The point is that readers will find ways you didn't an- ticipate to enter your hypertext work. Help these people out: At a minimum, provide a link back to your home page from every other page you put on the Web. Don't leave lost readers feeling more lost than when they entered.

GOOD READERS MAKE GOOD WRITERS

Hypertext works on the Web are living, growing structures. The best Web sites give you the feeling of visiting a real place occupied and maintained by an in- teresting community of people. Keep this in mind, and with a little prepara- tion, practice, and planning, your pages can grow and evolve as part of the World Wide Web.

The best preparation for writing HTML documents for the Web is reading Web HTML documents. Get a feel for what other authors have put on the Web and the approaches they've taken in organizing and formatting their work. Currently, somewhere around two-thirds of all people surfing the Web are using Netscape Navigator, and many Web pages are designed specifically for that browser and the expanded set of HTML elements it accepts. If you don't have Netscape Navigator, I highly recommend that you get it. Information on obtaining Netscape Navigator is available at http://www.netscape.com/.

Get some other browsers as well. NCSA Mosaic and CERN's Arena browser are also important standards. Microsoft's Internet Explorer (www.microsoft.com), as well as America Online and CompuServe's browsers are handy for checking your Web pages.

Most browsers come set to load a default home page—usually a home page of the manufacturing company or organization. This is a good place to start your study of Web pages. Another good starting place is one (or more) of the many search engines now on the Web. Almost all have a "What's New" and/or a "What's Cool" page of links, updated daily. One of the most popular is Yahoo (at www.yahoo.com), with its excellent subject-oriented catalog. Among the other leaders in the fairly crowded search engine field are AltaVista (www.altavista.com), Lycos (www.lycos.com), and Excite (www.excite.com). They each have a different flavor; try them all.

Most graphical Web browsers allow you to view and save any page on the Web in its original form (in computer terms, the "source code") as an HTML file. It is then a simple matter to open that file in a text editor to see how the author used HTML to create the page seen in the browser's window. (Depending on your browser, you may have to set an option or preference to use your favorite text editor instead of the default viewer provided.) As practice in writing HTML documents, edit these files and change the tags. Select the Open Local choice under your browser's File menu to view the edited pages and see your changes. After looking at a number of HTML documents and playing with the different elements of HTML, you should start to have an idea of what you can do with your own applications. But before you start, it's good to review a few principles that apply to computer projects in general but have special application to writing HTML documents for the World Wide Web.

KEEP IT SIMPLE

The first principle is to keep it simple. Emphasize content over form. You have little control over the typography and layout your document will have when viewed by the various browsers readers have at their disposal. Keep your pages as simple as possible and they will look good everywhere. Spend your time making the content—the information you want to convey to the reader—clear and compelling. Your pages will grow and change over time. It's better to start simply and have the evolving content drive the design of the page than to have an over-designed page constrain the evolving content. If the typography of a document must be exact, consider providing alternative versions on your Web server in formats that readers can download and display offline—a Microsoft Word document in RTF (rich text format) or an Adobe PostScript or Acrobat file, for example.

Make sure the images on your Web page are informative. A small picture of you on your home page provides readers with information that words alone cannot convey. A picture of your computer, unless you've done something extraordinary by transforming it into a work of art, does not. Avoid putting up Web pages that emulate automated teller machines with large graphical buttons for links. They take too long to load and are harder to maintain. Instead use an HTML list or table element to organize any set of links; doing so creates a more consistent style between Web sites. You can use small icons to decorate the page, adding personality and visual clues for navigation.

A Web page should not look like a magazine cover, either. Readers will choose to link to your page because they are browsing related information. A Web page does not have to depend as much on eye-grabbing graphics and promotion to reach readers as do magazines sitting on a shelf. I don't mean to imply that you shouldn't try to create "cool" Web pages. Yes, by all means, do so. This is a new medium and pushing its design limits is a big part of the fun, and a great way to learn.

The Internet—and the Web in particular—is growing so fast that many Internet experts are worried that bandwidth (essentially the network's capacity to handle traffic) is starting to get scarce. So it's considered polite practice (good "netiquette") to keep to a minimum the amount of data you're asking others to move across their networks on your behalf. Large graphic elements and long sound samples eat up bandwidth. Such objects should not be forced on readers without their informed consent. One approach commonly found on the Web is to use a small version of a graphic, often called a thumbnail, as a link to a larger version. For example, this bit of HTML

```
Click <A HREF="Large_AE.GIF"> Albert
<IMG SRC="Small_AE.GIF" ALT="Einstein" ALIGN=middle></A>
to see a large (90K bytes) picture of the scientist.
```

creates the display shown in Figure 4.1.

The relative URL addressing (using a partial URL to refer to the location of a file relative to the URL of the current page) used in the HTML for Figure 4.1 requires that the two image files referenced in the HTML anchors— Large_AE.GIF and Small_AE.GIF—must be in the same directory as the Web page containing the links. The name Albert and the small image are together the anchor of a link to the larger image file, Large_AE.GIF. Clicking on either one will fetch the larger file and pass it to a helper application (or to your browser itself if you are using it as an image viewer) to display it in a separate window as an external image. By telling readers in the text how large the image file is, you provide them with the information they need to estimate how long

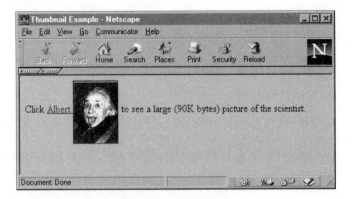

Figure 4.1: Using a thumbnail to access a larger picture

it will take to download the image. Note the use of the ALT attribute in the IMG tag to direct nongraphical browsers to display the text "Click Albert Einstein to see a large (90K bytes) picture of the scientist."

LINK UP!

Above all, use the power of hypertext to clarify your information. Hypertext allows you to serve content to your readers in simple chunks; the hypertext structure reveals additional relationships in the information and allows your readers to choose a level of complexity suitable to their own needs. You can't assume that all your readers are at the same level of comprehension. As a statistician friend of mine is fond of saying, "Only half of the people are smarter than average."

GOOD WORK IS NEVER DONE

Only after you make your information available on the Web will you begin to understand what it was you wanted in the first place. You should expect to frequently update and revise much of the work you put on the Web. As you add to and expand the information on a page, you'll have the opportunity to work with its structure, improve its looks, and replace any dead URLs—links to Web pages or servers that no longer exist. You'll also have the benefit of feedback from other people who have read your work. It's a good idea—in fact it's an accepted Web convention—to include your signature and e-mail address on your work. And feel free to ask your readers for comments.

A decade ago, a speaker at a computer language conference I attended formulated this principle into the following law, which he named after himself. Here is Biddlestone's Law:

The requirements of any system are a function of the experience gained installing that system for the user.

One thing this implies is that whatever information you have, just go ahead and mark it up into a Web page. Don't spend a lot of time planning out the design: Just take the content, do a simple markup, check it out with your favorite browser, make whatever adjustments your need, and upload it to your server. Now you can really look at it, and test the links to explore how your page fits in the context of the Web site and the Web at large. Many pages on the World Wide Web are "Under construction" or "Work in progress." You should not be ashamed to place unfinished information on your Web pages, as long as you inform your readers of the situation.

THE MOST IMPORTANT RULE IN HTML
Have fun :-)

GOOD CODING STYLE

As the Web continues to grow, it becomes more important to write HTML that conforms to certain guidelines and styles. Right now there are dozens of different Web browsers available (counting all the available versions). The major on-line services provide Web browsers as part of their offerings and current releases of the most popular operating systems (UNIX, Microsoft Windows 95, Macintosh System 7.5, and OS/2 Warp) have built-in Internet connectivity. The growth of the Web user community shows no sign of slowing. It's critical to write HTML that will look good on any client, now and in the future, not just on Netscape, Explorer, and the current generation of browsers.

This section offers some guidelines about the dos and dont's of writing good HTML documents: pages that are easy to maintain and produce presentable results on any browser. Bear in mind that there's no authority that dictates what is and what isn't good HTML style. These guidelines reflect the lessons learned by many Web authors—that is, the many authors who share their experiences using newsgroups and mailing lists. Check Appendix C for a list of these resources and make it a practice to visit them regularly. The Web is still in its adolescence and no one knows what it will grow into.

COMMON CONVENTIONS

Although most browsers are very forgiving of how you code — neither tags nor attributes are case sensitive — servers, especially UNIX servers, are completely unforgiving when it comes to filenames. For example, if you refer to a image in your HTML source code like this:

```
<IMG SRC="earth.gif">
```

but your file is named Earth.GIF on your server, your browser will not be able to find the file and you will see the symbol for a broken image when you access that page. Moreover, some FTP programs automatically make your filenames lowercase as they transfer the files to the server. Therefore, it's best to keep all your filenames, including HREFs and SRCs, in lowercase, both in your code and on your system.

It is a good idea to sign and date all pages you put on the Web so that your readers can form some impression of the authority of the page—how recent it is and how reliable the source of the information is. On a home page or any page that serves as an introduction to a hypertext work, your signature should include your full name and e-mail address so readers can send you comments on your work. You can make a link from your name back to your personal home page. On less important pages of the work, your signature can just be your initials linked back to the authorship information on the home page. When developing a new Web site, it's a good idea to put the URL of each page at the bottom so that printed versions of the pages are readily identifiable. Later, when the pages are more stable, you can comment out the identifying URL.

Remember that your documents are going on a *World Wide* Web, so, when writing dates, use a long format with the name of the month spelled out or abbreviated — in other words, July 4, 1997, or 4-Jul-97. Formats such as 7/4/97 can be ambiguous in some cultures. The same holds true for monetary amounts. Other countries such as Canada and Australia use the dollar sign. Make it clear which currency you mean by writing US$19.95 or $19.95 USD, for example, instead of just $19.95.

COMMON MISTAKES

Probably the most prevalent kind of error in HTML is the misuse of paragraph breaks. In part, this comes from working so much with one browser that you begin to accept its handling of white space as common. It also comes from the syntax change from an empty paragraph tag in HTML2 to a container in HTML 3.2. Because HTML 3.2 is backwards compatible with HTML2, you can use either form of the tag. In either case, avoid the temptation to adjust the spacing of

page elements by placing extra paragraph tags where none are necessary—
around headings, lists, blockquotes, or address blocks, for example.

Trust the readers' browsers and forget about making such "adjustments" to
the layout. You'll be better off. Because it's cleaner, I recommend using the
HTML 3.2 container form of the paragraph element, especially when including an attribute. For example, use

```
<H3 ALIGN=center>WWW Menu Specials</H3>
<P ALIGN=center>
Hong Kong Flu<BR>
Beijing Duck<BR>
Turkish Taffy<BR>
French Farce
</P>
```

to create the centered menu effect of Figure 4.2.

Figure 4.2: A centered menu

Another common error is not properly closing an HTML element. With
container tags, don't forget the closing tag. With character entities, this means
forgetting the trailing semicolon or having spaces separate the character entity
from the rest of the text. You should write a level 2 heading introducing your
professional experience without space as:

```
<H2>R&eacute;sum&eacute;</H2>
```

Don't take a shortcut and write

```
<H2>Resume</H2>
```

which is just encouragement to continue. It's also easy to forget that the ampersand is the escape character. Make sure you write AT&T and not
AT&T. Forgetting one of the double quote marks that should enclose a URL is

also a common error. Some browsers don't care if a URL is in quotes, but many do, and most will have a problem if one quotation mark is there and the other isn't. To be absolutely correct, you should place all attribute values within quotes. It has become a general practice, however, to omit the quotes if the attribute value is a simple number or constant, as in this image tag:

```
<IMG SRC="images/boop.gif" ALIGN=top BORDER=2>
```

With tag elements, errors can occur when the closing right angle bracket (>) is missing. Many browsers will properly render strings that contain a single right angle bracket with no matching left bracket (<) as if that character were part of the text. For example,

```
&lt;This is not a tag>
```

will be displayed as:

```
<This is not a tag>
```

However, it is recommended that you use the character entity &gt for the right angle bracket

```
&lt;This is not a tag&gt;
```

because if there are any other tag errors in the document, having an extra > around will only make matters worse.

With containers, forgetting the slash (/) that begins the ending element will cause errors, as will having spaces on either side of the slash. Browsers are very forgiving. In most cases, they will ignore an incorrect ending tag and continue applying whatever tag was in effect to the following text, possibly to the end of the page.

You should nest tags with care. As a general rule, tags that define styles should be inside of tags that create structure. Without enumerating all the possible combinations, here are a few guidelines.

Avoid nesting other tags inside of a heading. The exceptions to this rule are the line break tag, <BR>, image tags, and anchors marking the heading as a hypertext link. Headings should never contain any tags that imply paragraph breaks. This includes other headings, paragraph tags, horizontal rules, list structures, blockquotes, addresses, tables, and preformatted style tags. If you want to create a multiple-line heading, use the line break tag <BR>. Likewise, headings should never be used inside tags other than <FORM></FORM>, <TABLE></TABLE>, and <DL></DL>, and, of course, the <BODY></BODY> and <HTML></HTML> tags that define the document. Enclosing headings within any other tags doesn't make sense, and the results are unpredictable.

You shouldn't use style tags to change the rendering of a heading except when you want to affect a small part of the heading text, for example:

```
<H3>Some <STRONG>Important</STRONG> phone numbers</H3>
```

Instead of enclosing the whole sentence in the <STRONG> tags you would be better off changing the heading setting from <H3> to <H2>.

You can use image tags inside of a heading to provide a graphic aligned to the heading text. The key to understanding the behavior of inline images in a heading, or anywhere on a page, for that matter, is in the word "inline." That is, an image is just like a big fat character in a line of text. It moves and word-wraps with the text. There are no implied paragraph breaks, line breaks, or even word breaks separating the image from the text unless you explicitly supply them with paragraph tags, line break, tags, or spaces.

If you want to create the effect of a button bar, as in Figure 4.3, you must specify the image tags defining the buttons without spaces between the tags:

```
<A HREF="top.html"><IMG SRC="top.gif" BORDER=0 ALT="[TOP]"></A>
<A HREF="page3.html"><IMG SRC="prev.gif" BORDER=0 ALT="[PREV]"></A>
<A HREF="page5.html"><IMG SRC="next.gif" BORDER=0 ALT="[NEXT]"></A>
```

Placing the image tags one per line in your HTML source:

```
<A HREF="top.html"><IMG SRC="top.gif" BORDER=0 ALT="[TOP]"></A>
<A HREF="page3.html"><IMG SRC="prev.gif" BORDER=0 ALT="[PREV]"></A>
<A HREF="page5.html"><IMG SRC="next.gif" BORDER=0 ALT="[NEXT]"></A>
```

may look neater, especially if each image is enclosed within an anchor tag, but the browser will interpret the carriage returns as word breaks and insert spaces between the buttons.

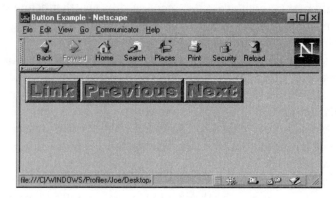

Figure 4.3: A clean button example

Most of the time you can write HTML without worrying about how you lay out your tags and content, but as you see, you have to be a little more careful with anchors. Many authors unwittingly create anchors with "tails." For example, this code may look reasonable:

```
<H2>Netscape Navigator
<A HREF="http://www.netscape.com/">
<IMG SRC="NN_logo.gif">
</A>
</H2>
```

but, as shown in Figure 4.4, the blue underscoring marking the anchor extends one space beyond the image. It comes from the carriage return in the HTML text after the image tag but before the close of the anchor with </A>. Most browsers will remove a leading blank following an actual or implied paragraph break, but the trailing word break that is put in place of the carriage return is kept as part of the anchor.

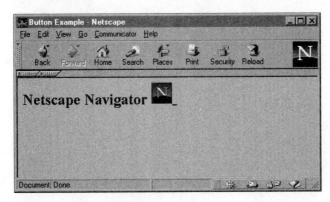

Figure 4.4: Example of the "tail" problem

It would have been better to write the HTML:

```
<H2>Netscape Navigator
<A HREF="http://www.netscape.com/"><IMG SRC="NN_logo.gif"></A>
</H2>
```

One last point with regard to tags is that, if you are copying elements from other pages on the Web, avoid using any obsolete elements (tags that were in earlier versions of HTML but are now superseded by other HTML 3.2 elements). These obsolete elements include <PLAINTEXT></PLAINTEXT>, <XMP></XMP>, <LISTING></LISTING>, <HP></HP>, and <COMMENT></COMMENT>. The first three should be replaced with the preformatted tags <PRE></PRE>; <HP></HP> (highlighted phrase) should be replaced with appropriate style tags; and <COMMENT></COMMENT> should be replaced with SGML comments, which are enclosed by the strings <!-- and -->.

HTML 3.2 browsers accept most HTML2 tags. There are a few tags, however, that have fallen out of use. They are not recommended for use in new documents and few browsers will render them distinctively. These include the list forms, <DIR></DIR> and <MENU></MENU>, some style tags, such as <CODE></CODE> and <KBD></KBD>.

URL errors are a different matter. A URL error won't affect the rendering of the page in a browser's display, but a badly composed URL will be incorrectly interpreted and you'll get an unknown server error or a file not found error. Relative URLs have strong advantages: They're shorter and they make a collection of documents portable. However, you should use relative URLs with care, because the URL does not contain all the information necessary to construct the link. The browser takes the missing server and path information from the URL of the document that contains the link. What is always safe is a relative reference to a file in the same directory as the current page. Files in a subdirectory can be safely referenced by using slash—a forward slash (/), not the backslash (\) used in DOS path names—as in:

```
our clerk, <A HREF="accounting/Cratchet.html">Bob Cratchet</A>
```

Refer to the parent directory of the directory containing the current page by using two dots (..). However, this may not work with a parent directory of a parent directory, as in:

```
<A HREF="../../officers/Scrooge.html">my boss</A>
```

A single dot refers to the current directory, thus,

```
<A HREF="./accounting/Cratchet.html">Bob Cratchet</A>
```

is the same as:

```
<A HREF="accounting/Cratchet.html">Bob Cratchet</A>
```

A URL beginning with a single slash (/) is the entire path, including the name of the drive, to the file:

```
<A HREF="/staff/accounting/Cratchet.html">Bob Cratchet</A>
```

Most browsers let you set the default home page URL. If you are not permanently connected to the Internet, it's a good idea to set this to a file on your own machine using the "file:" URL method. On a Windows system, for example, a URL pointing to the index file in the local copy of your Web site on your C drive might look something like this:

```
file:///C:/WINDOWS/WWW/HTML/INDEX.HTM
```

Notice the three forward slashes after "file:". Because this a local file, there is no server name or IP number after the first two slashes. The third slash is necessary to show that the path begins at the root. The hard drive designation "C:" is considered a subdirectory of the root. The rest of the URL must point to an actual file because there is no server running to establish a default.

Note: Netscape Navigator and some other browsers will provide an FTP-style directory listing if the URL ends in a directory name. This feature is useful for development and maintenance. This feature is also the default action of some servers if no file with the proper default name (index.html) is found, so it's a good idea to have a file with the default name in your Web site. Even if you never link to it, it prevents readers from browsing your directories.

Finally, be aware of the different file naming conventions. DOS, Windows 3.1, and Windows NT have the most restrictive scheme: up to eight characters for the filename plus a three-character extension. Most Web servers are UNIX based, where filenames can be up to 255 characters and contain any character except the forward slash used to separate directories. Macintosh and Windows 95 filenames can be up to 31 characters in length, cannot contain a colon (:), and are not case sensitive. Remember that UNIX filenames are sensitive to case, so a link that works locally on your Macintosh or your Windows system may not be valid when the files are moved to a UNIX server because of capitalization errors.

The best advice is not to mix cases in your file and directory names, keep them eight characters or fewer in length (or at least unique within the first eight characters), and don't use any characters other than letters, numbers, the period (.) and the underscore (_). Although other characters will probably not cause problems, if you must include them, it's a good idea to code them in hexadecimal notation using the percent character (%) followed by two hexadecimal digits. For example, this link to the file, "r&d rept.txt"

```
<A HREF="r%26d%20 - rept.txt">Research and Development</A>
```

uses the sequence "%26" for the ampersand and "%20" for the space character. Check the back of your modem manual; there's probably an ASCII reference chart there that you can use to look up the hexadecimal equivalents for special characters. Naturally, you can find it on line; the Best Business System site at www.bbsinc.com/symbol.html is one source.

These are only some of the more common sources of error. Developing a good HTML style is a matter of practice, studying the work of others, and finally, good common sense.

Planning a
Web Site

VISUALIZING THE SITE

FINDING THE RIGHT MODELS

PAGE LAYOUT AND DESIGN

SITE SECURITY

TEAM WORK

Chapter
5

Any time you spend designing your Web site is time well spent. You get a firmer grasp of the various individual elements that are involved: the necessary text, graphics, and links. In addition, you have an opportunity to create the overall "look-and-feel" of the site. Any Web site—in fact any Web page—can benefit from a unified style, whether you are creating it for a client or for yourself.

As mentioned, Web pages are living, changing documents. In the planning stage, you can enhance this viability, and make it easier on yourself, if you plan for growth. Although this could mean developing a multistage implementation plan, it can also simply mean maintaining good coding habits and designing your pages carefully.

Playing the "What if..." game—that is, imagining how your pages might need to evolve—lets you give your site room for expansion and helps it avoid that "tacked on at the last minute" look. Try asking yourself a few questions like these:

- ▶ What if we want to add a chat room to the site? How would users get in and out of it?

- ▶ What if we want to increase the feedback from the site? How can we get the users involved?

- ▶ What if we want to highlight an upcoming event? How could we integrate that into the home page without detracting from the existing components.

Throughout this chapter, you'll learn various methods for preparing to build your Web site. One good strategy is to remember that new technologies can still benefit from old dictums. "Form follows function" is still an excellent rule to follow when designing a Web page from scratch. Three key questions help you define which form to follow:

- ▶ **What's your message?** Describe the idea for your Web site in one sentence—for example, "This Web site is the home of the stock research firm, Undiscovered Equities."

- ▶ **Who's your audience?** Determining your primary target will help you define the structure of your Web site. Ask yourself whether you expect your visitors to spend a lot of time at your site, or just download the vital information and move on.

- ▶ **What's your budget?** Here "budget" refers to three things. First, it means the time that you can devote to creating the site. If you're doing it for yourself, you can count on your own part-time, long-term involvement; if, however, you are building the site for a client who wants to be online in two weeks with full interactive programming, your budget is a lot tighter. Second, budget can refer to the physical storage space a particular Web site will take, if your site is hosted on a remote system. Often, you can store only 15 to 25 megabytes of information without incurring additional charges. Third, budget can mean "How much can we spend." Designing a cutting-edge Web site with up-to-the-minute revisions for a client who says the sky's the limit is far easier, but also far more unlikely.

Asking yourself these three questions, and understanding the limits you're under, will help you to build a more efficient site.

VISUALIZING THE SITE

When you think about your upcoming site, what do you see? Visualizing your Web site allows you not only to imagine its look and feel, but also its purpose on the Web.

One of the primary differences between the Internet and the World Wide Web is use of graphics on the Web. Often, when first trying to envision a Web site, designers get stuck on the look of it. Remember that the Web is content driven: People enter **Alzheimer's** as the search engine criteria, not "cool animated graphics on Alzheimer's." Try to imagine how content will be sought out and how best to convey it, and focus on the completeness and accessibility of that information.

Ask yourself what kind of visitors your site will draw? Will they be savvy net surfers who can figure out the most arcane navigational system or will they be first-time newbies requiring some straight-forward hand-holding? This parallels the question of how users will approach your site. Will they come through the front door or through another link to some other part of your Web site? This chapter will help prepare you to handle the possibilities.

Finally, what overall impression do you want your site to convey? Is it a fun, raucous party or is it a site for serious inquiry with many levels of in-depth knowledge. Often, Web designers err on the side of jazzed-up business when a few well-chosen images work better. Again, it all comes down to content.

APPROACHES TO WRITING WEB PAGES

The way you approach creating a Web site for the World Wide Web depends on what kind of information you want to serve and how much of it is already in digital form. Broadly speaking, there are two approaches: top-down and bottom-up. If you are starting a work from scratch and there is little or no information available in digital form, work from the top down by building your home page first. If there is already a lot of information that needs organizing, or if there's an existing work to be converted to hypertext, start from the bottom, and work your way up. Of course, not all hypertext applications fall easily into one of these two categories. Most real-world projects are a combination of new work and existing material. This is especially true in organizations that already make use of electronically distributed information.

A third approach you might find useful is stealing. Well, borrowing, anyway. If you find something you like, figure out how the author did it and copy it. You may prefer to think of this as borrowing ideas; if so, you should pay back the ideas with interest. Please, only copy the structure and the hypertext links to other, external Web sites, not the content from somebody else's Web page. You don't want a Web site that's a "look and feel" clone of someone else's either, so don't copy background patterns or distinctive icons. Avoid copying anything from pages that have explicit copyright or trademark statements. When in doubt, ask for permission. And give credit where it's due.

Once you've decided on your approach and have put up a few pages to test out your design ideas, take some time to plan the entire Web site. Even a Web site centered on a personal home page can quickly grow to encompass three or four dozen files. Mapping the connection between conceptual areas of a Web site and the physical layout of directories and files can be critical to the site's maintenance and growth. Figure out which pages will reside at the root of the Web site and which will be in subdirectories. It's a good idea to put images in their own subdirectories. Images that are used across several pages should be in a subdirectory at the root. The same applies to sounds, graphics, and other multimedia files.

Many Web servers use a default filename such as index.html for the home page of a Web site, or Web site subdirectory if none is provided in a URL. Take advantage of this default to shorten the URLs of the main entry points into your Web site. For example, my Web site is on my current Internet service provider's system under my userid, laronson. My file, index.html, is a simple annotated listing with links to the principal pages, with my personal home page, homepage.html, listed first. On my business card, I list my URL as:

```
http://www.interport.net/~laronson/
```

Consider also placing a file at the root and in each subdirectory of the Web site with a file name such as index.txt. Use this file as a database of information about the Web site or subdirectory. Include the file name and title of each Web page, the author(s) of the page, creation and update dates, lists of the images used on the page, and whatever else you and others might need to maintain that Web site. The advantage of using a text file is that you can maintain the indexes to the Web site with the same editor you use to write the Web pages.

IDENTIFYING ENTRANCE POINTS

The truth is that any page on your Web site is a potential entrance point. This openness stems from search engine "spiders," which go out on the Web and index sites based on content. Although you can and should specify keywords for your site by using the META tag described in Chapter 3, you don't really have any control over where and how your Web site will be referenced elsewhere on the Web. What you can do, however, is recognize the potential of this exposure and design for it.

Suppose you are building a site that publishes reviews of consumer electronics, and a review of a particular scanner is now in the archives section of your site. Someone who is thinking about buying a scanner might visit a search engine such as AltaVista and, after entering **scanner**, get the following search engine results:

▶ *Crest point extraction on a skull (3D **scanner** data)*—Perspective views showing two positions of the skull, where the gray level corresponds to the number. *www-syntim.inria.fr/syntim/recherche/richard/crests.htm*

▶ *Scanner II*—Alan Rath's **Scanner** II with its probing eye is on display at the Contemporary Arts Museum. *http://www.chron.com/content/interactive/special/finearts/art/rath2.html*

▶ *GadgetBoy*—Reviews with attitude in all consumer electronic categories, including audio/video equipment, **scanner**s, etc. *http://www.gadgetboy .com/gbpast/CES/*

▸ *PDF 120 Portable Data File CCD* **Scanner**—The Economical Way to Bring the Benefits of PDF417 Symbology to Your Office. The PDF417 "portable data file" is... *http://www.symbol.com/ST000090.HTMStoryboarding Typical Paths*

...and many others. Users who click on the GadgetBoy site will finds themselves in middle of a review published last year on the latest scanners previewed at the Consumer Electronic Show. Providing a link back to the main page allows someone who "stumbled" into your site to see it from the beginning and get a complete grasp of what you are trying to achieve. Any additional navigational aids should be keep content specific and nongeneric. Stay away from "Next" and "Back" buttons, which don't convey any real information about where the links will lead. In this case, links to "Main," "More Reviews," and "Links to Manufacturers" would be appropriate.

In extremely long pages, consider including same page links that take the viewer to the top and/or bottom of the page—where the navigational links are located. Use the HREF=#NAME attribute of the anchor tag to achieve this effect, as here:

```
<HTML>
<HEAD>
<TITLE>JoeBob's Catalog of Catalan Cuisine</TITLE>
</HEAD>
<BODY>
<H1 NAME="TOP">Welcome to JoeBob's Catalog of Catalan Cuisine</H1>
<P>Following are a collection of my mother's Catalan recipes...
...
...
<A HREF="#TOP">Top</A>
</BODY>
</HTML>
```

FINDING THE RIGHT MODELS

Web sites exist in three separate realms:

▸ **Content** What the site actually has to say

▸ **Intent** What the site hopes to accomplish.

▸ **Structure** What the user's experience is of the site

It is best to clarify all three early and often. A successful Web design most often combines them so that they are mutually supportive.

A purpose statement can help you design the Web site to be consistent with all your client's needs, even if you are your own client. A purpose statement should include the overall goal and the intended audience. For example, a site developed by a publisher specializing in information on managed health care could have the purpose statement, "To market newsletter subscriptions and special reports to physicians and health care industry professionals." From this statement, you can glean the intent (to sell), the content (market-specific newsletters and reports), and the audience (doctors and managed care industry leaders). Such information should influence the look-and-feel of the site (a more professional as opposed to a mass market approach) and give clues about how the site might break down structurally (individual pages for each of the newsletters and the reports as well as a subscription order form).

Metaphors in Web design are powerful tools that make new technology easier to understand and provide a unifying look and feel. Let's say a publisher wants to market children's, preteen, and teenage books on the Web. Rather than just listing the company name and its separate divisions, the Web site can use the metaphor of an amusement park. Now, the young romance readers can visit the "Tunnel of Love," the ghost story aficionados can go to the "Haunted House," and the younger children can check out "Toon Town." The site can provide the same content within an overall fun, inventive setting.

CHOOSING A NAVIGATIONAL MODEL

How people navigate to your site is crucial. Depending on the design of the site, the user can investigate it in many ways, without any overt control by the designer. How a user interacts with a site contributes greatly to the site's overall effectiveness and the user's impression of it.

The Linear Model The most basic navigational model is a linear one. The Web site starts with a home page and then, instead of providing links to various pages throughout the Web site, offers one navigational option: "Next Page." A linear Web site is basically an online multimedia book with one page following another in a booklike fashion. Pages after the first one might add a "Previous Page" button to take viewers to the page they had just encountered. Figure 5.1 illustrates the concept.

Figure 5.1: Linear Web site model

The linear model is a very rigid structure that tightly controls the user's impression of the Web site. Although this approach might be effective in a slide-show presentation for a captive audience, it can potentially be extremely frustrating to the viewer. If you have ever been stuck following a voice mail labyrinth where you must push button after button to search for your information, you have experienced an electronic linear structure. Keep in mind that this is often called "voice-mail hell."

The linear navigational method is only recommended for extremely short Web sites with a narrow purpose. Within a larger site, some designers use the linear model for their entrances and exits when they must lead the viewer through several screens to make their point. In such circumstances, it might be preferable to use the HTTP-EQUIV="Refresh" attribute of the META tag to achieve the slide show effect.

The Hierarchical Model   A slightly more sophisticated approach is the hierarchical navigational model. Here, you again start with a home page, but now you allow readers to branch to several pages, which in turn can take them to several other pages, and so on. See Figure 5.2 for a sample hierarchical model.

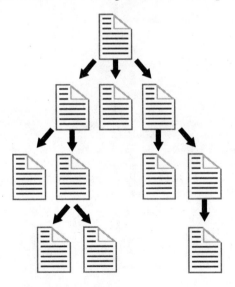

Figure 5.2: A hierarchical Web site model

It is considered good practice to include a link to the home page, an index page, or both on every page. This makes it easy for your visitors to orient themselves and lets you emphasize your primary message simply by having it on your home page.

As mentioned, you can include a linear navigational section as part of a larger site and meld the hierarchical and linear models for carefully defined areas. Just remember, after the linear scenario, to allow for further forward branching as well as a jump to the home page.

The Spoke-and-Hub Model   The next step up the evolutionary ladder is the spoke-and-hub navigational model. As the name implies, the home page is the center spot from which all the primary pages are accessible. This method is the most web-like of any of the navigational techniques.

Figure 5.3 shows a Web site based on the spoke-and-hub model. It illustrates an outline or storyboard for a bar that wants to promote its premium beers and liquors. From the central opening page containing basic contact information, you can follow your preferences: regular draught beers, hand-pumped beers, bottle beers, or liquors. Then the site incorporates some hierarchical elements to break down the larger categories of bottle beers on a per country basis and the liquor by type.

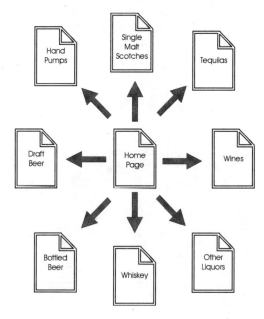

Figure 5.3: A spoke-and-hub Web site model

The only thing to be careful of when using the spoke-and-hub model is the possibility of the user getting lost in a large, complex site. The solution, once again, is to provide a link to the home page so that users can orient themselves and jump to the top if they want.

The Full Web Design The next extension of these navigational models is the full Web design. Here, once you enter the site's home page, you can get to any page. Furthermore, any page can take you to any other page. When you use this model, user's can get extremely disoriented, even in a moderately intricate site. Figure 5.4 illustrates the potential complexity of a full Web design.

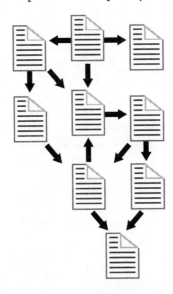

Figure 5.4: Full Web design navigational model

Don't discard the full Web model because of its complexity, however. Although providing a link to every page might (and probably should) be outside of the scope of the home page, it is perfectly acceptable for an index page where all key terms are hypertext links that enable you to jump to the specific page. Moreover, you can reference such an index page on the home page to maintain a clean look while providing high-end accessibility.

ESTABLISHING A CONSISTENT STYLE

There's a very good reason for establishing a consistent style, or base style, for your Web site. Although your browser remains a constant, there is no standard user interface from Web site to Web site. So, each time you visit a new site, you'll probably have to adjust to a whole new user interface. When creating a Web site, the best you can do is to provide a consistent interface for all the pages within the site.

There are many ways to give a site a uniform look and feel. You can and should reuse logos and fundamental graphics on separate pages. This unifies the site, and significantly cuts down on user download time because the graphics are reused from the client's cache rather than reloaded. Moreover, you can dynamically resize graphics through HTML code by using the HEIGHT and WIDTH attributes of the IMG tag, which provide for graphic variations with no additional download time, as you learned in Chapter 2.

The primary way to achieve a consistent interface, however, is to establish a consistent style, or template, to be used across the board. When you do so, your palette, background, and overall page design remain the same, with minor variations, for every page. Using a Web page template makes it easy for first-time visitors to quickly adapt to your site. It also cuts down tremendously on both the decisions you have to make and your graphics work load. Figure 5.5 illustrates how a template is used.

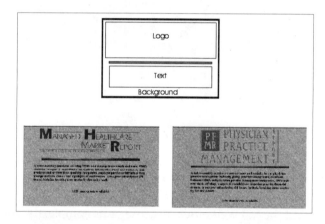

Figure 5.5: A template in use

CREATING THE RIGHT LOOK

One of the tools you can use to determine the right look for your Web site is the purpose statement. The more clearly defined the goal, the easier it is to achieve. You can measure the appropriateness of any given design against the intent of the site and the profile of the anticipated audience.

When developing a new Web site, I first look at a client's existing marketing material, if any. This includes catalogs, brochures, press releases, signs, stationery, and advertisements. This can provide good source material, and can also give you a feel for what has worked for the client in the past. Next, I conduct a survey of the client's current market base or, if the Web site will be used to promote a new service or product, their hoped-for audience. The same process holds true for nonprofit organizations, such as schools, and for-profit companies. Determine who you are trying to reach and what you are trying to tell them.

Once you have determined the general appropriate style for your audience, the next decisions are all a balancing act.

- ▶ Balance the content with the download time. Filling a page with large graphics dramatically increases the downloading time. The primary question to ask yourself is, "Is it worth waiting for?"

- ▶ Balance the text and the graphic elements. Although there are extremes in both areas—all-text and all-graphics sites—most sites combine the two elements. Discretely placed graphics can break up and illuminate a site heavy with text; too many graphics can overshadow the content and keep user's from getting to the core of the matter.

- ▶ Balance the foreground and the background elements. HTML lets you use various background colors or images, over which the text can flow. Be careful to use contrasting colors for the text and various link states so that everything is legible. If you use a multicolored background image, make sure the text color stands out against the entire range of colors.

PAGE LAYOUT AND DESIGN

The best Web design is the one that stays true to your purpose, conveys your message, and relates to your audience. A text-only site aimed at cancer researchers that describes the latest vitamin-oriented treatment can be just as successful as a graphics-intensive Generation X site like that of Wired magazine. There are five general types of page layout styles: all text, mixed text and graphics, graphic-centric, column based, and frames based.

ALL-TEXT LAYOUT

All-text page layouts have their roots in the earliest Internet sites. Many sites featuring straight documentation employ this style. The text can be formatted fairly extensively using HTML text and paragraph-level commands such as the various heading sizes (<H1> to <H6>) and <BLOCKQUOTE>. You can break up the text with bulleted and numbered lists (use the unordered <UL> and ordered lists <OL> tags, respectively). You can use the horizontal rule, <HR>, to separate sections of the document. Navigational links rely on the default browser style to stand out (usually blue and underlined). Figure 5.6 shows an example all-text site.

One of the major advantages of all-text sites is access time. By far, this page layout displays the fastest on the client machine. Because no additional images, applets, or other elements have to be downloaded (that is, transferred from the host system to the client computer), the text renders as fast as it can be read.

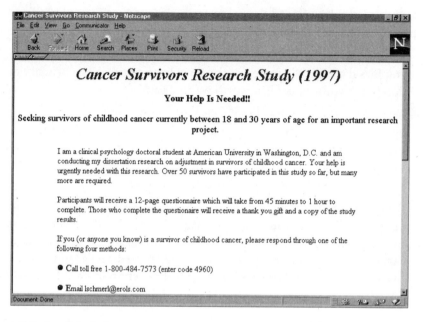

Figure 5.6: An all-text site

MIXED TEXT AND GRAPHICS LAYOUT

The HTTP protocol and the Web allowed you to mix color graphics and text on a single page. In fact, inline graphics are responsible for the popularity of the Web. There are no shortage of mixed text and graphic page layouts on the Web. Figure 5.7 gives one example.

Most mixed text and graphic layouts involve several blocks of text wrapped around small graphics. White space is used liberally to isolate the text/graphic groupings. The default bullets and horizontal rules supplied by HTML commands can be replaced by small images, usually in GIF format. There is a small cottage industry in Web clip art, including navigational graphics, buttons, bullets, and rules. A personal favorite is PixelSight (www.pixelsight.com), which allows you to create personalized imagery through a series of "Manglers." Appendix C includes a list of other graphic elements.

GRAPHIC-CENTRIC LAYOUT

The opposite of all-text sites are graphic-centric ones. Although these sites are not devoid of text, they make imagery paramount. They rely heavily on the imagemap technique-defining different areas of the same picture as separate hyperlinks.

In the example in Figure 5.8, from www.drinkgoodstuff.com, each of the bottle caps links to another page in the site. The marble backdrop is a separate file used

Figure 5.7: A mixed graphic and text site

as a background image in the BODY tag. The match book and bottle caps are another graphic file—a GIF with the transparency turned on, allowing the individual elements to "float" on top of the background. The HTML code looks like this:

```
<BODY BACKGROUND="marble.jpg">
<IMG SRC="dbapic.gif">
```

The background extends as far as necessary to include all elements, unifying the page.

The obvious drawback to a graphic-centric approach is the increased time it takes for pages to download. Chapter 6 discusses techniques for decreasing the download time. But even if you compress the files, you must balance the impact of design with time spent accessing it. In other words, "Is it worth the wait?"

COLUMN-BASED LAYOUT

The column-based layout is essentially a subtype of the mixed text and graphic layout. Graphic designers have influenced the design of Web pages, but it was difficult to apply print-oriented design techniques until the TABLE element was included in HTML 3.2 (this element is covered in detail in Chapter 7). This tag allows you to organize your pages into column-based layouts like the one shown in Figure 5.9.

Figure 5.8: A graphic-centric site

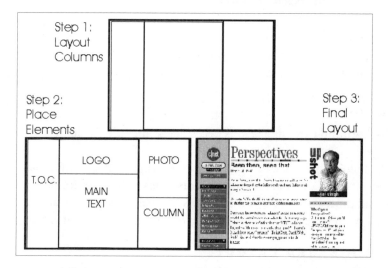

Figure 5.9: A column to table illustration

The column-based design provides a tidy solution to the vexing problem of Web page navigation. Placing the links to other pages in the Web site at the bottom of the page often requires the user to scroll down to see them; novices might not know they're there if they are not immediately visible. Putting them at the top of the page gives them too much emphasis and encourages visitors to jump immediately without fully viewing the page. Column-based layouts let you put the navigational buttons to one side where they are always accessible, but don't distract from the main point of the text. Figure 5.10 shows an example of this technique. Notice that the navigational buttons on the left are in one column, the text under "Perspectives" is in a second column, and the text under the photo is in a third column.

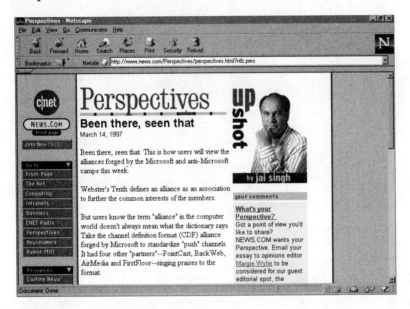

Figure 5.10: A table navigation example

FRAME-BASED LAYOUT

The frame-based design is a variation on the column-based layout. Unlike the other layouts, frame-based layout doesn't work in any media other than the Web. This is because each separate rectangular frame element is separately scrollable and independent of every page element.

Frames, an HTML element described in Chapter 8, allow a link in one section to change the display in another. The navigation technique discussed in the section on column-based layout is used extensively in the frame-based design, but with a hyperlink twist. Click on any of the navigational buttons and only the frame with the content changes. In the example in Figure 5.11, clicking on "Technology" will bring up that page in the center frame and leave the top and left elements unchanged . Using the frame-based layout, you can even display a variety of Web sites while keeping the same main navigation window open.

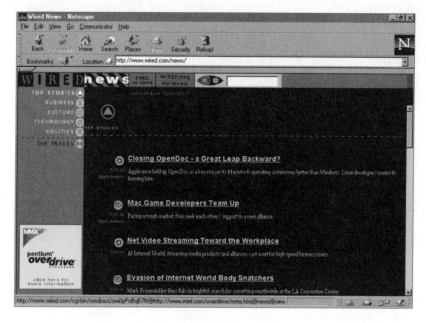

Figure 5.11: Frame-based layout example

SITE SECURITY

An unfortunate reality of the times is that because all Web sites are publicly accessible, they all face some security risk. Web sites can be altered without the webmaster's approval or knowledge—an intruder just needs to know a password to gain access to the site. Sites that link to active databases can find private data subject to scrutiny. There are simple and not-so-simple techniques and tools to protect Web sites and intranets from varying forms of attack.

PASSWORD PROTECTION

Publishing your Web pages on the Internet is straightforward. You dial into your domain using an FTP (file transfer protocol) program, log in, and begin updating your HTML files and graphics. There is only one detail protecting your directory on the server: the password.

Like many computer-related transactions, your FTP account on the Web server will be password protected. It goes without saying that you should protect your password as much as you can. This means letting the fewest people possible know it. It also means changing your password frequently. Although this is often recommended and rarely done, changing your password often is the best, and perhaps the only, protection against unauthorized alteration of your Web site.

FIREWALLS

To an architect, a firewall is a heavy metal wall used to prevent the spread of flames. In computing, a firewall also protects your system from danger, but here the danger is from unwanted intrusion. A firewall is a system (usually a computer, although it can be a single-purpose networking device called a router) designed to control access between two networks—generally an organization's and the Internet.

As an access control device, the firewall can prevent unauthorized outsiders from getting in, and can also keep unauthorized insiders from getting out. A firewall can restrict Internet and Web access to those employees who have a demonstrated need.

The larger threat, by far, is that of an unsavory individual invading your computer network and gaining access to your information for malicious purposes. It could be a hacker who wants to prove him or herself by getting into your system or it could be an industrial spy out to do real damage to your business.

In addition to limiting entry into your network, a firewall can store information intended for public consumption so that your public material can be safely isolated from your private material.

Firewalls are largely a hardware solution that does not affect HTML design. However, in the case of an intranet with an external Web presence, the HTML design must appropriately designate which pages go where. Don't put your Human Resource Department's evaluations outside the firewall, for example.

SECURE SOCKETS LAYER (SSL)

Another form of protection comes in the form of a protocol called SSL, short for Secure Sockets Layer. SSL is a security standard designed by Netscape and released into the public domain for the Internet community. Based on encryption technology that scrambles messages as they pass between client and server, SSL enables either side to unscramble the information using a series of software keys and digital signatures.

SSL is implemented on a server-by-server basis. Such secure servers have URLs that begin with "https" rather than the usual "http." When you file an order form with such a server, if you are running a security browser such as Netscape Navigator or Microsoft Explorer, a certificate of authenticity is passed to your machine. This verifies that you are dealing with the company you think you are dealing with. This also sets up a series of security keys. The details of SSL implementation are beyond the scope of this book, but you can get a sense of the security features by examining Figure 5.12, which shows a sample document information screen from a Netscape order form.

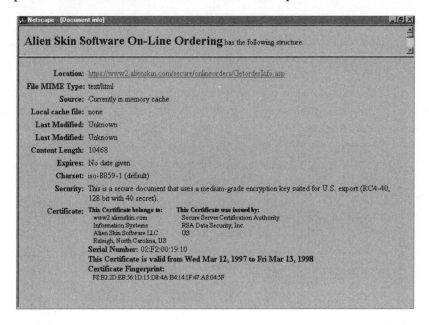

Figure 5.12: SSL document information

Team Work

You might be responsible for all aspects of the design and implementation of a Web site. But, if you are working on a site of any size, chances are that you are working with additional people. Although you might be working with an additional graphic designer or another HTML programmer, at the very least you will be working with a client who is providing the bulk of the content and the focus of the site. This section describes how to work effectively as a team to develop your Web site.

GATHERING CONTENT

One of the first questions you ask a prospective Web site client is, "What sort of material do you have that we might use in the Web site?" Include in this category marketing brochures, press releases, product descriptions, database information, logos, photographs, and anything else you can lay your hands on. Each individual piece may not be exactly right for the site, but all of the material collectively will give you a clearer idea of what the organization is and how they wish to be perceived.

Generally, the more material the client can provide the faster you can build the Web site. After you have the bulk of the material, begin to sketch out the separate pages. If a major piece is missing—such as a "Welcome from the President"—construct the page around it, place an "Under Construction" notice on the page, and go on. Make it clear to the client that, although you can post the page in this unfinished state, it is up to them to provide the content.

PRODUCTION SCHEDULING

Building a successful Web site from start to finish consists of six steps, some distinct, some overlapping, and some ongoing:

1 **Planning** Devoting a lot of time to designing the Web site will save you more time later, correcting and modifying the site. Pay special attention to the purpose of the site and the intended audience.

2 **Analyzing** This is an ongoing process, vital in the beginning stages of any Web project. Once the site design is completed, you should assess whether the site does what it's supposed to do and should also check the audience response.

3 **Designing** Creating an overall look and feel unifies the site and makes it easier to use. You must also strike a balance between conveying the content and making the page visually appealing.

4 **Implementing** This step involves doing the actual HTML and other coding, whether it be CGI scripting or Java applets. Code needs to be precise and, at its best, easily modifiable. Because Web pages are often updated by nonprogrammers, the HTML code should be commented heavily with a generous use of white space.

5 **Promoting** The Web can be a terrific marketing tool, but only if other people know about your site. After the site is up and running, advertise its address. A good way to do this is by listing the site on as many of the Web's search engines as you can. A bad way to do this is by e-mailing every one in creation an announcement—a practice known as "spamming."

6 **Upgrading** The last thing a Web site should be is stagnant. The Internet is constantly evolving, and a site can best serve its mission and its users by staying in touch with the state-of-the-art Web technologies and techniques. This doesn't mean upgrading for its own sake, but rather using new tools judiciously to make the content easier to reach for a chosen audience.

TESTING, TESTING

Software debugging is an art form that few want to practice. Unfortunately, testing your site is an ongoing necessity. There are a several strategies to keep in mind when you start to run your site through its paces.

First, organize your local site the same as your remote site. Make sure that you have the same directory and subdirectory structure set up on your C drive as on the server you will be FTPing your files into. This will help eliminate the "File Not Found" errors that can occur. This strategy applies not only to the HTML files in your site but to all the additional support files as well: the graphic files (.GIF and .JPG), sound files (.WAV and .MID), video files (.AVI), and so on. If you are using any CGI scripts, you must put them in the cgi-bin directory on your server, and on your local drive for proper testing.

If you are a beginning Web site builder, be sure to choose a Web hosting service that features technical support. Be sure to check out their Web site; often they will have areas known as FAQs (Frequently Asked Questions) that address the most common problems. It is a good sign when a Web hosting site has a comprehensive list of answers already posted.

Be prepared to test as much after you have uploaded the site to the server as during the local building of the page. Pages that loaded smoothly locally could cause location and name recognition errors when you first test them on a remote system. You'll also notice a significant time lag in loading your pages off a server versus loading them off your hard drive. Welcome to the World Wide Wait.

With this loading lag is mind, you can begin to fine-tune your page where necessary. You can speed up graphics by making them smaller and/or reducing the number of colors they use. There are a number of good utilities for this very purpose; check Appendix C for the details.

Test your pages on various browsers and different systems. Although the cutting edge of technology is moving onto 56 Kbps and faster modems, most of your audience is, at best, experiencing the Web with a 28.8 or 14.4 modem. Different browsers have varying offsets also; what looks like exactly 2 pixels in on your browser could be 20 on another. Remember that Web page design is not about the precise delivery of an exact page to every browser, but rather the rendering of your content across a wide platform.

Finally, have complete novices try out your Web page whenever possible. Although you might think that you can try every possible combination, the truth is all programmers make certain unconscious decisions as they test their programs. They might overlook some elements altogether, and unknowingly avoid others. Time and again, the programmer will be convinced that the system is absolutely bug-free, and the first time a complete outsider uses it, an error appears. Furthermore, watching a "Net newbie" visit your site for the first time will teach you reams about computer interface design. The next chapter will give you some advanced HTML tools to make your Web site easier to use and more state-of-the-art.

Advanced Design

PAGE BACKGROUNDS

ADVANCED INLINE GRAPHICS

IMAGEMAPS

MULTIMEDIA

Chapter 6

T his chapter takes up some of the techniques that really make Web pages distinctive. The basic HTML information you learned about earlier lets you get your content across. The procedures introduced in this chapter will broaden your palette and give your Web site a facelift.

First you'll learn about page backgrounds: how to set page and text colors and how to use an image to pattern the page. Then you'll find out more about controlling images, including animated graphics and hyperlinked graphics known as imagemaps. Next, you'll examine one of the latest innovations in HTML: frames. Finally, a section on multimedia explains how to put sound and video and even virtual reality links on your page.

Page Backgrounds

The default background (the "paper" on which your text and images are laid out) for most browsers is either white or a light gray. Although this default is perfectly acceptable, HTML 3.2 lets you alter the color of the page and even embed an image on it.

PAGE AND TEXT COLORS

There are six attributes that you can use in the <BODY> tag to control the general look of a page. Two of the attributes, BACKGROUND and BGCOLOR, control the look and color of the "paper" upon which the content is "printed." Remember, BACKGROUND sets a background image; BGCOLOR gives the entire document a uniform background color. The other four attributes— TEXT, LINK, VLINK, and ALINK—control the color of the various text states.

What are these states? Well, the value of the TEXT attribute specifies the color of ordinary text which, by default, is almost always black. The value of the LINK attribute specifies the color of links, which are usually blue. VLINK is for the color of visited links (purple in Navigator and Internet Explorer) and ALINK is the color of active links—that is, the color you see if you hold down the mouse button while the mouse pointer is positioned over the link.

The BGCOLOR attribute and the four text color attributes take RGB values, which were covered in Chapter 2. Remember that an RGB value is a triplet of red, green, and blue values—a universal method of specifying colors because any color in the visual spectrum can be expressed as a combination of these colors. If you want to use a color outside of the 16 named RGB colors (for example, "white", "black", "cyan", and so on), you must specify a color like so:

`#rrggbb`

using the pound sign, and then two characters each for the red, the green, and the blue values.

Each red, green, and blue value is a hexadecimal number between 0 and 255. Hexadecimal. Yikes! Okay, I know, your eyes glazed over in that "Introduction to Computers" class when they talked about hexadecimal, or base 16, arithmetic. Don't panic; in this context, it's not that difficult. For example, each of the two "r" characters representing the red value is a symbol standing for a number from 0 to 15. The first "r" is the number of "16s" and the second "r" is the number of "1s." Thus, hexadecimal 42 is four 16s (64) and two 1s, or decimal 66. The symbols used are the ordinary digits 0 through 9 for the numbers zero to nine and the letters "A" to "F" for the numbers 10 to 15.

Still Can't Think in Hex?

Most computers come with an onscreen calculator that can convert numbers from decimal to hexadecimal. Suppose you're trying to match a particular shade of green in a image to use as the background. Pull up your favorite graphics package and open the image in question. Most graphics programs have a tool known as an "Eyedropper" that lets you pick a particular color on screen. Click on the green shade with the Eyedropper tool and then jot down the RGB numbers found in the color palette. Open your calculator, make sure it is in decimal mode, and plug in your first (red) value. Then switch to hexadecimal mode and, voilá, your magic decoder ring has done the trick! Complete the process by putting in the green and blue values and now you can complete the RGB triplet.

The color black is the RGB value #000000, and full white is #FFFFFF. Any value that has identical rr, gg, and bb parts is a shade of gray. A body tag specifying a blue background is written

```
<BODY BGCOLOR="#0000FF">
```

Mixing colors on a computer is an additive process—larger values mean more light is going into the final color. That's why #7F7FFF is light blue and not mud. Unfortunately this is a black-and-white book, so I can only give you the names of the colors corresponding to the values in the following table of common RGB values.

Color	Dark	Medium	Bright
Red	#400000	#7F0000	#FF0000
Yellow	#404000	#7F7F00	#FFFF00
Green	#004000	#007F00	#00FF00
Cyan	#004040	#007F7F	#00FFFF
Blue	#000040	#00007F	#0000FF
Magenta	#400040	#7F007F	#FF00FF

Here is a body tag specifying a light yellow page background with dark green text. Linked text is rendered in bright pink that changes to a medium gray to indicate that the link has recently been taken:

```
<BODY BGCOLOR="#FFFF7F" TEXT="#004000" LINK="#FF00A0" VLINK="#A0A0A0">
```

What do you think would happen if the values of the BGCOLOR and VLINK attributes were the same? For example,

```
<BODY BGCOLOR="#C0C0C0" VLINK="#C0C0C0">
```

Hint: don't do it. If you do, you won't be able to see links once you've visited them.

If you want to change the color and size of individual text elements within the page body, you can use a recent HTML 3.2 addition, the <FONT></FONT> tags. You should use this element like other inline style elements, such as emphasis, inside of enclosing HTML structural elements. It has two attributes: SIZE and COLOR. The value of SIZE is a signed number from -3 to +3 indicating how much smaller or larger, relative to the current font size, to set the font size(s) of the enclosed content. The COLOR attribute takes an #RGB value, as described earlier. For example, the following bit of HTML will be rendered in red type, moderately larger than corresponding elements on the rest of the page.

```
<P><FONT SIZE=+2 COLOR="#FF0000">!! Hot Sites !!</FONT></P>
```

When viewed on a color display, the text should be red and a couple of point sizes larger than normal paragraph text. The color applies only to normal text. It won't change the color of linked text.

BACKGROUND PATTERNS

The BACKGROUND attribute's value is the URL of an image file, usually a small one in GIF format. For example,

```
<BODY BACKGROUND="images/bkground.gif">
```

When the page is loaded, the image is downloaded to the reader's disk just like any ordinary inline image. However, the browser repeats the image across and down the page, forming a background pattern, as shown in Figure 6.1.

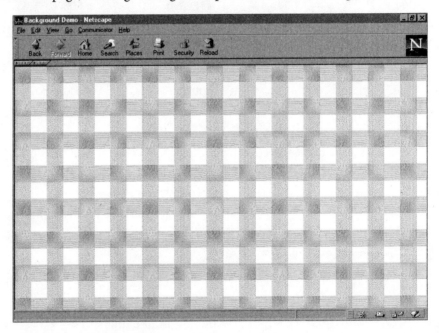

Figure 6.1: Repeating background pattern

Background patterns can be very attractive, providing effects ranging from watermarks to fields of stars, and they're very easy to install. On a Macintosh, you can copy a pattern out of the Desktop Patterns control panel, paste it into a graphics application or utility, and save it in GIF format. In Windows, you can open a bitmap file (the filename ends in .bmp) in a graphic application or utility and similarly save it in GIF format. Just for fun, experiment with background images that are 1 pixel high.

There are a couple of things to be aware of when using a GIF as a background pattern. First, keep it small. The smaller it is, the faster your page will load. Second, use as few colors as possible. Some operating systems allow only a limited number of colors to be used in a page and many people are still browsing the Web on 16-color and even grayscale machines. If the total number of colors used on a page exceeds the capacity of the reader's display device, the extra colors will be changed to colors in the existing set and the results can look quite ugly. So, be sure to check out your backgrounds at different color depths. Make sure your page is readable on those 16-color Windows systems and grayscale laptops. Color mapping across systems is problematic at best. If you have photographs on your page and you want them to look their best, avoid using background patterns.

Test your Web pages with screens of different resolutions. If you build your site while using a 640x480 screen and then look at it on an 800x600 screen, your background might be noticeably different. A common problem is that the background image is too narrow and the browsers tile it to fill out the larger screen. For example, if you want a column to run down the left side of your page, you might use a graphic with a slice of the column, as shown in Figure 6.2. If placed as a BACKGROUND, this graphic will fill out a 640x480 display perfectly (Figure 6.3); however, when you view it with a 800x600 resolution, two columns appear (Figure 6.4). If you don't want this effect, a workaround is to use an image wide enough (close to 800 pixels) that the browser won't tile it.

Advanced Inline Graphics

An inline image behaves on a Web page as if it were a large character of text. It is inserted into the content at a specific point in the text. I mention this again because it is the key to understanding how to use images on a Web page. First of all, it means that, anywhere you can put a character of text, you can put an inline image. Second, inline images are bound to adjacent characters or other inline images the same way as letters are bound into words. This means that

```
<IMG SRC="...">
<IMG SRC="...">
<IMG SRC="...">
```

is not the same as

```
<IMG SRC="..."><IMG SRC="..."><IMG SRC="...">
```

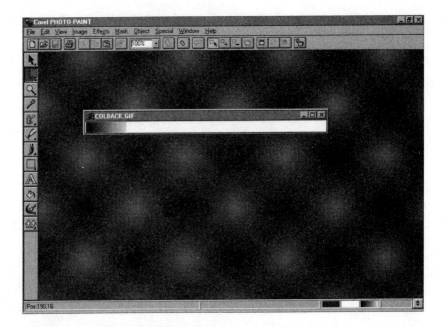

Figure 6.2: The original graphic

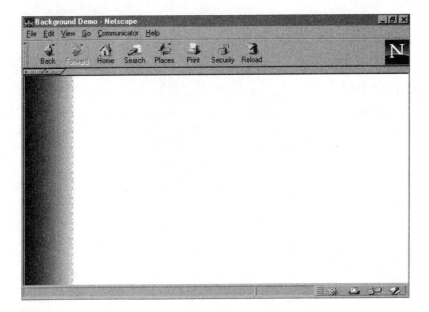

Figure 6.3: The background at 640x480 resolution

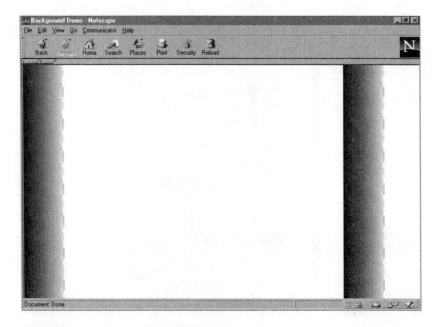

Figure 6.4: The background at 800x600 resolution

In the former case, the carriage returns ending each line in your HTML source file appear as spaces between the images. In the latter, there are no spaces whatsoever between the images.

A large image, especially one that's wider than it is high, should be placed by itself, either by enclosing it in line break tags, or better yet, an HTML element that can take the ALIGN attribute, such as a division, heading, or paragraph. The following HTML, for example, centers an image over a "caption":

```
<H3 ALIGN=center><IMG SRC="images/300-8.gif"><BR>
Cover of the Current Edition</H3>
```

Figure 6.5 shows how this would be rendered.

CONTROLLING IMAGES

For images that are taller than they are wide, you often want text to flow around the image, either on the left or the right side. There are two approaches in HTML for doing this. The first method was introduced by Netscape as an extension and later incorporated into HTML 3.2.

HTML 3.2 extended the ALIGN attribute so that it recognized the values "right" and "left". ALIGN="left" means that the image is rendered to the left of the text, and ALIGN="right" means that the image is rendered to the right of

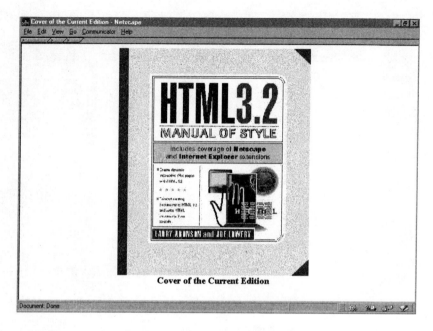

Figure 6.5: Image centered over text

the text. This is distinctly different from the values of "top", "middle", and "bottom", which specify how the image should be aligned with the baseline of the text. When the ALIGN attribute has a value of "right" or "left", the image is no longer inserted at a specific point like a character that word-wraps with the rest of the text. The image now behaves as a container. There is no ending image tag, </IMG>, to signal the end of the container; rather, any HTML element with the CLEAR attribute stops the text from flowing around the image. Because the image is not tied to a specific point, you should be careful about placing it inside other HTML elements; headings, for example.

Figure 6.6, generated by the following HTML, shows a right-aligned image.

```
<HTML>
<HEAD>
    <TITLE> Right Aligned Image</TITLE>
</HEAD>
<BODY>
<HR>
<IMG SRC="images/300-8s.gif" ALIGN=right ALT="cover">
<H3><CITE>HTML Manual of Style</CITE>,</H3>
Published by Ziff-Davis Press, was one of the very first books on World Wide Web
```

```
publishing. It's now in its fifth printing and available in several foreign
translations.<BR CLEAR=right>
<HR>
</BODY>
</HTML>
```

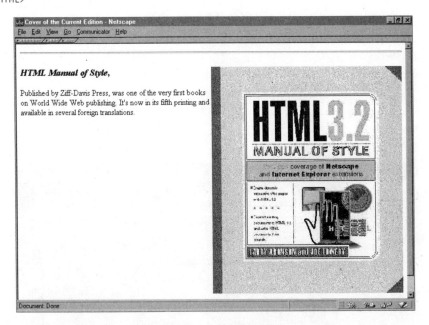

Figure 6.6: A right-aligned image

The line break tag specified with CLEAR=right in the preceding example instructs the browser to space down the page, if necessary, until the current right margin is clear before placing the next HTML element, in this case, a horizontal rule. There are no restrictions on what other HTML elements can be inside the content that flows around an image. You can have headings, lists, tables, and even other images. For example, Figure 6.7 shows what happens when you use the same image with both left and right alignment. It's generated by the following HTML.

```
<HTML>
<HEAD>
<TITLE>Image Alignment</TITLE></HEAD>
<BODY>
<HR SIZE=6 CLEAR>
<IMG ALIGN=left SRC="images/column.gif">
<IMG ALIGN=right SRC="images/column.gif">
```

```
<PRE></PRE>  <!-- force a little spacing at the top -->
<H3 ALIGN=center>Between the Columns</H3>
<HR ALIGN=center WIDTH=50%>
<H5 ALIGN=center>An</H5>
<H3 ALIGN=center><Illustration</H3>
<H5 ALIGN=center>of</H5>
<H3 ALIGN=center>Left and Right Image Alignment</H3>
<H3 ALIGN=center>Made Possible</H3>
<H5 ALIGN=center>by</H5>
<H3 ALIGN=center>Extensions</H3>
<H5 ALIGN=center>to the</H5>
<H3 ALIGN=center>Image Tag</H3>
<HR SIZE=6 CLEAR>
</BODY>
</HTML>
```

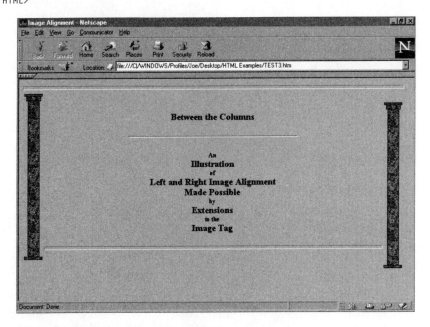

Figure 6.7: Left and right image alignment

Adding Space around Graphics For a little more image control, HTML 3.2 recognizes the additional attributes, HSPACE and VSPACE. These attributes take a numeric value specifying the number of pixels of padding that should be placed between the image and the text that flows around it. HSPACE is the space on the right or left side of the image, VSPACE is the amount of space above and below the image.

Generally speaking, the larger the image, the more HSPACE and VSPACE you'll want. Typical values are from 5 to 15 pixels. This is different from the BORDER attribute, which applies only when the image is inside an anchor tag. When it's obvious that an image is a button that the reader may click on, or the border is distracting, you can suppress the blue border indicating that the image is a link by adding BORDER=0 to the image tag.

Resizing Graphics   The HEIGHT and WIDTH attributes, another set of HTML 3.2 image extensions, also take values in pixels, but their function in the image tag is performance-related. If you specify the HEIGHT and WIDTH attributes, HTML 3.2–compatible browsers preallocate a rectangle of that shape in the appropriate place on the page. This allows the browser to continue formatting the page while the image is being downloaded, speeding up the download process. It also gives your viewers something to look at while waiting for the file to download.

   You should give the HEIGHT and WIDTH attributes values that are the exact vertical and horizontal size of the image. If you provide values that are different than the actual size of the image, HTML 3.2 attempts to scale the image to that size; however, it doesn't use a very sophisticated algorithm. So, if you want to change the size of an image, it's better to do so in PhotoShop or some other graphic application.

Mixing Low- and High-End Images   HTML 3.2 has one more image tag attribute to improve loading performance, LOWSRC. This attribute, which takes a URL in the same manner as the SRC attribute, loads an image before the image specified by the URL of the SRC attribute. Suppose you have an image that's 300x400 pixels (large.gif). You can use a graphics utility to create a smaller copy (small.gif) that has the same proportions, say, 30x40 pixels. Write the image tag as follows:

```
<IMG LOWSRC="small.gif" SRC="large.gif" WIDTH=300 HEIGHT=400>
```

   When HTML 3.2 processes this tag, it will download small.gif first and scale it up to 300x400 pixels. Because the file is small, it will load very fast. It will appear as a low resolution image, because when you originally scaled it from 300x400 pixels down to 30x40, you threw out 90 percent of the data. HTML 3.2 can continue to load and format the rest of the page's content. Then, when large.gif is completely downloaded, it replaces small.gif.

Image Attributes in Action This next example shows how to combine many of the image attributes. It's the two by three table of images and text shown in Figure 6.8. Here's the HTML:

```
<HTML>
<HEAD>
<TITLE>Image Table</TITLE>
</HEAD>
<BODY>
<TABLE CELLSPACING=1Ø>
<TR>
<TD><IMG SRC="images/A.gif" ALIGN=left HSPACE=5 HEIGHT=72 WIDTH=6Ø>
    Athena<BR>Anubis<BR>Ariel<BR>Aphrodite</TD>
<TD><IMG SRC="images/B.gif" ALIGN=left HSPACE=5 HEIGHT=72 WIDTH=6Ø>
    Baal<BR>Bragi<BR>Bubastis<BR>Bigfoot</TD>
<TD><IMG SRC="images/C.gif" ALIGN=left HSPACE=5 HEIGHT=72 WIDTH=6Ø>
    Cassiopeia<BR>Cronus<BR>Cupid<BR>Ceres</TD>
</TR>
<TR>
<TD><IMG SRC="images/D.gif" ALIGN=left HSPACE=5 HEIGHT=72 WIDTH=6Ø>
    Diana<BR>Dionysus<BR>Demeter<BR>Doctor Who</TD>
<TD><IMG SRC="images/E.gif" ALIGN=left HSPACE=5 HEIGHT=72 WIDTH=6Ø>
    Ea<BR>Eros<BR>Elvis<BR>Electra</TD>
<TD><IMG SRC="images/F.gif" ALIGN=left HSPACE=5 HEIGHT=72 WIDTH=6Ø>
    Fatima<BR>Flora<BR>Freya<BR>Frankenstein</TD>
</TR>
</TABLE>
</BODY>
</HTML>
```

Interlaced GIF Files Another technique for dealing with the World Wide Wait is to use interlaced GIF files. Web surfers can get very frustrated waiting for a file to completely download before it displays—not only because of the time it takes, but also because nothing is happening on the screen. Interlaced GIFs appear gradually, almost as if they were developing before the viewer's eyes.

Here's how it works. First, the graphic is saved in GIF89A format, which allows both transparency (which allows one color to appear to be invisible) and interlace modes to be turned on. If a picture is saved with the interlace option, it displays the entire graphic with the lowest amount of information first. Gradually, additional data is added, sharpening the picture and "developing" the image. When a picture is saved without the interlace option, the image displays either all at once, after your browser has completely downloaded the file, or one line at a time, depending on your browser settings. Whether you use interlace mode or transparency mode is purely a design choice—some images you want to come into focus slowly, others you want to pop on the page.

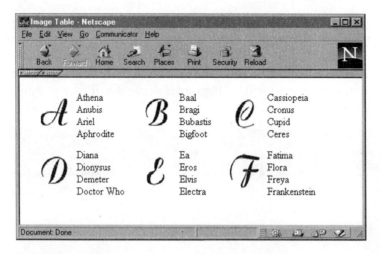

Figure 6.8: Images in a table

ANIMATED IMAGES

One of the most fun innovations in recent Web history (that is, the last 9 months or so) is inline animation. Just as you can include any graphic in line with text, now you can also include any moving graphic, using GIF animations.

You create GIF animations by combining single GIF images one after another, much like a flip book. Both are made up of single drawings that give the illusion of movement when viewed in rapid sequence. The best thing about GIF animation in HTML is that it's easy. Simply call the file the same way that you would call any image, by using the IMG tag. For example,

```
<IMG SRC="ball.gif">
```

will load and run an animation entitled ball.gif.

The Basics of GIF Animation   Although the actual animation steps are too program-specific to describe here, the basic steps are the same. Let's build that bouncing ball animation as an example. It's best to create the frames of your animation with a drawing program, such as CorelDraw or Adobe Illustrator, that lets you position each object independently.

First, create a small square filled with a background color. This will be a bounding box that keeps your animation moving only where you want it to move, much like traditional animators used pegs to keep each page in place. Next, draw a small ball in one corner of the screen; that's the first frame. Then select the box and the ball and create a duplicate of it off to one side—this is to be frame two. In frame two, move only the ball, in the direction that you want to ball to travel. Duplicate frame two to make frame three and again move the ball slightly. Continue creating new frames in this way until you have bounced the ball around a bit. Film uses 24 frames per second of animation and video uses 30 frames per second, so you can see that the more frames you use the smoother your animation will be. Figure 6.9 shows a sequence of frames of my bouncing ball.

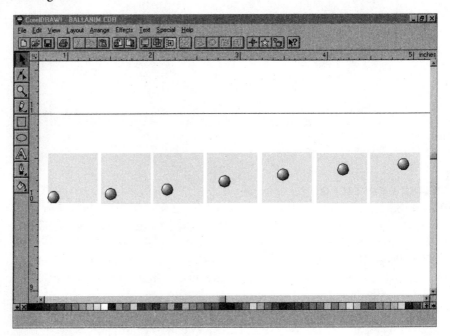

Figure 6.9: The bouncing ball frames

When you've completed all your frames, you need to save each section individually as a GIF file. If you have 24 frames, you'll initially have 24 files. Then, you bring all the frames together with a GIF animation builder such as GIF Construction Set or Microsoft's GIF Animator. You can choose to have the animation play once or loop indefinitely. If you want to have your animation float on top of your page, be sure to turn on the transparency option for the GIF89A files. When you're finished selecting your various options, save the file; this is your final compiled result.

Animation File Sizes GIF animation files pose the same problems as other graphics on the Web, only multiplied by the number of frames. A single animation that starts with a 12K image can inflate to over 1,150K for a 4 second, 24 frames per second moving image. There are two approaches to keeping the file sizes acceptable: first, keep your animations as physically small as possible; the smaller each graphics file is the better. Second, use fewer frames per second. Frame rates of 10 to 12 frames per second are perfectly acceptable for small images. As with graphics, include animations only when they add to the Web page and can successfully answer the question, "Is it worth the wait?"

Animation Tools   There are a growing number of software programs and Web sites devoted to GIF animations. We've mentioned a couple of the most popular programs already. GIF Construction Set, shareware developed by Alchemy Mindworks, Inc., works by allowing you to insert commands that control the transparency and interlace properties. Microsoft GIF Animator is a relatively recent addition, but its no-nonsense approach has won many advocates. GIF Animator takes your individual GIF frames and makes them into an animation, allowing you to control the animation's timing.

IMAGEMAPS

Imagemaps are an important extension to the concept of document linking. An imagemap is an ordinary image or figure upon which a set of subareas have been defined, each of which can link to a different URL when clicked on. There are currently two different methods of designating such subareas: the original HTML2 method and a set of HTML 3.2 extensions to the image tag. Imagemaps created with the HTML2 method are referred to as server-side imagemaps, because they require a special program called Imagemap residing on the server. Imagemaps generated with the other method are called client-side imagemaps, because they don't require any processing on the server, and, unlike the HTML2 method, can be developed and tested locally.

A third method for using imagemaps has emerged from Java, the Internet programming language developed by Sun Microsystems. Because this technique requires a Java-enabled browser, imagemaps created in this way can be viewed by the fewest browsers. However, it does add some functionality: In a Java imagemap, you can program the image to highlight or change to show hidden submenus when a mouse passes over it. See Figures 6.10 and 6.11 for a before and after picture. You'll learn more about Java in Chapter 7.

SERVER-SIDE IMAGEMAPS

Server-side imagemaps are supported by most browsers that can display images. To implement a server-side imagemap you have to have root access to the

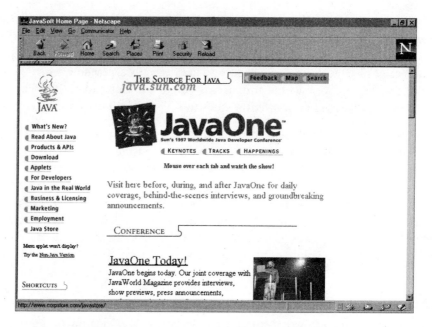

Figure 6.10: Java imagemap

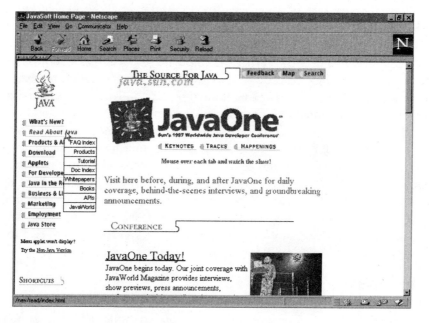

Figure 6.11: Java imagemap in action

server, so you'll probably need the assistance of your webmaster or systems administrator.

The key to creating server-side imagemaps is to include the attribute ISMAP in an image tag enclosed in an anchor tag that calls the server's Imagemap program. This passes a pointer to a map file defining the subareas of the image and their associated URLs. Unfortunately, the exact syntax of all the various pieces of this process differs slightly depending on the type of server software being used. Here's an example that uses the syntax appropriate to NCSA's UNIX-based http server:

```
<A HREF="http://www.yerserver.com/cgi-bin/imagemap/demo">
<IMG SRC="images/demo.gif" WIDTH=300 HEIGHT=200 ISMAP></A>
```

The special directory cgi-bin exists at the root of most Web servers. It's the repository of cgi (Common Gateway Interface) scripts. Imagemap is the name of one such script supplied with most server software. See the documentation at http://hoohoo.ncsa.uiuc.edu/cgi/overview.html for more information.

Readers with some UNIX experience would think the URL in the preceding example referenced a file named demo in a directory named Imagemap, but it doesn't. Web servers will interpret demo as extra path information that is passed to the Imagemap program, in an environmental variable (PATH_INFO). The Imagemap program treats this information as a symbolic name, which it looks up in a special configuration file (imagemap.conf). This information allows it to find the actual path and file containing the information that maps subareas of the image to specific URLs. This file is called a map file. By convention, it has the same name as the image file but ends in .map instead of .gif. It can be located in your Web site, so you can change the imagemap's subareas just as long as you don't change the name or location of the map file.

The map file is an ASCII text file with one line per image subarea specifying the shape of the subarea, the URL linked to that subarea, and the subarea's coordinates. In the example, it would be called demo.map, and a line in this file defining a 50x50 pixel subarea in the upper-right corner of the 300x200 image would look something like:

```
rect    http://www.someplace.com/somepage.html    249,0 299,49
```

"rect" says that the shape of the subarea is a rectangle and that the coordinates (x,y x,y) are the offset of the upper-left and lower-right corners, inclusive, from the upper-left corner of the image. The URL should always be specified in its full format. Other entries can be "circle," with coordinates referring to the center and any point on the circumference; "poly," with n sets of coordinates specifying the vertices of a polygon with n sides; and "default," with no coordinates providing a URL to link to when the reader clicks outside of any defined subarea. Subareas can overlap, in which case the first entry matching the coordinates of the reader's mouse click is used.

CLIENT-SIDE IMAGEMAPS

Client-side imagemaps are much easier to implement than server-side imagemaps, but they are newer and not yet universally supported. There is an elegant implementation of client-side imagemaps that's flexible and can be used in conjunction with server-side imagemaps for browsers that don't support these extensions. Either in place of or in addition to the image tag's ISMAP attribute, you can code the USEMAP attribute, the value of which is a URL pointing to a map specification element. This element can be in the same file as the image tag with the USEMAP attribute, in a separate file by itself, or in a file with other map specifications. Here's an example of a "button-bar" with a three-button map in the same file as the image tag:

```
<IMG SRC="images/bbar.gif" WIDTH=150 HEIGHT=30 USEMAP="#bbar">
   .

   .
<MAP NAME="bbar">
<AREA SHAPE="rect" HREF="top.html" COORDS="0,0,49,29">
<AREA SHAPE="rect" HREF="prev.html" COORDS="50,0,99,29">
<AREA SHAPE="rect" HREF="next.html" COORDS="100,0,149,29">
</MAP>
```

The USEMAP attribute takes precedence over an ISMAP attribute. In other words, if a reader's browser does not support such client-side imagemaps, it will ignore the USEMAP attribute and the <MAP></MAP> and <AREA> tags and process the imagemap using the HTML2 server-side mechanism. Note the differences in syntax between server-side and client-side map specifications. The latter uses relative URL addressing and requires a comma between the upper-left and lower-right coordinates.

As in server-side imagemap processing, the first <AREA> specification that matches the coordinates of the reader's mouse click will be the one taken. To provide a default URL for reader clicks outside any defined subareas, simply provide a final <AREA> with coordinates encompassing the entire image area. If you want such a default to take no action—that is, that no link be made—use NOHREF in place of HREF="*url*".

The HTML 3.2 specification provides a different way of implementing client-side imagemaps. Within the content contained in the HTML 3.2 AREA element, anchors can have the additional attribute, SHAPE, which takes a set of coordinate values. This encourages authors to provide descriptive links in the text corresponding to the subareas defined in the figure for non-complying browsers. This technique works nicely for many simple application interface screens. However, it can get awkward when the imagemap has many subareas—on a state map of counties, for example. In that circumstance you would use the DEFAULT shape. For example, to implement the button bar in the preceding example, you would code:

```
<MAP NAME="TheButtons">
<AREA HREF="top.html" SHAPE="Default" Coords="0,0,49,29">
<AREA HREF="prev.html" SHAPE="Default" Coords=50,0,99,29">
<AREA HREF="next.html" SHAPE="Default" Coords=100,0,149,29">
</MAP>
```

An earlier HTML2 browser will not recognize the MAP tag and no image or anchor text will appear on the page.

IMAGEMAP TOOLS

More and more of the full-featured Web page creation programs include tools for creating imagemaps. Currently, however, not all support both client-side and server-side imagemaps: Macromedia's Backstage Designer outputs only server-side imagemaps; Microsoft's FrontPage 97 works with client-side imagemaps; Adobe's PageMill can be configured for either client-side or server-side.

There are also numerous single-purpose imagemap editors. An excellent utility, Map This! by Todd Wilson of Molly Penguin Software, is freeware available on the Web. An enhanced version published by Mediatech, Inc. as LiveImage is commercially available. Web Hotspots by IAutomata is a more full-featured editor with a free-form tool that gives you more precise control over irregularly shaped imagemaps. All of these editors will output both client- and server-side imagemaps. Check Appendix C for URLs that will help you find out more about these and other Web tools.

MULTIMEDIA

Increasingly, Web pages are reaching beyond text and graphics to include a wide range of other media: sound, video, animation—in other words, multimedia. Just as the integration of inline graphics and text made the Web immensely popular, much of the power of multimedia stems from its integration into Web pages. You might log onto a popular singer's Web site, click on the image of the latest album, and listen to it while watching a clip from the music video.

Despite the seeming complexity of multimedia Web pages, there's really not much to learn about coding them in HTML. The process of creating multimedia objects, on the other hand, is very involved, platform specific, and beyond the scope of this book.

To include a multimedia object on your Web page—be it a sound bite, or a video clip, or whatever—just create a normal anchor link to the binary file containing the object, like this:

```
<A HREF="videoclip.avi"><IMG SRC="videostill.gif"></A>
```

It is up to the reader to configure his or her browser to recognize the object by the filename extension and associate it with a suitable plug-in or helper application on her computer. A *plug-in* is a program that extends the capability of the basic browser for displaying or playing the data downloaded; *helper applications* do the same thing, but open a window separate from the main browser. Some browsers are beginning to include the most popular plug-ins for hearing sound or watching video clips. Other plug-ins are easy to download as needed.

It is considered polite to inform your readers when a link is to some object other than a Web page, and to provide the size of the object so the reader can estimate how long it will take to download. For example, on the page containing information on the First Family in the White House (the one in Washington DC, USA) Web site, there is an image (an audio icon) that links to a sound file of the first feline's (Socks's) meow:

```
<A HREF="../audio/socks.au">
<IMG SRC="/White_House/images/audio_button.gif"
ALT="[AUDIO: Socks, the First Family's cat]"></A> (~36K)
```

MIME TYPES

There are a large number of file formats for text, images, sound, and video—not to mention specific applications and the list grows longer every day. So that Web users could easily exchange information no matter the form, there needed to be a system that allowed the data to stay in its original format and still be accessible. That system is called MIME (Multipurpose Internet Mail Extensions); it was developed much like the Web itself, by a consortium of developers, when the need for such a standard became apparent.

Each file format is known by its MIME type and subtype; the Web server sends this information to the browser so that the browser can interpret it correctly. For example, when an HTML page is sent from a Web server to your machine, the server begins its transmission with a declaration of what's coming, in this case, the content following is HTML text. The actual coded line looks like this:

```
Content-type: text/html
```

How does the Web server know the file type? It uses the filename extension. If the extension is .html or .htm, the server knows that the file is a text file of HTML subtype. Today's operating systems also use the file extension to know, for example, that .doc signifies a Word document and .wpd stands for a Word-Perfect file. Because you can define a MIME type for your browser, you could specify that any .doc file downloaded would be read by Microsoft Word. MIME types are a very powerful tool for expanding the multimedia flexibility of your Web site or intranet because you can incorporate new file types as they are developed.

Table 6.1 shows some current MIME types, subtypes, and the file extension associated with each.

Table 6.1: Popular MIME Types and Extensions

Type	Subtype	Extension
text	html, htm	.html, .htm
	plain	.txt
application	mac-binhex40	.hqx
	msword	.doc
	pdf	.pdf
	zip	.zip
image	jpeg	.jpeg, .jpg, .jpe
	gif	.gif
	tiff	.tiff, .tif
audio	basic	.au, .snd
	x-aiff	.aif, .aiff, .aifc
	x-wav	.wav
video	mpeg	.mpeg, .mpg
	quicktime	.qt, .mov
	x-msvideo	.avi
	x-sgi-movie	.movie

PLUG-INS

Plug-ins extend the capability of a program. Browsers can read any type of file, display any image, play any sound, and so on—as long as there is a plug-in for the file available to the browser. Plug-in technology for the Web was pioneered by Netscape, but Internet Explorer also accepts plug-ins of a special type, ones using ActiveX controls.

Generally, the major file formats for the Web—like GIF and JPG for images, and AU and SND for audio—are handled natively by each browser. Currently, there are over 100 plug-ins covering a wide range of file types, and more companies hop on the plug-in bandwagon all the time.

Installing a plug-in is extremely simple. Download and uncompress the file. Save the file in the plug-in folder for your browser. When you start your browser it will make note of all available plug-ins and load them as needed.

It's considered good HTML programming practice to place a notice on a Web page if visiting that site requires a specific plug-in. Moreover, many Web developers provide a link for downloading the plug-in on the same page so you don't have to search the Net for it. That way, if your viewing public doesn't have the necessary tool, they can easily find it.

Plug-ins have become extremely important in intranets. Using this technology, a company can make very specific documents available to be viewed through the browser. For example, an architectural firm might have thousands of Autocad files it could make available in-house, but converting them to JPEG or GIF format would be prohibitively time consuming and would also lose valuable detail. By employing an Autocad plug-in called WHIP, firm members can view their drawings alongside text descriptions.

Shockwave One of the best general-purpose animation and sound plug-ins on the Net is Shockwave. Shockwave was developed by Macromedia as a method of displaying multimedia files created by their popular Director program. Director uses a special utility called AfterBurner to turn Director movies into Shockwave files.

Because Director is a full-featured interactive presentation development tool, some of the coolest sites on the Web are those that have been "Shocked." Shockwave is available for free from the Macromedia Web site (www.macromedia.com) and comes in several flavors: Flash for small animations and Essentials for full Shockwave compatibility. Shockwave has recently added a streaming feature to its plug-in. Normally, a file—whether it is video or animation—needs to download completely to your computer before it can play. If a file is streamed into your system, it begins displaying as soon as the first playable bytes arrive. This speeds up apparent file transfer tremendously. Shockwave also supports streaming audio for playing music and sounds.

RealAudio and RealVideo   One of the prime innovators of streaming technology is Progressive Networks, creators of RealAudio and, just introduced, RealVideo. When you install their RealPlayer plug-in, just click on a RealAudio file embedded on a Web page and you can hear stereo sound using modem speeds of 28.8 kilobits per second (abbreviated as "Kbps") and near-CD quality at higher bit rates; the sound degrades to AM radio quality at 14.4 Kbps. The RealPlayer also handles streaming video when it is in the RealVideo format. Progressive Networks claims to achieve "Newscast-quality video" at rates of 28.8 Kbps and full-motion at higher modem speeds. The images are $1/4$ screen size and come in at about 15 frames per second (full-motion is 30 fps).

From the programmers end, again, implementation is easy. Simply reference the filename through the HREF attribute. When selected, the file will begin downloading to the client; next, it invokes the player and begins to play while continuing to download. However, to use RealAudio or RealVideo files, your Web site must reside on a compatible server. When designing sites, be sure to ask potential hosts what streaming systems they support, if any. RealPlayer is available for free from www.realaudio.com. There is a higher end version called RealPlayer Plus; it costs about $30 and you can order it from the same site.

Adobe Acrobat   Adobe Acrobat gives you instant access to documents in their original form, independent of computer platform. With the Acrobat Reader, you can view, navigate, print, and present any Portable Document Format (PDF) file. Current versions of the Acrobat Reader (3.0 and higher) act as a plug-in rather than as an outside helper application.

Again, installation is straightforward. Download the Reader (free from www.adobe.com/acrobat) and open the executable file. It will uncompress the Reader program and place it in your plug-in folder. You need to quit and restart your browser to properly load the Reader. Acrobat Reader starts and a new toolbar appears in the browser's window, allowing you to control the PDF file with standard VCR-like controls on your screen, as you can see in Figure 6.12.

Specialty Plug-Ins   Plug-ins don't just help you to decode the major software formats. The specifications for building a plug-in are available at no charge from Netscape (www.netscape.com); from a C++ programmer's viewpoint, the implementation is trivial. It's no surprise, then, that there are many specialty plug-ins designed to read data from specific programs. Here's a brief list:

- ▶ **Argus Map Viewerfrom Argus Technologies, Inc.** The first geographic viewer for the Internet that allows you to view dynamic maps with high-quality vector graphics.

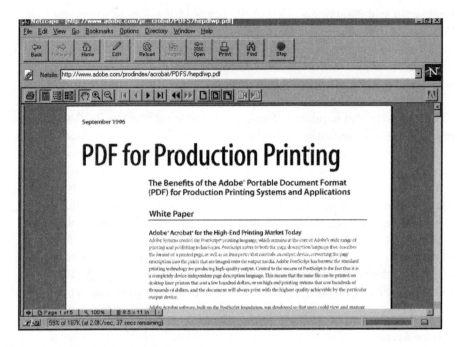

Figure 6.12: The Adobe Acrobat plug-in

- **Chemscape Chime from MDL Information Systems.** This plug-in allows scientists to view chemical information from many of the popular 3D display formats such as the Brookhaven Protein Databank (PDB) format.

- **EarthTime from Starfish Software.** EarthTime shows you the local time and date in eight global locations.

- **EchoSpeech from Echo Speech Corporation.** This plug-in plays high-quality compressed speech.

- **PointCast from PointCast, Inc.** The PointCast Network broadcasts personalized news, stock quotes, weather, and more, directly to your computer screen; a free service.

A good site for catching up on the latest in plug-ins is The Plug-In Plaza at www.browserwatch.iworld.com/plug-in.html. You can browse the plug-in list (and their associated links) by category (multimedia, graphics, sound, document, productivity, and Virtual Reality Markup Language) or alphabetically. They also maintain a full ActiveX list.

AUDIO TECHNIQUES

The Web is very visually oriented: You read text, view graphics, and even watch animations. However, you can enhance your Web pages with music, sound bites, and digitized speech. All it takes is a link to a sound file on one end and a Web surfer with the right equipment (sound card and speakers) on the other.

There are a handful of sound formats in use on the Web today. The most common are

- ▶ MIDI for playing instruments through the sound card
- ▶ AIFF (Audio Interchange File Format) developed by Apple
- ▶ AU files, the NeXT/Sun audio format
- ▶ WAV, the Waveform Audio File Format, developed by Microsoft and IBM for use in Windows
- ▶ RA or RAM, the RealAudio format for streaming audio.

The hardest part about getting sound and music into your Web page is converting the analog sound to a digital format. Many newer computer systems now come with microphones and input jacks on the sound cards to record your sound source, but users of older systems will have to buy additional hardware to digitize the sound.

With sound files, as with image files, you need to balance quality and file size. As with graphics, the more realistic the sound, the larger the file. With audio the resolution of the sampling rate is the determining factor, not the number of colors. When sound is digitized it is said to be sampled. The sampling rate is measured in the number of times per second, or kilohertz (KHz), the audio signal is captured. Sample rates range from 8KHz (about telephone quality) to 48KHz (CD quality), and, naturally, the higher the rate the larger the file size.

Background Sound   To date there is no standardized way to play a sound when you first encounter a site. However, Microsoft has advanced the use of sound in its Internet Explorer software with the BGSOUND tag. A HTML file containing the following code:

```
<BGSOUND SRC="elvisc.wav" LOOP="Infinite">
```

will play a digitized sample of Elvis Costello for as long as you remain on the Web page. BGSOUND supports WAV, AU, and MIDI sound types.

Audio Tools   There are a wide range of audio tools available today. Depending on how involved your sound plans for your Web site are, you might be able to use the free or shareware versions on the Net. For very demanding jobs, Sound Forge 3.0 is a solid tool, as is Sound Foundry. Both can handle the full range of recording and editing chores you might need, and both output to any of the popular file formats.

A relatively full-featured shareware sound editor is GoldWave (http://web.cs.mun.ca/~chris3/goldwave/), programmed and supported by Chris Craig. GoldWave can open and play .AU files found in Java applications and on Web pages. It can convert to and from many sound formats including WAV, VOC, AFC, AU, and binary data. Special effects such as Doppler, distortion, echo, flange, and transpose can alter and enhance your audio files to create new and unique sounds.

One of the drawbacks of RealAudio is that it requires special server software to be installed. There are several alternatives, however. TrueSpeech from the DSP Group, Inc. offers a free streaming player and the files work without any additional server software. Microsoft bundles their encoder-the device that takes analog sound signals and converts them to digital—in Windows 95 and NT with their Sound Recorder.

Of course, you don't have to "roll your own" when you are thinking about including sound in your Web pages. Just as there is a mountain of clip art available, there are thousands of digitized sounds and music scores available on the Web. Appendix C lists many other sound resources, including audio archives.

VIDEO TECHNIQUES

As you discovered in the GIF animation section, moving images create huge files. When the images are photorealistic, as with videos, the resulting file size can be astronomical for even the briefest movie. However, streaming technology has made it possible to include small videos on your Web site without having prohibitive download times.

The file formats used in video are

▶ AVI is for Windows environments.

▶ MOV or QT is the QuickTime format developed by Apple; it now has players available on many platforms.

▶ MPG or MPEG was developed by the Motion Picture Expert Group; it's similar to the JPG format.

QuickTime movies have the widest support, although Microsoft supports an additional attribute, DYNSRC, for the IMG tag that allows the playing of an AVI file. You can control the number of times the video clip plays with the LOOP attribute.

Streaming video is in its infancy on the Web and no mechanism enjoys universal or even widespread use. The ones to watch are the RealPlayer from Progressive Networks, which handles RealVideo files, and VDOLive from VDOnet Corporation (www.vdolive.com). VDOLive is available both as a Netscape plug-in and as a Microsoft Internet Explorer ActiveX control. Figure 6.13 shows an example of the RealVideo output.

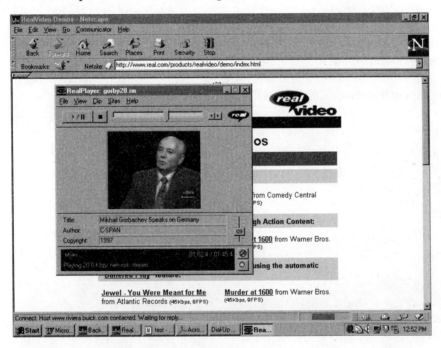

Figure 6.13: The RealVideo Player

Video Tools   To convert regular video or film for use on a computer, you have to digitize the images. This process requires a video capture card or a digital camcorder (these have just been released to the market). In addition, you need a very large, very fast hard drive to hold and access the vast amount of data produced by digitizing a video.

Once you've processed the footage, there is a healthy selection of software video tools for editing your work. Many come integrated with hardware such as the systems from NewTek, Matrox, Avid, and Pinnacle. Video editing software is also available from Corel, Microsoft, and Macromedia, among others.

A good starting place for the full range of video information on the Web is The Film and Broadcast Page (www.interlog.com/~proeser/), with its links to Broadcasters, Film Studios, Audio Resources, Manufacturers and Services, FAQs, Regulators, Associations, Festivals, Newsgroups, Educational Programs, and Other Media Related Resources.

INLINE VRML

Tired of your ordinary two-dimensional HTML world? Take a step into VRML—Virtual Reality Markup Language. Virtual reality uses 3D modeling techniques to let the participant enter a computer-generated environment, move about in it, and interact with the objects found there. VRML takes those concepts and applies them to the Web.

Although a full examination of VRML is beyond the scope of this book, the recent emergence of VRML plug-in modules makes it worth a look. Microsoft's Internet Explorer supports VRML through its Virtual Explorer plug-in module. You insert an addition to the IMG tag like this:

```
<IMG SRC="no3d.gif" VRML="gallery.wrl" HEIGHT=300 WIDTH=300">
```

Netscape uses the EMBED tag that is covered in the next chapter. Both allow peeks into a fascinating realm of interactive futuretech, as you can see from Figure 6.14.

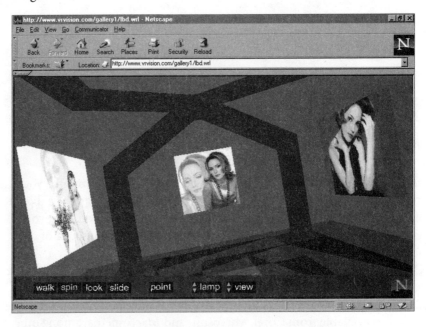

Figure 6.14: A view from the Virtual Gallery (www.vrvision.com)

Interactive Pages

Forms

CGI: Common Gateway Interface

Scripting

Objects

Dynamic Documents

So far, most of the material in this book has been directed towards publishing on the World Wide Web in the traditional sense of the word. You put a fixed amount of information on a "page" and present it to the reader. The Web, from this point of view, is the whole world's shared disk drive, with a graphic, hypertext-based file system. Although this advance alone makes the Web the hottest thing since the first video game, Pong, in the future the true value of the Web will be as an environment for *interactive* pages. In this environment, the reader—through his or her Web browser—will exist in a virtual space interacting with others online.

We're not quite there yet. Currently, most interactive Web applications use a server-side process called the Common Gateway Interface. However, there are several technologies that will download a small program to your browser when you click on a link. This program will modify the current page in response to your input. Such client-side programs are known as "applets" or "objects." In their present stage of development, applets are written by programmers in special computer languages. This chapter provides an overview of several such approaches: Java from Sun Microsystems, ActiveX and VB-Script from Microsoft, and JavaScript from Netscape. First, however, you'll learn how you can use HTML in an interactive environment.

FORMS

A form is a designated area of an HTML page containing input fields and other interactive objects, such as pop-up menus, check boxes, and buttons.

Interactive forms allow you to obtain information from your readers. A form on a Web page is very much like a reader reply card bound into a magazine. The reader types information into fields on the form. Then the contents of the form are posted somewhere for processing—either to an e-mail address or to a program on a server.

Sending the contents to a server has advantages—the information can be checked and processed in real time and a custom reply can be generated (possibly containing another form) and returned to the reader. But if you have the contents sent to an e-mail address you don't need to run a server to test the form and you don't have to write a program to process the input. Such programs, known as Common Gateway Interface (CGI) scripts, are written in various languages for different operating systems. Writing them is more complicated than creating Web pages. CGI scripts are discussed in more detail later in this chapter. The examples in this section post the contents to an e-mail address.

Forms begin and end with the tags <FORM> and </FORM>. The <FORM> tag can take three attributes: METHOD, ACTION, and ENCTYPE, although only the first two are commonly used. METHOD indicates how the form's content will be presented to the script or e-mailer. There are two possible values for METHOD: "post" and "get". Always use the value "post" to specify that the content is presented as standard input. The other value, "get", is obsolete. It specifies that the form's content is sent to the server in the form of a URL. Some older servers limit the length of data passed this way, so use "post".

The ACTION attribute specifies what should be done with the information entered by the reader. The ACTION attribute takes a URL as its value—either the URL of a CGI script or a "mailto" URL, as here:

```
<FORM METHOD=post ACTION="mailto:president@whitehouse.gov">
```

(Be aware that some older browsers may not support mailto URLs and that a browser must be properly configured for this process to work properly. Here again, it's a very good idea to test on multiple systems and platforms.)

The third attribute for <FORM> specifies the encoding type and is called ENCTYPE. Technically speaking, this attribute specifies the MIME media type used to encode the *name=value* pairs for the form processing program. In other words, it dictates how the submitted information will be presented to the recipient—in the preceding example, e-mail to The White House.

What actually gets mailed to the address? It's a string with each input field presented as *name=value* separated from other input fields with an ampersand. The name is from the <INPUT> tag's NAME attribute and the value is from the reader's input. If I had typed my name and e-mail address in a sample form and then added a comment, "Just checking!", the body of an e-mail message sent to mybox@myplace.com would contain:

```
name=Larry+Aronson&addr=laronson@acm.org&comment=Just+checking%21
```

Trailing spaces are trimmed from the input field and the plus sign is substituted for any internal space. Special characters, such as the exclamation point at the end of the comment, are represented by hexadecimal values begun with the percent sign (%21 = decimal 33 = ASCII "!").

There are many tools on the Web that can shape this information into a more useable format. A good one is WebParse, which you can get from Informatik (www.informatik.com). This shareware program will lay out your responses in a readable form, stripping out the plus signs, and so on. In addition, it will put the information into a simple database.

Keep in mind that you can use other HTML elements—both structure tags like <P> and style tags like <EMP>—freely inside and outside the form. You can use virtually any other HTML command—including those for graphics, lists, and tables—to provide additional content by including it within the <FORM></FORM> pair. You can even include a hypertext link inside the form, although this isn't advisable; after all, you want the form completed before your visitor jumps to another page.

Let's build a sample form, one element at a time. Here is basic code for a very simple form:

```
<FORM METHOD="post" ACTION="mailto:mybox@myplace.com">
<P>Please Enter Your Name:
<INPUT TYPE="text" NAME="name" SIZE=30>
</P>
<INPUT TYPE="submit"><INPUT TYPE="reset">
</FORM>
```

Figure 7.1 shows the result.

The first line starts the form, sets the post method, and selects a URL that will mail the information to an e-mail address. The next line starts a paragraph with the <P> tag and gives the user some instructions. Next is a key concept in developing a form, the input field.

INPUT FIELDS

<INPUT> tags are empty. <INPUT> tags insert objects (such as text boxes and radio buttons) in line with other text, just like <IMAGE> tags. This means that your browser will draw the box inline with your surrounding text until it meets either a structure tag or the <BR> tag. You can isolate the code

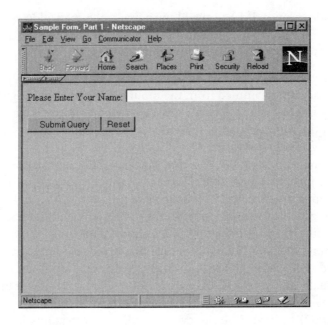

Figure 7.1: Simple form

on its own line (the example does this with the <P> tags) and still have it appear next to the description. The TYPE attribute of the <INPUT> tags in this example has the value, "text", creating a text box—a single-line field whose length in characters is determined by the SIZE attribute (30 characters in the example). Each input tag must have a NAME attribute with a unique value within the form; the example uses the apt name, "name".

You can set a default value in your INPUT="text" box by using the VALUE attribute. If, for example, you included a "Country" field, and you knew that 90 percent of your respondents were from the U.S., you might use the following code:

```
<INPUT TYPE="text" NAME="country" VALUE="United States" SIZE=40>
```

This would putting the words "United States" in your Country field initially, but would let anyone filling out the form type in new information.

<INPUT> tags don't have to be text. In a moment, you'll learn about other types of input such as radio buttons, check boxes, and drop-down lists.

At the end of the form are two buttons created by the tags <INPUT TYPE="submit"> and <INPUT TYPE="reset">. Clicking on the submit button tells the browser to take the action specified in the FORM tag—sending the contents of the fields to the specified e-mail address. Clicking on the reset button clears all input fields within the enclosing <FORM> tags.

By default, the "submit" and "reset" types create buttons that say "Submit Query" and "Reset," respectively. You can change that by using the VALUE attribute. To make your buttons say "Send Form Now" and "Clear Form Now," use the following code:

```
<INPUT TYPE="submit" VALUE="Send Form Now">
<INPUT TYPE="reset" VALUE="Clear Form Now">
```

The <TEXTAREA> Tag   You use the TYPE="text" attribute for any single-line field, such as Address, City, State, or Zip. But what if you want to solicit more general feedback and allow readers to enter more than a single line of text? HTML 3.2 includes a special tag for this circumstance, <TEXTAREA>. The <TEXTAREA> tag creates an input area with a specified number of rows and columns, allowing the reader to enter free-form text.

Like the <INPUT> tag, <TEXTAREA> requires a NAME attribute, unique within the form. Again, this tag labels whatever text is submitted and processed. Unlike the <INPUT> tag, however, the <TEXTAREA> tag is not empty. Any text between it and the ending tag, </TEXTAREA>, goes into the text area by default, and can be edited by the reader.

You determine the size of the <TEXTAREA> box by using the ROWS and COLS attributes. Both attributes take numeric values—COLS=n specifies how many characters wide the text box will be and ROWS=n indicates how many lines high it will be. This height and width does not limit the amount of text that can be entered: If you enter more text than fits within the box, horizontal and vertical scroll bars appear, allowing you to see any text that doesn't display initially. In other words, the box created by <TEXTAREA>'s COLS and ROWS attributes is just a window for viewing that text.

The example shown in Figure 7.2 is a simple form application to request a comment from the reader; it puts together all the commands you've learned so far:

```
<HTML>
<HEAD>
<TITLE>Form Example</TITLE>
</HEAD>
<BODY>
<H1>Comments Please</H1>
<P>We would like to hear from you. Please use the following form to submit any
comments on our service.</P>
<FORM METHOD="post" ACTION="mailto:mybox@myplace.com">
<P>Please enter your name:
<INPUT TYPE="text" NAME="name" SIZE="30"><BR>
```

```
and your email address:
<INPUT TYPE="text" NAME="addr" SIZE="30"></P>
<HR>
<P>Use the input area below to enter any comments you like.<BR>
Click the "Send Form Now" button when you are done.</P>
<TEXTAREA NAME="comment" ROWS=6 COLS=40></TEXTAREA>
<P>Thanks for your input.
<INPUT TYPE="submit" VALUE="Send Form Now">
<INPUT TYPE="reset" VALUE="Clear Form Now">
</P>
</FORM>
</BODY>
</HTML>
```

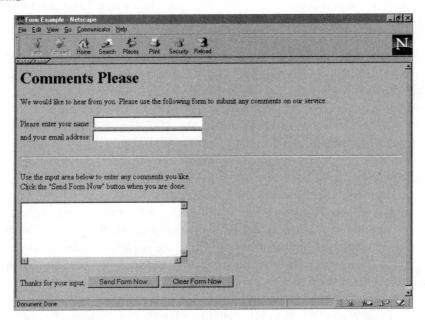

Figure 7.2: A sample form

Radio Buttons and Check Boxes When you want the reader to choose from a finite number of options, you can use radio buttons, check boxes, and pop-up menus.

Radio buttons work in a set; when one is selected, all other buttons in the set are deselected. Use radio buttons when you want the reader to choose one-and-only-one value from a small set of mutually exclusive values. You define each button with a separate <INPUT> tag; however, the NAME attribute has the same value for all buttons in the set. For example:

```
<H3>Annual Income Level:</H3>
<P>
<INPUT TYPE="radio" NAME="income" VALUE=1> $0 to $19,999<BR>
<INPUT TYPE="radio" NAME="income" VALUE=2 CHECKED> $20,000 to $59,999<BR>
<INPUT TYPE="radio" NAME="income" VALUE=3> $60,000 and up
</P>
```

You use check boxes to let readers choose anywhere from zero to many values from a small set of nonexclusive values. Each box is defined with a separate input tag and, because check boxes are not grouped into sets, each has a unique value for the NAME attribute. For example:

```
<H3>Computers:</H3>
<P>
<INPUT TYPE="checkbox" NAME="C1" VALUE="W"> Windows
<INPUT TYPE="checkbox" NAME="C2" VALUE="M"> Macintosh
<INPUT TYPE="checkbox" NAME="C3" VALUE="U"> UNIX
<INPUT TYPE="checkbox" NAME="C4" VALUE="O"> Other
</P>
```

Hidden and Password Fields   There are two special-purpose TYPE values: hidden and password. Setting the TYPE="hidden" option allows you to embed information in the form without the user seeing it. This property becomes useful when each form contains information you want passed back to you. If, for example, your Web site has multiple forms, all mailing to the same e-mail address, you might want to label each form. Use the VALUE attribute to set the title. Here's one example:

```
<INPUT TYPE="hidden" NAME="title" VALUE="User Survey">
```

The hidden value is also used extensively to set parameters for CGI scripts, as you'll see later in this chapter.

Occasionally, you might want to provide an password input field. For password information, it's customary to mask the actual characters being typed by displaying asterisks instead. If you set the TYPE attribute to "password", you'll get this effect: Every input character appears in the text box as an asterisk (*), but the actual password information is passed to your variable specified by NAME. Here's a simple example:

```
<P>
Please enter your password:
<INPUT TYPE="password" NAME="pword" SIZE=30>
</P>
```

SELECT MENUS

You create pop-up menus with the <SELECT> tag. Pop-up menus are useful for letting the reader choose one option from a set of many. This tag is a container tag; you mark individual menu options with the <OPTION></OPTION> tags, as in this example:

```
<H3>Primary Application:</H3>

<P>
<SELECT NAME="prime">
<OPTION SELECTED>Word Processing</OPTION>
<OPTION>Graphics</OPTION>
<OPTION>Spreadsheet</OPTION>
<OPTION>Project Management</OPTION>
<OPTION>Games</OPTION>
<OPTION>Utilities</OPTION>
<OPTION>Programming</OPTION>
<OPTION>Database</OPTION>
</SELECT>
</P>
```

One of the options in a SELECT should have the SELECTED attribute; otherwise, by default, the first OPTION value is selected. You can specify multiple choices by adding the MULTIPLE attribute to the SELECT tag. The content of each OPTION is the value that will be posted should the reader choose that option—for example, prime="Project Management". This can be overridden by adding VALUE attributes to the OPTION tags, for example,

```
<OPTION VALUE="pman">Project Management</OPTION>
```

Figure 7.3 shows the radio buttons, check boxes, and pop-up menus built from the code examples in this section.

CGI: COMMON GATEWAY INTERFACE

The Common Gateway Interface (CGI) is the Web's standard for client-server application interfacing. Most HTML documents are static, meaning that they exist in a constant state over some period of time, from hours to years. A CGI program, on the other hand, generates HTML in real time. Its output is a dynamically generated Web page. It's a way to present information to your readers that isn't exactly known until asked for. This is how search engines generate their responses to a query.

CGI programs (or "scripts"—the terms are used interchangeably) perform many general Web functions. Imagemap, the CGI program that handles

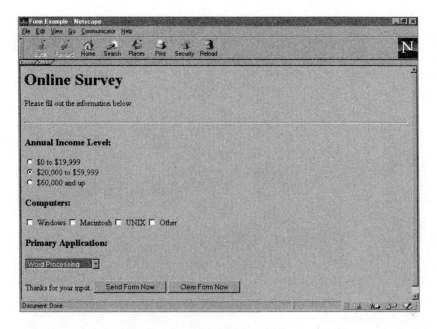

Figure 7.3: Radio buttons, check boxes, and pop-up menus

server-side imagemaps for many servers, is probably the most familiar. HTML forms typically require CGI scripts to do something with the information the readers enter. CGI scripts serve as the interface between a Web server and other computer applications, such as database managers and order processing systems. There's really no limit to what can be hooked up to the Web. The only requirement is that a CGI program must do its work quickly. Otherwise, the reader will just be staring at his or her browser waiting for something to happen.

For most servers, CGI programs need to reside in a special directory, usually called cgi-bin, so that the Web server knows to execute the program rather than download it to the reader's browser. This directory is usually located at the root of the system, and can only be modified by your site's webmaster. There are other ways to allow access to CGI scripts, but your webmaster has to set these up for you, too. A program in the cgi-bin directory is meant to be executed by anyone. There's no built-in protection in this interface, so the webmaster must have the final authority on the contents of that directory to keep the system secure.

CGI programs can be written in any language that allows them to be executed on the system hosting the Web server. Most are written in one of the following languages:

- C/C++
- FORTRAN
- PERL (Program Extraction and Report Language)
- TCL
- UNIX shell
- Visual Basic
- AppleScript

Certain languages such as C or FORTRAN are programming languages that need to be compiled before they can be run on a system. Scripting languages, like PERL or UNIX shell, use scripts that are interpreted at runtime by the related program. Because they are a little easier to follow, the examples use scripting languages.

PROCESSING OVERVIEW

In the simplest sense, information sent from the reader's browser goes to the CGI program as standard input, and whatever the program writes to standard output goes back to the reader. To understand it in more detail, it helps to understand a little more about Hypertext Transfer Protocol (HTTP), the set of formal rules that servers and browsers follow when talking to each other. The conversation begins when the reader clicks on a link, or a form's submit button. It proceeds in four steps:

1 A connection is made to the server at the Internet address and port number specified in the URL.

2 The browser sends either a request to *get* an object from the server, or a request to *post* data to an object on the server.

3 The server sends back a response consisting of status code and, usually but not always, response data.

4 The browser closes the connection to the server.

The request data sent by the browser to the server includes a modified URL. The URL method (for example, http:) and the server:port address are stripped from the beginning of the URL and a query string preceded by a question

mark (?) may be added to the end. When you click on a (server-side) imagemap, for example, the request sent to the server will look like this:

```
GET /cgi-bin/imagemap/mapname?x,y HTTP/1.0
```

where "mapname" is the symbolic name (see Chapter 5) of the image's map
file and (x,y) are the offset, in pixels, of the reader's click from the upper-left
corner of the image.

When the browser sends a request to the server using the POST method—
the recommended method to use for forms—the information is sent as MIME
data encoded in the standard URL format with spaces replaced by plus signs
(+), fields separated by ampersands (&), and special characters encoded in
%xx hexadecimal notation. For a typical guestbook form, the actual request
from the browser to the server would look something like this:

```
POST /cgi-bin/guestbook.pl HTTP/1.0
Accept: text/plain
Accept: text/html
        .
        .
        .
Accept: */*
Content-type: application/x-www-form-urlencoded
Content-length: 57

name=Larry+Aronson&addr=laronson@acm.org&loc=...
```

The script, guestbook.pl, would parse the data at the end of the request, append it to a file, or do something else with it and write a response to standard
output. The server will send the output back to the reader along with a status
code, such as 200 = "success", or 404 = "URL not found". To dynamically generate and return an HTML page, the output must begin with a MIME content
declaration followed by an empty line followed by the HTML content. For example, the following UNIX shell script (identified by the opening "#!/bin/sh"
line) can be called by the CGI script to send a reply back to a user who has submitted a form:

```
#!/bin/sh
echo "Content-type: text/html"
echo
echo "<HEAD><TITLE>Form Reply</TITLE></HEAD>"
echo "<BODY>"
echo "<H2 ALIGN=center>Thank You</H2>"
echo "<H3 ALIGN=center>for submitting your information.</H3>"
echo "<HR>"
```

```
echo "Return to our <A HREF=\"/homepage.html\">homepage</A>"
echo "</BODY>"
```

A SIMPLE CGI MAIL FORM

Although you must program in PERL, UNIX shell, or one of the other CGI-compatible languages to get the most out of CGI scripts, there are a lot of existing CGI scripts on the Web that you can use—either unaltered or adapted. This section shows you how to tailor a simple CGI script to your needs.

One of the most common CGI uses is the mail form. After a user fills out a form on your Web page and clicks on a submit button, a CGI mail form program checks for errors, parses the URL-encoded text, sends the information via e-mail to a specific address, and then gives the user some feedback. This section describes how to use a very simple mail form called mailer.pl.

Mailer.pl is written in PERL, one of the most powerful and common CGI languages. Most of the CGI scripts on the Web are written in PERL. One of the advantages of PERL is that it works with scripts that you can read and edit in a regular text editor. When your HTML code calls a PERL script with the AC-TION attribute, it is run by the PERL engine located on the server. You can find the full listing for mailer.pl and all the other programs in this section on this book's Web site at www.mcp.com/zdpress/features/5299/. Because it is a text listing, just go to its page in your browser and then use the Save As command to put it on your hard drive.

Here are the steps for using mailer.pl:

1 Open the mailer.pl file in your favorite text editor.

2 Look over the code. Lines starting with a hash mark (#) are comments; variables start with a dollar sign ($). Comments mark each of the seven subroutines in the script.

3 To personalize the code, you must set the first two variables, $mailprog and $recipient. $mailprog is the name and location of the mailing program that mailer.pl uses to send the data. The default, "/usr/lib/sendmail", is perhaps the most common, but check with your server's administrator to be sure. The second variable, $recipient, is the e-mail address of where the form information is to be sent. You must put it in the format "*yourname/@yourhost*.com"—the forward slash (/) causes the next @ to be read correctly.

4 Save your script.

5 Transfer your altered mailer.pl to the cgi-bin directory of your server. This is usually done with an FTP program such as CuteFTP for Windows

or Fetch on the Macintosh. (If you don't have an FTP program, check Appendix C.)

6 Open your HTML page with the form on it.

7 Change the FORM command to read:

```
<FORM METHOD="post" ACTION="http://www.yoursite.com/cgi-bin/mailer.pl"
```

8 Save and transfer your HTML page to the server.

That's it! You've just coded your first CGI script in PERL.

What can you expect to see when mailer.pl is run? Your users will see a brief reply informing them that their data has been sent. You will receive, via e-mail, a list of the NAMEs in each of your form input fields and the response submitted by the user; Figure 7.4 shows an example.

Figure 7.4: An e-mailed response from mailer.pl

Although it does the job, mailer.pl has some drawbacks. First, the reply to your user is pretty barren; it would be nice to indicate where the form information has been sent. Second, you only get what fields the user fills out. If the "Ask A Salesman to Call!" radio button is selected but the phone number field is empty, you're in trouble. It would be better to require certain fields. Third, the server has access to information, such as where the user called from, that could be helpful. The next CGI program you'll examine can fill your wish list and more—all from within the HTML document.

PASSING CGI VARIABLES

To get additional information, you need to tell the PERL program what you are looking for; you do this by passing variables. Passing variables is a basic computer programming technique that allows one program to set the specifications for another. In this case, you can use the general PERL program with different HTML programs without having to rewrite the PERL source code.

The PERL program you will be using is called formmail.pl. It was written by Matthew W. Wright and can be found at www.worldwidemart.com/scripts/ and on this book's site. Formmail.pl uses the <INPUT> tag with the TYPE="hidden" attribute to pass the variables behind the scenes.

You still have to modify the formmail.pl script as you did the mailer.pl script. You must verify that the mail program and its location are correctly identified with the $mailprog variable. You also have to set the @referers array to the domain name of the user, like this:

```
@referers = ('www.yoursite.com')
```

This ensures that your mail form script can only be used from your server. Otherwise, anyone on any server could point to the program and use it without your knowledge or permission. There are security issues concerning CGI scripts, as you'll learn a little later in this section.

What can formmail.pl do? This PERL program allows you to specify the recipient of the e-mailed form, specify a subject for the message header to identify the e-mailed response, require certain fields to be filled out before the form can be processed, sort the response fields alphabetically or in a particular order, and output a more informative reply to the users or redirect them to a specific HTML page of your own creation. Let's get started!

There is only one required variable to be passed for formmail.pl to work correctly. You must tell it whom the recipient of the e-mailed response is to be, as in this line to be included between <FORM> and </FORM>:

```
<INPUT TYPE="hidden" NAME="recipient" VALUE="you@yoursite.com">
```

You use this approach instead of having to alter the $recipient variable in the PERL script. All the other form fields are optional.

You specify the subject of the mail message sent to you in the same manner, using NAME="subject" and whatever text you want to appear assigned to the

VALUE attribute. To require certain fields to be filled out, include a line like this in your HTML code:

```
<INPUT TYPE="hidden" NAME="required" VALUE="name,phone,email">
```

In this example, if either the name, phone, or email field is not filled out, the user will be notified and asked to try again. In the value list, substitute your own field names, separated by commas.

You can use formmail.pl to sort the generated response either alphabetically or in a particular field order. To specify an alphabetical sort, include this line in your form:

```
<INPUT TYPE="hidden" NAME="sort" VALUE="alphabetic">
```

To set your own order for the response, use this code syntax:

```
<INPUT TYPE="hidden" NAME="sort" VALUE="order:field1,field2,field3">
```

Naturally, substitute your field names for those listed in the VALUE.

ENVIRONMENTAL VARIABLES

The server knows a fair amount about every transaction that takes place: the who, what, where, and when—although not the why (yet!). This information is stored in what are collectively called the environmental variables. You can include this information on the e-mailed response by setting the environmental variables within your HTML code.

There are over 20 environmental variables on a regular Web server. There's a full list of them at NCSA (www.ncsa.org). Here's a short list of the most useful ones:

- ▸ **REMOTE_HOST**   The username that is making the request
- ▸ **REMOTE_ADDR**   The Internet provider address of the user
- ▸ **REMOTE_USER_AGENT**   The browser being used; includes the software and the version number

To request this environmental report, use the following command in your FORM:

```
<INPUT TYPE="hidden" NAME="env_report"
VALUE="REMOTE_HOST,REMOTE_ADDR,REMOTE_USER_AGENT">
```

REDIRECTING THE USER

The final option covered with formmail.pl is redirection. Suppose you want to send your users to a special Web page after they have submitted the form, instead of sending them a default response. To do so, include another hidden type input variable with "redirect" as the name. Here's an example:

```
<INPUT TYPE="hidden" NAME="redirect"
VALUE="http://www.yoursite.com/newplace/newpage.html">
```

Notice that the full URL is used for the value. Although you can use relative addressing, absolute addressing is the safer alternative. If you move your site, however, be sure to update all absolute addresses.

You can do numerous other things with the formmail.pl script, and Matthew Wright has many other terrific CGI scripts. To learn more, check out www.worldwidemart.com/scripts as well as his upcoming book on CGI programming published by John Wiley & Sons.

There is, of course, much more to CGI scripting. There's a good online primer for learning more about CGI at http://hoohoo.ncsa.uiuc.edu/cgi/.

SCRIPTING

As mentioned, HTML 3.2 can extend its capabilities by accessing other programming languages. One of the most flexible extensions is the <SCRIPT> element. This tag allows for compatibility with today's and tomorrow's languages. This section examines the use of the <SCRIPT> tag, primarily through the language of JavaScript. Both the Navigator and Internet Explorer browsers are JavaScript-enabled to varying degrees. For this reason, JavaScript enjoys the widest support of any Internet scripting language today. You'll also find out a bit about Microsoft's VBScript and note some of its special qualities.

JAVASCRIPT OVERVIEW

JavaScript, developed by Netscape, was initially known as LiveScript. The language didn't really take off until Sun Microsystems joined the development team and LiveScript was renamed JavaScript. This was a marketing stroke of genius and a major source of confusion: JavaScript has almost nothing to do with Java except that they both can work with HTML.

A good way to think about JavaScript is to remember that it is part of a client-side process. Because CGI resides on the server, programs involving CGI are server-side processes. Therefore, the speed of any JavaScript process depends on the speed of the client's machine, and, given today's multitasking environments, what else is running on the system. Still, for many operations, JavaScript is apparently as fast as any process on the server side; the major trade-off being that almost all browsers can access CGI scripts and not all browsers are JavaScript-enabled.

<SCRIPT>: THE HTML-JAVASCRIPT CONNECTION

Including JavaScript code in your HTML page is very easy and familiar: you simply enclose your JavaScript code within the <SCRIPT> and </SCRIPT> tags. For added flexibility, <SCRIPT> takes one attribute, LANGUAGE, which you set to whatever script language you are using (the current choices are "JavaScript" and "VBScript"). Your HTML code with JavaScript included would look like this:

```
<HTML>
<HEAD>
<TITLE>First JavaScript</TITLE>
<SCRIPT LANGUAGE="JavaScript">
"Your JavaScript Code Here!"
</SCRIPT>
</HEAD>
<BODY>
...
</BODY>
</HTML>
```

Here, the sample JavaScript code (not the real thing) is in the HEAD section of the document, which is used for preloading graphics or other elements into memory. JavaScript can also go anywhere within the body of the document, where it will be treated as another inline element—that is, whatever the code is doing will appear there.

There is one other consideration to keep in mind when placing your Java-Script code: Not all browsers can read it. To hide the code from browsers that can't read it, enclose all the JavaScript within the HTML comment structure, after the <SCRIPT> tag, like this:

```
<HTML>
<HEAD>
<TITLE>First JavaScript</TITLE>
<SCRIPT LANGUAGE="JavaScript">
<!-- begin to hide
"Your JavaScript Code Here!"
// the hiding ends here -->
</SCRIPT>
</HEAD>
<BODY>
...
</BODY>
</HTML>
```

The double forward slashes (//) indicate JavaScript comments; anything following them will be ignored by JavaScript.

OBJECTS IN JAVASCRIPT

JavaScript is a relatively accessible object-oriented computer programming language. As far as HTML is concerned, object-oriented means that every element on a Web page can be defined as an object—every form, every heading, every image. Once you can identify an object on a page by name, you can alter its properties. Each object, depending on what it is, has different properties. Objects such as the check boxes found in forms can have a "checked" property while TEXTAREA objects can not.

You refer to an object according to its hierarchy. An address is a sort of reverse hierarchy: 151 1st Avenue, Apt. 16, New York, NY, USA. Instead of starting with the item at the top of the hierarchy (the country), addresses start with house number. JavaScript uses a top-down hierarchical system, separating each element with a period. The preceding address, in JavaScript, would look something like this: "USA.NY.NewYork.1stAvenue.151.Apt16."

At the very top of the JavaScript hierarchy is the window object—everything else that the viewer sees is part of the browser's window. Within the window object, the document object is of primary interest; this is the HTML page. The page (the document object) contains other objects, including links and forms.

Next you'll create a simple HTML page (which gathers document color info) to see how JavaScript objects are identified, and how you can start to use them.

```
<HTML>
<HEAD>
<TITLE>First JavaScript</TITLE>
</HEAD>
<BODY BGCOLOR="silver">
<H1>Simple Color Converter</h1>
<HR>
<SCRIPT LANGUAGE="JavaScript">
<!-- being to hide
document.write("This background is " + document.bgColor)
// the hiding ends here -->
</SCRIPT>
</BODY>
</HTML>
```

After setting the background color normally in the BODY tag and putting in a heading and horizontal rule, this code sets up one line of JavaScript code. The code, "document.write()", is a method used by JavaScript to write whatever is in the parenthesis on the screen. (More about methods in the next section.) In this case, it is the background color of the document, or, in JavaScript, the "document.bgColor". Note the exact spelling of each element; JavaScript is case sensitive and would not recognize "document.bgcolor". You can see the result in Figure 7.5.

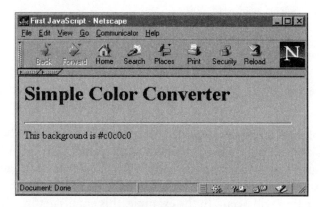

Figure 7.5: A simple JavaScript demonstration

METHODS, PROPERTIES, AND EVENTS

All objects in JavaScript come with a series of methods, properties, and events attached. Methods are what an object can do, properties describe what an object looks like, and events are what an object can respond to.

As noted, "document.write()" is a method. Methods can be thought of as commands. All methods are followed by parentheses. Depending on the object, there may or may not be a value within the parentheses: The window object close() doesn't need a value to operate; the alert() object displays a message box containing whatever is within the parentheses.

Most objects have a series of properties; these often correspond to the attributes that accompany HTML tags. For example, a document's properties include the bgColor, alinkColor, linkColor, and vlinkColor corresponding to the HTML page's BODY attributes BGCOLOR, ALINK, LINK, and VLINK. The difference is that with JavaScript's event handlers, you can alter the properties of almost any given object. Events are generally what the user does—clicking a button with the mouse, entering some text, or even moving her or his mouse over an object. Events are at the heart of JavaScript interaction. Here's a demonstration:

```
<HTML>
<HEAD>
```

```
<TITLE>A JavaScript Event!</TITLE>
<SCRIPT LANGUAGE="JavaScript">
</SCRIPT>
</HEAD>
<BODY>
<H1>Don't be shy, enter your name!</h1>
<FORM NAME="myForm">
<INPUT TYPE="text" name="theName" SIZE=30>
<INPUT TYPE="button" name="Button1" value="Hi There" onClick="alert('Hi ' +
document.myForm.theName.value)">
</FORM>
</BODY>
</HTML>
```

This example sets up a FORM named "myForm" and puts two INPUT fields into it. One, a regular text field, has the name "theName". The other is an additional type allowed by JavaScript: the button. The TYPE="button" attribute enables your first event handler, "onClick". When the user clicks on the button, the described action will occur. In the example, this entails getting the value from the text box, concatenating it to another text string ("Hi"), and putting it on screen in the form of an alert or message box. Figure 7.6 shows the result.

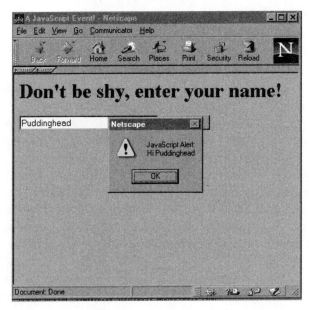

Figure 7.6: Interacting with JavaScript

You've only scratched the surface of JavaScript's potential. The best way for you as a beginning HTML programmer to proceed is to visit some of the many fine JavaScript sites on the Web, many of which are listed in Appendix C. There you'll find additional tutorials and examples.

VBSCRIPT

Much of what you just learned about JavaScript holds true for Microsoft's VB-Script. You start your VBScript code in the same way, but you set the LAN-GUAGE attribute to "VBScript" instead of "JavaScript". The same hierarchical principles of identifying objects are in place, as are similar methods, properties, and events. As you'll learn in Chapter 8, Microsoft has enabled a slew of attributes, especially in regards to the TABLE tag, that can all be addressed through VBScript properties.

Aside from its being specific to Internet Explorer, the only major difference between VBScript and JavaScript is a series of added objects known collectively as ActiveX controls. ActiveX controls allow you to add a host of graphic user interface elements such as timers, sliders, and multistate buttons. ActiveX controls are covered in the next section.

OBJECTS

As the multimedia and hypermedia nature of the Web expands, the original notion to mix text and graphics seems to pale by comparison. A streaming video feed could no more fit in an <IMG> tag than could an active spreadsheet. The image is becoming one of many HTML objects. HTML 3.2's ability to use objects counts as a major advance; it allows you not only to share a wide range of data types besides particular graphic and text formats, but also to transmit small programs. These small applications are best known as applets, and the computer programming language that made them popular is Java.

JAVA APPLETS

A lot of people are very excited about Java, Sun Microsystem's programming language for distributed applications, and the HotJava browser. Recent versions of both the Netscape and Microsoft browsers are Java-enabled. And still the excitement continues to grow.

What's so wonderful about Java? A lot: On a Web page, Java-enabled browsers can play inline sounds when a page loads, or supply ambient music for a page. A Java browser can play real-time video and generate simple animations. A Java browser should be able to do most anything an application program can do on your computer, including communicating over the Internet. Java, however, is much more than just the next hot Web browser. Java is a programming language for distributed applications. It is a method of transmitting executable content.

Without Java, the Web is a space filled with data objects—pages, images, sound clips, and so on. These objects can either be static, as files waiting to be downloaded, or dynamically generated by CGI scripts. Still, HTTP is only designed for moving data objects from here to there. With Java, objects traversing the Web can carry with them the necessary code for the object to interact with the reader. Such enhanced objects are called applets. Applets are platform-independent. A Java program will run equally well on any computer that has a Java-enabled browser. Java programs are compressed to a compact format called byte code, which is interpreted and executed on the fly by a Java-enabled browser.

Today, when a new data type is introduced to the Web—Real Video is a recent example—it takes some time for enough readers to download the helper application for that data type to be worthwhile for authors to use. This is unnecessary with Java.

There are three parts to the Java environment: a Java-enabled Web browser, a Java compiler to turn Java source code into byte code, and a Java interpreter to test and run stand-alone Java programs. Java is another object-oriented programming language, and the process of writing and testing a Java applet is the same as that of writing and testing C++ programs. Most of the resources for learning the language and the environment are listed on Sun's Java page at http://java.sun.com/. Some other Java development resources are listed in Appendix C.

The <APPLET> Tag   You add applets to Web pages with the <APPLET> </APPLET> tags, which describe the applet: its height and width, and any parameters. When a Java-enabled browser encounters an <APPLET> tag, it downloads the code for the applet and executes it. Here, for example, is the HTML to call a simple applet that will play in a 300x200 pixel rectangle:

```
<APPLET CODE="appname.class" WIDTH=300 HEIGHT=200></APPLET>
```

The CODE argument identifies the applet with a relative URL. In this example, the applet, appname.class, is in the same directory as the Web page that calls it. The <APPLET> tag is not an HTML structural element. No paragraph breaks are implied either before or after the applet. Like images and figures, an applet appears inline with other content and markup. In fact, most of the attributes and values that are used with the IMAGE and FIGURE tags—such as

ALIGN, VALIGN, HSPACE, VSPACE, and ALT—can be used in the APPLET tag. Microsoft's Internet Explorer allows similar use of its embedded Java elements, except the applet must be in the <OBJECT> tag rather than the <APPLET> one.

An applet can be on a different server from that of the referring page, even though you must use relative addressing in the CODE attribute. You can use the CODEBASE attribute to provide a base URL for the applet, as in:

```
<APPLET CODE="appname.class"
CODEBASE="http://applets_R_us.com/classes/"
WIDTH=300 HEIGHT=200>
</APPLET>
```

Any content that appears between the starting and ending <APPLET> tags is considered "alternate content." Alternate content can contain any HTML elements, including images and figures. This content is ignored when read by a Java-enabled browser. The <APPLET> tags are ignored by browsers that are not Java-aware.

Parameter Tags A well-designed Java applet will be configurable with a set of parameters controlling most of its important aspects. This allows HTML authors to customize an applet without having to edit and recompile any Java code. Because each applet recognizes a different set of applet parameters, you specify them by placing <PARAM> tags just after the beginning <APPLET> tag and before any alternate content. Each <PARAM> tag has NAME and VALUE attributes whose values are specific to the applet called. For example, a generalized applet that provides animation by repeatedly looping through a set of images might be written with <PARAM> tags that specify the image set and timings:

```
<APPLET CODE="animator.class" WIDTH=144 HEIGHT=216>
<PARAM NAME="images" VALUE=8>
<PARAM NAME="frameset" VALUE="duke">
<PARAM NAME="pause" VALUE=1000>
<IMG SRC="duke.gif" ALT="Sun's Java mascot, Duke">
</APPLET>
```

In this HTML, <PARAM> tags stipulate the number of images in the animation, the location of the images, and how many milliseconds the animator applet should pause between frames. An image of Duke, Sun's rather strange-looking Java mascot, is the alternate content in this example.

Java is a general programming language, not just a Web scripting language. In fact, Corel recently unveiled an entire suite of programs written in Java. Java lets you do just about anything you can do with a traditional programming language like C++. In fact, Java is very similar to C, although much easier to use and cleaner in design. Because it's platform-independent and distributed on the Web, Java might well become tomorrow's language of choice for personal programming.

ACTIVEX CONTROLS

One of the drawbacks to Java is that each applet is distinct and cannot interact with any other applet. In Java, each component has to be totally self-contained because the applets are compiled as one program. What is needed is a collection of network-savvy, platform-independent objects that can work together. Enter ActiveX.

Microsoft's ActiveX technology stands on the shoulders of its Object Linking and Embedding (OLE) development, which allowed applications to share data—you could include a spreadsheet in a word processing document, for example. This sharing of data is at the heart of the ActiveX controls. The controls themselves are a series of objects that can be embedded in your HTML documents to increase the Web page's functionality. The basic controls are similar to the command buttons (like "Submit" and "Reset"), check boxes, and radio buttons that were in the <FORM> tag; however, the ActiveX versions can interact right on the page and don't require data to be processed by a server. Moreover, there are some very sophisticated controls that can emulate almost any interfaces available in a regular desktop application.

ActiveX and HTML   Let's look at how a sample control is incorporated into your HTML code. (Don't be put off by the initial code; later you'll see how to generate it automatically.)

```
<HTML>
<HEAD>
<TITLE>ActiveX Button</TITLE>
</HEAD>
<BODY>
<P>
<OBJECT ID="cmdStart"
CLASSID="clsid:D7053240-CE69-11CD-A777-00DD01143C57" BORDER="0"
WIDTH="96" HEIGHT="32">
<PARAM NAME="Caption" VALUE="Start Button">
<PARAM NAME="Size" value="2540;847">
<PARAM NAME="FontCharSet" value="0">
<PARAM NAME="FontPitchAndFamily" value="2">
<PARAM NAME="ParagraphAlign" value="3">
<PARAM NAME="FontWeight" value="0">
```

```
</OBJECT>
</P>
</BODY>
</HTML>
```

This code will create a simple button like the one shown in Figure 7.7.

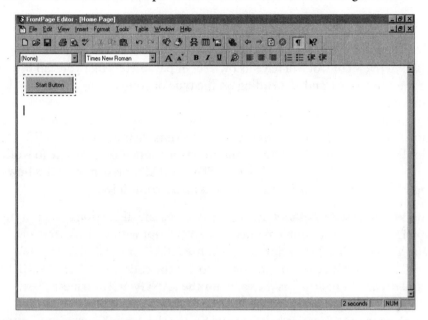

Figure 7.7: A simple ActiveX button

Notice that the ActiveX code goes between the <OBJECT></OBJECT> tag pairs (just as the Java code went between the <APPLET> tags). Within the opening <OBJECT> tag are a number of attributes that specify the ActiveX control being inserted. ID gives the control a name in the HTML document, CLASSID is a unique number registered with Microsoft to identify this control, and WIDTH and HEIGHT allow the browser to quickly draw the element. The easiest way to insert the CLASSID number (and the rest of the identifying code) is to use a tool like the ActiveX Control Pad available separately from Microsoft (www.microsoft.com) or built into Microsoft's Web site development tool, FrontPage. Again, check Appendix C for a full list of resources.

All the other statements in the <PARAM> element are, as with Java, parameters that are passed to the control.

- ▸ "Caption" is the name that appears on the button.

- ▸ "Size" is the width and height specified in twips $(1/20^{th}$ of a point or $1/1440^{th}$ of an inch).

- ▸ "FontCharSet" denotes the font (0 is the default, Times New Roman).

- ▸ "FontPitchAndFamily" sets the style for the caption.

- ▸ "ParagraphAlign" aligns the caption within the button.

Each ActiveX control will have its own set of parameters that you can use to alter the appearance and, depending on the type of control, the interactive elements of the control.

Controls by themselves do nothing. In Microsoft's parlance, they have to be "activated." Although you can use JavaScript to enable the interaction, VBScript is a better match for ActiveX and there are more tools available to work with the ActiveX/VBScript combination. The next section demonstrates how a sample VBScript can make your ActiveX controls come alive.

Using VBScript with ActiveX If you've followed the discussions so far in this chapter, you'll have no problem integrating VBScript with ActiveX controls. Again, VBScript, like JavaScript, can go in the HEAD or the BODY section of the HTML page. Once you decide where to put the code, insert the <SCRIPT> tag and declare "VBScript" as the value for the LANGUAGE attribute. Next, start the HTML comment command ("<!--") to stop older browsers from printing your code. Here's a brief example using the ActiveX command button set up in the previous example:

```
<HTML>
<HEAD>
<TITLE>ActiveX Button</TITLE>
</HEAD>
<BODY>
<P><SCRIPT LANGUAGE="VBScript">
<!--
Sub cmdStart_Click()
cmdStart.Caption = "Activated!"
end sub
-->
</SCRIPT>
<BODY>
<P>
<OBJECT ID="cmdStart"
CLASSID="clsid:D7053240-CE69-11CD-A777-00DD01143C57" BORDER="0"
WIDTH="96" HEIGHT="32">
```

```
<PARAM NAME="Caption" VALUE="Start Button">
<PARAM NAME="Size" value="2540;847">
<PARAM NAME="FontCharSet" value="0">
<PARAM NAME="FontPitchAndFamily" value="2">
<PARAM NAME="ParagraphAlign" value="3">
<PARAM NAME="FontWeight" value="0">
</OBJECT>
</P>
</BODY>
</HTML>
```

VBScript can use subroutines (as can JavaScript), just like most programming languages. In this instance, the first part of the subroutine label ("cmd-Start") identifies which control is being used and the second part ("Click()") gives the event that will start the code—that is, the code will run whenever the user clicks on this button.

The code itself consists of one line:

```
cmdStart.Caption = "Activated!"
```

Here, as you saw before in JavaScript, a hierarchical naming convention is being usedcmdStart. Caption translates to "the caption of the button named cmdStart". In this case, the code will change the caption from "Start Button" to "Activated!"

This is a very basic demonstration of the capabilities of using VBScript with ActiveX controls. There are a growing number of resources for ActiveX controls and VBScript. A good place to start is CINET's ActiveX Web site (www.activex.com). This site contains basic tutorials and information, as well as a large collection of ActiveX controls.

DYNAMIC DOCUMENTS

Browsers are generally driven by user input. The reader clicks on a link and a Web page is downloaded to the browser for viewing. Netscape, in release 1.1 of their Navigator browser, introduced a concept called dynamic documents. They come in two forms: client-pull and server-push. When a reader links to a client-pull page, it is downloaded and displayed as usual. If, after a specified period of time, the reader has not clicked on a link or otherwise exited the page, a second page is automatically sent to replace the first. A server-push document is a page, some part of which is continually refreshed by a server-side CGI script. Server-push provides a means for enhancing pages with inline animations. Let's look at client-pull pages first.

CLIENT-PULL

In client-pull dynamic documents, a special tag in the head section of the document tells the client what to do after some specified time has elapsed. In the simplest case, the page is just automatically reloaded on a regular basis. For example, save the following HTML in a file:

```
<HTML>
<HEAD>
<META HTTP-EQUIV="Refresh" CONTENT=5>
<TITLE>Page One</TITLE>
</HEAD>
<BODY>
<H1>This is PAGE ONE!</H1>
Put some stuff here, maybe an image.
</BODY>
</HTML>
```

Then load it into Netscape or some other browser that supports client-pull (not all browsers do). You will notice that the page reloads itself once every five seconds.

It's the <META> tag in the head section that is, in effect, "pulling" a new copy of the page from the server every five seconds. The META tag simulates an HTTP response five seconds after being read by your browser. To the server, this response contains the request to reload the current page, just as if you had clicked on the reload button. Each time the page is reloaded, the refresh directive is also reloaded. In other words, the page reloads itself every five seconds, until the reader intervenes and exits the page by clicking on a link, or the home button, or by closing the page's window.

A client-pull page need not be a static page. If a process on the server periodically updates the HTML file with time dependent content, the page is dynamically updating itself.

You can also use the <META> tag to cause another page to replace the current page in so many seconds.

```
<META HTTP-EQUIV="Refresh" CONTENT="60; URL=http://yersite.com/page_2.html">
```

Note that a fully qualified URL is used and that a semicolon separates the two parts of the CONTENT attribute. This page can also be a client-pull page, making it possible to present a sequence of pages to the completely passive reader. Because not all browsers support the META tag, it's a good idea to explain near the top of the page that it might go away in so many seconds or minutes (or that it might not), and encourage your reader to click on one of the links provided.

SERVER-PUSH

In server push, a server-side CGI script sends down a chunk of data, which the browser displays normally. However, the HTTP connection is kept open, allowing the server to send additional data whenever it wants to. The connection is held open for an indefinite period of time, with each block of data replacing the previous until either the server decides enough is enough, or the reader interrupts the process or exits the page.

In a typical application, the block of data is a new HTML page, with some small part—a table of data read from a database (enclosed in <PRE></PRE> tags)—differing from the previous page. This is like client-pull except that the control and timing are handled on the server side. It's also more efficient because the connection is opened and closed only once. However, it can use up considerable CPU resources on a server.

A Netscape extension provides another use: animation. The data sent by the server script can be a series of GIF images that are the frames of an animation. In the HTML for the page displaying this animation, an ordinary image tag is used; ordinary except that the URL of the SRC attribute is a CGI script instead of a GIF file. For example, this image tag points to a CGI script on Netscape Communication's Web server:

```
<IMG WIDTH=64 HEIGHT=64 SRC="http://www.netscape.com/cgi-bin/doit.cgi">
```

doit.cgi is a small C program written by Rob McCool. You can get the source from: http://home.netscape.com/assist/net_sites/mozilla/doit.c. Like a CGI script, it begins with a MIME content type/subtype declaration. However, instead of the usual "text/html," it writes the special declaration:

```
Content-type: multipart/x-mixed-replace;boundary=ThisRandomString
```

Typically, an HTTP response is only a single piece of data. However, the MIME standard has a facility for sending many pieces of data in a single response. So, the MIME type is "multipart" and the subtype says the data is of an experimental, mixed type that replaces previous data sent. The boundary argument provides a string that separates the data blocks. Each data block has its own MIME content type/subtype declaration—"text/html" for an HTML page, and "image/gif" for images, as in this case.

What doit.cgi does is run a timed loop that, during each iteration, writes out the boundary string, a MIME declaration, and GIF data. Each iteration creates one frame of the animation. The output of doit.cgi looks like this:

```
Content-type: multipart/x-mixed-replace;boundary=---ThisRandomString
--ThisRandomString
Content-type: image/gif
```

```
{ GIF Data for the first frame }
--ThisRandomStringContent-type: image/gif
{ GIF Data for the second frame }
 .
 .
 .
--ThisRandomString
Content-type: image/gif
{ GIF Data for the last frame }
--ThisRandomString--
```

The final two dashes (--) appended to the boundary string signal that the last block has been sent and the connection can be closed. No matter how slow the loop is, as long as the reader doesn't interfere, the browser will keep the connection open, waiting patiently for each block of data to be sent to replace the previous one.

SERVER-SIDE INCLUDES

Server-side includes is a method of having the server insert content into a Web page as it is downloading it to the reader. Such content can be marked up text from another HTML file—a common banner for the top of every page in a Web site, for example. The included content can also come from environmental variables set by the server and from information in the HTTP request block sent by the browser requesting the page. The content can even be generated by a CGI script.

Not all Web servers support server-side includes—NCSA's and Netscape's servers can but CERN's cannot—and many sites turn the feature off or restrict its use. There are two reasons for doing this. First, parsing every document requested, looking for includes, and patching the content eats up a lot of processing time. Second, there are security concerns when anyone can execute commands and launch programs just by downloading a page from your server.

Web sites that do support server-side includes usually restrict the parsing of documents to files with the special extension .shtml instead of .html or .htm. Very few public sites support the execution of commands or scripts from server-side includes declarations. Check first with your systems administrator to see what features are available for you to use.

The mechanism for specifying server-side includes uses a special form of the SGML/HTML comment:

```
<!--#command arg1="value1" arg2="value2" -->
```

The arguments are written in the same *keyword=value* format as tag attributes. There cannot be any spaces separating the opening left angle bracket (<), the exclamation point (!), dashes (--), and pound sign (#). There also cannot be any extra text. It may look like a comment, but it isn't.

The include command is one of the following:

▸ **include** Inserts content from another file at the given point in the document

▸ **echo** Inserts the value of a CGI environmental value at the given point in the document

▸ **exec** Executes a shell command or a CGI script and inserts the output at the given point in the document

▸ **fsize** Inserts the size, in bytes, of a specified file; useful for annotating links to files that vary in size, such as mail archives

▸ **flastmod** Inserts the last modified timestamp of a specified file; useful for annotating links to files that are updated irregularly

Include, fsize, and flastmod take one of two arguments specifying the file to be included or reported on. That file must be on the same Web server as the page containing the include. For example, this include

```
<!--#include virtual="~www_admin/includes/logo_head.html"-->
```

uses the virtual argument and specifies the file by giving its path relative to the Web server. The tilde (~) is a UNIX shortcut meaning "the home directory of userid:". Here it is the file logo_head.html in a subdirectory, called includes, of the home directory of the userid, www_admin. The other way of specifying the include file is with the "file" argument identifying a file relative to the parsed document's location. For example,

```
<!--#include file="my_buttons.html"-->
```

references an HTML file in the same directory as the HTML file containing the include. When you use the file argument, the referenced file must be in the same directory or in a subdirectory of the file containing the include. It cannot be in a higher level directory.

The "echo" include command has one argument, var, which has as its value the name of an environmental variable. What follows is an example using three echo includes. The set of available environmental variables differs from one site to another as well as from one browser to another, so I won't list them all. Check with your webmaster to see which, if any, are available at your site.

```
<P>Welcome <!--#echo var="REMOTE_USER"--> to our Home Page.<BR>
It is now: <!--#echo var="DATE_LOCAL"-->.<BR>
This page was last modified on: <!--#echo var="LAST_MODIFIED"-->.</P>
```

The exec include command has the single argument, cmd, with a value of a shell language command or the name of a CGI script. As mentioned, Web sites rarely enable this feature because it eats up too much processing time and carries with it serious security concerns. Given the choice, most Web site administrators would rather have readers link directly to a script that dynamically generates an entire page rather than have the system include dynamically generated content into static, parsed pages.

PERSISTENT HTTP COOKIES

Cookies are another Netscape enhancement. This one addresses the general problem inherent in the Web's architecture: Servers have no memory. That is, without extensive programming on the server to gather and store information about each reader and what he or she is doing at any given time, it is very difficult to tie Web pages together into an application. On the Web, a server simply handles requests from readers who, once they get the page they want, go away. With an online service, the situation is the opposite: The service knows who you are, has your billing information, and is paying attention to every key you hit. An online service is a better environment for integrated applications.

Enter cookies. Netscape says they decided to call them "cookies" for no good reason whatsoever. A cookie (think of the fortune kind) is a packet of arbitrary information sent to the browser by a server-side script. A cookie has an expiration date and the browser will hang on to that cookie until it expires. The cookie also has a list of URLs (usually scripts), and the browser will send the contents of the cookie should the reader link to an URL in that list.

Say you visit a page that contains a form, enter some information, check some boxes, and click on the submit button. The script processing the information from the form sends a cookie back to the browser. The cookie contains information from the form as a set of strings in the format *keyword=value*, where the keywords are the names of the form fields and the values are what you typed in and selected. The script can include additional information in the cookie, such as a temporary customer id. After some time, but before the expiration date of the cookie, you visit a second page that also has a form, which you fill out and submit to a script whose URL is in the list of URLs associated with the cookie. The browser will send the cookie to the script in the HTTP header, giving this second script access to all the information you entered into the first form, and more. All this happens without the server having to do any work at all to store that information.

This is an important enhancement. For example, imagine a college registration system, with each department and class having its own page on the Web.

As you select your courses by selecting items from forms on the pages, server scripts can spot conflicts and check availability. You are free to rearrange your course schedule as often as you like because the server does as little work as possible until you reach the cashier's page and provide payment.

Likewise, if you visit a cybermall, the cookies can be the items in your "shopping basket" that you carry from department to department before you get to the "checkout" page. You can freely leave the store (go to WebLouvre or Hot-Wired, or check out a manufacturer's site, for example) and return days later to continue shopping—without needing a password!

For the complete syntax of HTTP cookies, see Netscape's description at http://www.netscape.com/newsref/std/cookie_spec.html.

Beyond HTML 3.2

Next Generation Tables

Frames

Cascading Style Sheets

Dynamic HTML

Cougar: The Next HTML Version

Today's Web designers must keep their feet firmly planted in the present while reaching into the future. To reach the widest audience, Web pages must comply with the standard HTML syntax. However, industry leaders bring out new features at an ever-increasing pace due to the "browser wars." Often the new capabilities stem from working drafts of HTML developed by the World Wide Web Consortium as it tries to enhance modern telecommunication. No matter where the HTML improvements come from, it is safe to say that the future is here to stay—and you have to be aware of the options to decide what to incorporate and when.

This chapter describes features that technically are "beyond HTML 3.2," but are nonetheless in common use today. Chief among these are advanced tables and frames. Close behind are Cascading Style Sheets. At the end of this chapter, you'll look at the exciting, just-released capabilities of Dynamic HTML and, finally, peek at the next release of HTML 3.2, code-named Cougar.

NEXT GENERATION TABLES

Tables have become a major Web site design tool. You can use them to keep elements aligned, giving your Web pages a clean, well-organized look. You can organize diverse, complex data into a coherent whole by using the <TABLE> element commands covered in Chapter 3. This chapter expands your palette with additional tags and attributes to enhance the backgrounds, borders, columns, and rows within tables.

Most of the tags and attributes in this section currently only work with Microsoft Internet Explorer. Remember, a number of commands proposed for HTML 3 didn't make it into the final version of HTML 3.2, including <THEAD>, <TBODY>, <TFOOT>, <COL>, and <RULES>. These and more work in Internet Explorer but are ignored by any other browser. However, these table modifications are under consideration for the next version of HTML. In addition, if you are designing an intranet site where Internet Explorer is the browser of choice, you can use these features today.

ENHANCED BORDER CONTROL

The standard HTML 3.2 BORDER attribute is fairly limited. After you turn it on, the only modification you can make is to specify its width in pixels. For instance, BORDER=5 globally turns on a 5-pixel wide border, surrounding the table and separating each individual cell. Internet Explorer lets you control the inside and outside borders separately; however, you must set up your table properly to do so.

Table Structure   The advanced table structure is divided into head, body, and foot elements. Think of a written page with a header at the top, text body in the middle, and a footer along the bottom; the header and footer repeat as the text body changes. Likewise, the new table structure features tags for the head, body, and foot of the table.

The <THEAD></THEAD> pair marks the heading section of the table. You can include one or many rows in this area. As in the HTML document, the body section of the table, separated with the <TBODY> and </TBODY> tags, contains the bulk of the table material. Finally, the <TFOOT></TFOOT> tags delineate the footer section of the table. This element often has nothing between the opening and closing tags and is used simply to signal the bottom of the table.

This code shows the placement of these new table elements:

```
<HTML>
<HEAD>
<TITLE>Table Divisions</TITLE>
</HEAD>
<BODY>
<TABLE>
<THEAD>
    <!--Your Table Header Goes Here-->
</THEAD>
<TBODY>
    <!--Your Table Body Goes Here-->
```

```
</TBODY>
<TFOOT>
    <!--Your Table Footer Goes Here-->
</TFOOT>
</TABLE>
</BODY>
</HTML>
```

Presently, these settings are only used to set up the enhanced border control you'll learn about in the next section. However, they potentially could permit the header and footer sections to stay fixed while the body section scrolls, both on a Web page and when printed. This advancement is currently in discussion with the W3C organization.

Internal and External Borders   Once you set up a table with the <THEAD>, <TBODY>, and <TFOOT> tags, you can use it do some fancy borders. Two new attributes for the <TABLE> tag give you independent control over the external and internal borders. FRAME manages the outside borders and RULES manages the inside. To initialize them, you must use the BORDER attribute within the <TABLE> tag.

With the FRAME attribute, you can specify a border around any or all of the outside of a table. The syntax for this attribute is FRAME="value," where "value" can be any of the following:

- **border** The default, where all sides have a border (same as **box**)

- **void** No outside borders

- **above** Only the top border is shown

- **below** Only the bottom border is shown

- **hsides** Both the top and bottom border (the horizontal sides) are shown

- **vsides** Both the left and right border (the vertical sides) are shown

- **lhs** Only the left border is shown

- **rhs** Only the right border is shown

Compared to the all-or-nothing situation with borders in standard HTML 3.2, this is a big improvement.

For inside borders, you can use the RULES attribute to set a similar set of options:

- **none** No internal borders

- **all** Each cell has a border

▸ **groups** Borders separate the <THEAD>, <TBODY>, and <TFOOT> sections

▸ **rows** Borders separate each row

▸ **cols** Borders separate each column

As an example, here's a simplified version of the planetary table from Chapter 3, with enhanced border attributes.

```
<HTML>
<HEAD>
<TITLE>Table Test</TITLE>
</HEAD>
<BODY>
<TABLE BORDER FRAME="none" RULES="groups">
<CAPTION ALIGN="bottom"><I>The Inner Planets - Revised</I></CAPTION>
<THEAD>
<TR>
 <TH><BR>Planet</TH>
 <TH>Distance from Sun<BR>Kilometers*</TH>
 <TH>Year<BR>Length</TH>
 <TH>     Day     <BR>Length</TH> </TR>
</THEAD>
<TBODY>
<TR><TH>Mercury</TH>
 <TD ALIGN="center">57,900,000</TD> <TD>88 days</TD> <TD ALIGN="right">59
days</TD></TR>
<TR><TH>Venus</TH>
 <TD ALIGN="center">108,200,000</TD> <TD>225 days</TD> <TD ALIGN="right">243
days</TD></TR>
<TR><TH>Earth</TH>
 <TD ALIGN="center">149,600,000</TD> <TD>365 days</TD> <TD ALIGN="right">24
hrs</TD></TR>
<TR><TH>Mars</TH>
 <TD ALIGN="center">227,900,000</TD> <TD>687 days</TD> <TD ALIGN="right">24.6
hrs</TD></TR>
</TBODY>
<TFOOT>
<TD COLSPAN=4>*Distances are approximate.</TD>
</TFOOT>
</TABLE>
</BODY>
</HTML>
```

Figure 8.1 shows what the browser renders when the external border is turned off with FRAME="none" and the internal border is set to separate only the table divisions with RULES="groups".

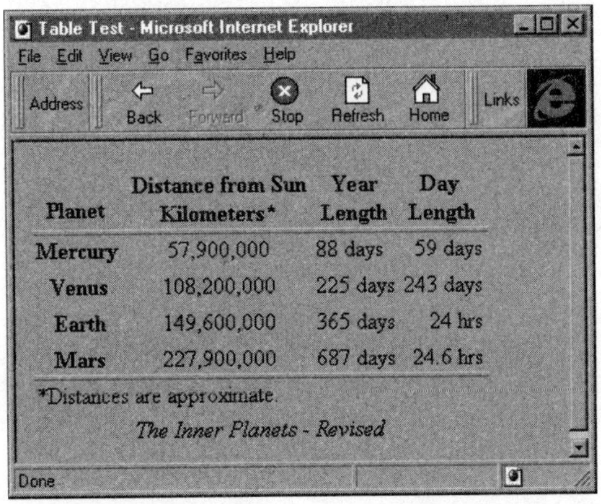

Figure 8.1: Table using the FRAME and RULES attributes

A major advantage of this technique is that you can easily test a variety of borders by simply replacing the two values for FRAME and RULES. One caveat: Using COLSPAN or ROWSPAN in the table can lead to unpredictable results with these new attributes. This is an acknowledged bug that is being worked on.

Colored and Shaded Borders   Standard HTML 3.2 uses a browser's defaults when drawing any border; a three-dimensional gray is the most you can expect. New <TABLE> attributes available in Internet Explorer let you specify any color as well as giving you extra command over the three-dimensional shading. All of the following attributes are in the opening <TABLE> tag and take the same color names or RGB hexadecimal triplet values as the BG-COLOR attribute that was covered in Chapter 2.

The main attribute for altering the color of the border is BORDERCOLOR. Like FRAME and RULES, BORDERCOLOR must go in the TABLE tag for border coloring to work. The syntax for the new attribute is like what you have seen before: BORDERCOLOR=#rrggbb or BORDERCOLOR=*colorname*. If you used this code,

```
<TABLE BORDER BORDERCOLOR="red">
```

any borders will be red.

You can use two other attributes to control the shading of a three-dimensional border. BORDERCOLORDARK sets the color for the darker sides of a three-dimensional border, usually the bottom and right edges; and BORDER-COLORLIGHT does the same for the lighter sides, usually the top and left edges. Of course, this means that you can reverse the normal shadowing effect by putting a lighter color in the BORDERCOLORDARK attribute and a darker color in the BORDERCOLORLIGHT attribute. To see this effect more clearly, increase the SIZE attribute of the border.

GRAPHIC TABLES

A standard text table with its structured columns and rows is a graphic element by itself. HTML 3.2 tables can include an image (or even another table) in any cell, to which you can add a border of a thickness that you determine. In enhanced tables, you can have colored or image backgrounds for the entire table and/or individual cells. In this section, we'll build a table that includes both options.

Multicolored Tables   Like borders, table color is an all-or-none proposition in standard HTML 3.2. The BGCOLOR attribute of the <TABLE> tag can turn on a color background for the whole table in HTML 3.2. That's nice, but the major use for color in tables is to highlight certain rows or columns, and for that you need much more control. Current versions of Netscape Navigator and Internet Explorer extend the color control to individual cells.

You can set the background color for an entire table or for an individual cell by using the BGCOLOR attribute—what is changed depends on where you place the attribute. To color an entire table, place the BGCOLOR="value" attribute in the <BODY> tag. (Remember that the value can be either a hexadecimal triplet in the form #rrggbb or one of the color names.) To color an individual cell, put BGCOLOR="value" in the table data (<TD>) tag. Here's a simple example that alternates plain and colored rows for easy reading.

```
<HTML>
<HEAD>
    <TITLE>Colored Table Example</TITLE>
</HEAD>
<BODY>
<H2 ALIGN="center">The Stegosaurus</H2>
<TABLE BORDER="1" WIDTH="100%">
<TR>
<TH>CATEGORY</TH>
<TH>DESCRIPTION</TH>
</TR>
```

```
<TR>
<TD BGCOLOR="yellow">Period</TD>
<TD BGCOLOR="yellow">Middle Jurassic To Late Cretaceous (100 Million To 65
Million Years Ago)</TD>
</TR>
<TR>
<TD>Size</TD>
<TD>Approximately 20 Feet From Head To Tail (6 Meters)</TD>
</TR>
<TR>
<TD BGCOLOR="yellow">Locale</TD>
<TD BGCOLOR="yellow">North America, Europe, Africa, Asia</TD>
</TR>
<TR>
<TD>Diet</TD>
<TD>Herbivore</TD>
</TR>
</TABLE>
</BODY>
</HTML>
```

Figure 8.2 shows a grayscale version of the results.

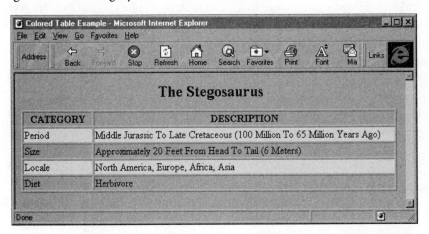

Figure 8.2: Colored cells in a table

Images in Tables   As already, standard HTML 3.2 can use an image in any cell of a table. However, these are only foreground images. Internet Explorer uses an enhanced <TABLE> attribute to permit background images as well, in both the whole table and any single cell. The attribute, BACKGROUND, is the same as the BACKGROUND attribute used with the <BODY> tag, but you place it in the <TABLE>, <TH>, or <TD> tag.

Remember how a background image is tiled to fill an HTML page? The same repetition occurs in tables. This can have the effect of unifying a table. Here's what the code would look like:

```
<TABLE BORDER="8" BACKGROUND="Gray_Marble30C0.gif">
```

Moreover, you can mix both the BACKGROUND image and the BG-COLOR if the image is a GIF file with the transparency turned on; the background color supplied by BGCOLOR will show up in the transparent areas of the GIF. To override an image in a cell, use a solid BGCOLOR in either a table header (<TH>) or table data (<TD>) tag.

You include images in a table with the same <IMG> tag you use for regular inline graphics. The code for a table data cell with a graphic would look like this:

```
<td align="center">
<img src="stego.jpg" width="275" height="200">
</td>
```

Finally, as noted earlier, you can also include a table inside a table. This is referred to as "nesting" because one group of tags is "nested" inside another. Make certain that you completely surround the inside table with the <TR></TR> tags, which you should in turn surround by the outer <TABLE></TABLE> tags. Here's a brief example using the previous table.

```
<HTML>
<HEAD>
    <TITLE>Table in A Table Example</TITLE>
</HEAD>
<BODY>
<TABLE BORDER=1> <!-- This is the start of the outer table -->
<TR>
<TD><H3>This text is in one cell of the outer table</H3></TD>
<TD>
<TABLE BORDER="1"> <!-- This is the start of the inner table -->
<TR>
<TH>CATEGORY</TH>
<TH>DESCRIPTION</TH>
</TR>
<TR>
<TD BGCOLOR="yellow">Period</TD>
<TD BGCOLOR="yellow">Middle Jurassic To Late Cretaceous</TD>
</TR>
<TR>
```

```
<TD>Size</TD>
<TD>Approximately 20 Feet From Head To Tail (6 Meters)</TD>
</TR>
<TR>
<TD BGCOLOR="yellow">Locale</TD>
<TD BGCOLOR="yellow">North America, Europe, Africa, Asia</TD>
</TR>
<TR>
<TD>Diet</TD>
<TD>Herbivore</TD>
</TR>
</TABLE> <!-- This is the end of the inner table -->
</TD>
</TR>
</TABLE> <!-- This is the end of the outer table -->
</BODY>
</HTML>
```

I've indented the code for the interior table to better illustrate where one table lets off and the other begins; indents like this make your code easier to follow as your pages get more complex. Figure 8.3 shows what the browser sees.

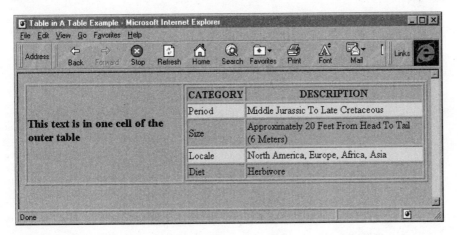

Figure 8.3: A table within a table

The following example brings together all of the advanced table elements. It combines a background image for the entire table, a graphic in a cell, a table within a table, separately colored cells, borders specified using FRAME and

RULES, and even a colored border with the dark and the light border color chosen. Whew!

```
<html>
<head>
<TITLE>Full Graphic Table</TITLE>
</head>
<BODY BGCOLOR="white">
<H2 ALIGN="CENTER">The Dinosaur Table</H2>
<TABLE BORDER="8" WIDTH="100%" BACKGROUND="Gray_Marble30C0.gif"
bordercolor="#C0C0C0" bordercolordark="#008000"
BORDERCOLORLIGHT="#00FF00" FRAME="border" RULES="none">
    <TR>
        <TD ROWSPAN="3" WIDTH="25%"><P ALIGN="center"><FONT
        SIZE="4" FACE="ARIAL"><B>Major Dinosaur Families</B></FONT></P>
        <ul>
            <LI><H4 ALIGN="left"><FONT SIZE="4"><B>Saurischia</B></FONT></H4>
            </li>
            <LI><H4 ALIGN="left"><FONT SIZE="4"><B>Prosauropods</B></FONT></H4>
            </li>
            <LI><H4 ALIGN="left"><FONT SIZE="4"><B>Ornithischia</B></FONT></H4>
            </li>
            <LI><H4 ALIGN="left"><FONT COLOR="blue"
SIZE="4"><B><U>Stegosaurians</U></B></FONT></H4>
            </li>
            <LI><H4 ALIGN="left"><FONT SIZE="4"><B>Ankylosaurians</B></FONT></H4>
            </li>
        </ul>
        </td>
        <TD ALIGN="RIGHT" COLSPAN="2"><H1 ALIGN="center">Stegosaurus</H1>
        </td>
    </tr>
    <tr>
        <TD CELLPADDING="2"><P ALIGN="left"><FONT SIZE="4"><STRONG>In
        the Jurassic period, the main group of armored dinosaurs
        was the stegosaurians, the most familiar of which is
</STRONG><STRONG><I>Stegosaurus</I></STRONG><STRONG>.
        This dinosaur had a double row of upright triangular
        plates that ran down its back, followed by four spikes on
        its tail. </STRONG></FONT></P>
        </TD>
        <TD ALIGN="center"><P ALIGN="left"><IMG
        SRC="../../../../../webtest/test1/stego.jpg" WIDTH="275"
        height="200"></p>
        </td>
    </tr>
```

```
<tr>
    <TD ALIGN="right" COLSPAN="2"><DIV ALIGN="right"><TABLE
    border="1" width="100%">
        <tr>
            <TH ALIGN="left" BGCOLOR="white">Category</TH>
            <TD BGCOLOR="white"><STRONG>Description</STRONG></TD>
        </tr>
        <tr>
            <TD BGCOLOR="yellow">Period</TD>
            <TD BGCOLOR="yellow">Middle Jurassic to Late
            Cretaceous (100 million to 65 million years ago)</TD>
        </tr>
        <tr>
            <TD BGCOLOR="white">Size</TD>
            <TD BGCOLOR="white">Approximately 20 feet from
            head to tail (6 meters)</TD>
        </tr>
        <tr>
            <TD BGCOLOR="yellow">Locale</TD>
            <TD BGCOLOR="yellow">North America, Europe,
            Africa, Asia</TD>
        </tr>
        <tr>
            <TD BGCOLOR="white">Diet</TD>
            <TD BGCOLOR="white">Herbivore</TD>
        </tr>
    </table>
    </div></td>
</tr>
</table>
</body>
</html>
```

As you can see in this code and in Figure 8.4, a white background color was added to the inner table to alternate with the yellow rows.

FRAMES

You learned a bit about frames in Chapter 6, in the section on frame-based layouts. In this section, you'll dive into the details. Frames are subdivisions of a Web page, each of which can scroll and be updated independently of any other frame. Frames on Web pages are not standard HTML 3.2, but are accessible through current versions of Netscape Navigator, Microsoft Internet Explorer, and Sun's HotJava browsers. Some Web designers swear by frames and some swear *at* them. It is true that frames are relatively difficult to implement

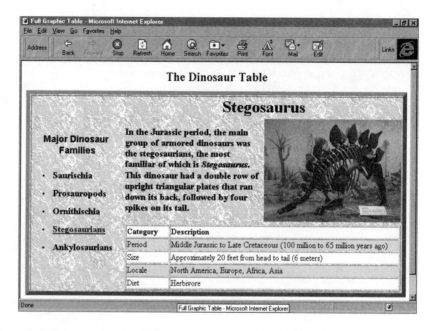

Figure 8.4: Enhanced table with background and embedded table

(compared to the rest of HTML) and they can make browser navigation very tricky. Nonetheless, in some circumstances, frames are the ideal choice and every Web designer should have them in their toolbox.

This section illustrates various frame structures, describes the available resizing and border options, and explains how to avoid frame pitfalls like recursion. But first, you need to set up your frame by using the <FRAMESET> element.

THE <FRAMESET> ELEMENT

You set frames off from the rest of the HTML document with the <FRAMESET></FRAMESET> tags, just as you typically use the <BODY></BODY> tags to separate the main section. In fact, the FRAMESET section generally replaces the BODY section in a HTML page using frames. Here's the normal structure for a frame page:

```
<HTML>
<HEAD>
<TITLE></TITLE>
</HEAD>
<FRAMESET>
```

```
...
</FRAMESET>
</HTML>
```

    <FRAMESET> takes several attributes that you've seen before, such as BOR-DER=*n* and BORDERCOLOR=#rrggbb|*colorname* (the "|" symbol means "or"). However, the actual layout of the frame is determined by two other attributes: ROWS and COLS.

Columns and Rows   Within the <FRAMESET> tag, you must declare whether the frame is to be divided into columns or rows. This is not as limiting as it sounds because you can subdivide each column or row—using another <FRAMESET> tag—into other columns or rows. First you'll learn the syntax for the COLS and ROWS attributes and then you'll see some examples.

    You set both COLS and ROWS to a list of values (representing either a percentage or a fixed value), separated by commas, indicating the number and the size of the subdivisions. If your frame is made up of two columns of equal size, your opening <FRAMESET> tag will read like this:

```
<FRAMESET COLS="50%,50%">
```

    Likewise, if your frame consists of two rows, equal in size, your code would look like this:

```
<FRAMESET ROWS="50%,50%">
```

    To make a frame with three rows, where the middle row is twice the size of either the top or bottom row, use this code:

```
<FRAMESET ROWS="25%,50%,25%">
```

    If you leave off the percent sign, your value will be interpreted in pixels. If you wrote "50" instead of "50%" in the preceding example, the FRAMESET command would create two columns each taking up 25 percent of the browser window's width and a third column only 50 pixels wide.

    This is not to say that you cannot mix percentages and absolute values. In fact, you can even use a special character in the ROWS and COLS attribute to make such design work simpler. You can use an asterisk (*)to indicate "the balance of the window." For example, suppose you want a three-column frame where the first column is exactly 150 pixels wide, the second column is 50 percent of the window, and the third column is whatever is left over. Here's the <FRAMESET> tag for such a design:

```
<FRAMESET COLS="150,50%,*">
```

An easy way to do a frame that has two rows of equal height is to use the asterisk twice, like this:

```
<FRAMESET ROWS="*,*">
```

The asterisk has one other use with COLS and ROWS. When used with an integer—that is, $n*$, that frame will be allocated n times the space it would have received otherwise. To split a frame into two columns, where one column is twice the size of the other, you can use this code:

```
<FRAMESET COLS="*,2*">
```

THE <FRAME> TAG

The next step in building your frame involves learning to use the <FRAME> tag. You use this tag within the <FRAMESET></FRAMESET> pair to point to the URL of that particular frame. Much like the image tag <IMG>, the <FRAME> tag uses the SRC attribute to identify the URL. It's also common to use the NAME attribute to give the FRAME a name that can be referenced by other hyperlinks.

Here's some typical code for a frame that has three rows:

```
<FRAMESET ROWS="25%,50%,25%">
<FRAME SRC="top.html" NAME="top">
<FRAME SRC="middle.html" NAME="middle">
<FRAME SRC="bottom.html" NAME="bottom">
</FRAMESET>
```

Frames made up of just rows or just columns are fairly straightforward. Combining rows and columns is more complex, but also much more interesting from a design standpoint. You do this by nesting <FRAMESET> and <FRAME> elements.

Let's take the previous three-row example, but split the middle row into two columns. Start with the same code as before and substitute a new FRAMESET for the middle FRAME, like this:

```
<FRAMESET ROWS="25%,50%,25%">
<FRAME SRC="top.html" NAME="top">
<FRAMESET COLS="*,2*>
    <FRAME SRC="midleft.html" NAME="midleft">
    <FRAME SRC="midright.html" NAME="midright">
    </FRAMESET>
<FRAME SRC="bottom.html" NAME="bottom">
</FRAMESET>
```

This code produces a layout like that illustrated in Figure 8.5. The COLS="*,2*" syntax in the inner FRAMESET yields twice as much space for the right column as the left.

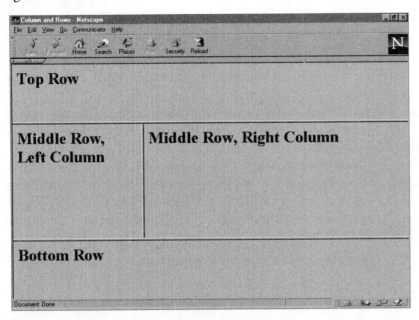

Figure 8.5: Combined rows and columns table

Note that there are now five HTML documents being used to generate this one page—one with the FRAMESET layout and one for each of the <FRAME> tags.

Scrolling and Resizing Options   One of the distinguishing features of frames is the scroll bar. When an HTML page is too big for a frame, you can add a scroll bar to let the viewer see the overflow material.

The SCROLLING attribute of the <FRAME> tag takes one of three values: "yes", "no", and "auto". As you would expect, SCROLLING="yes" enables the scroll bar and SCROLLING="no" disables it for the specific frame. The "auto" option is the default; it leaves the scroll bar display to the discretion of the browser. Both Navigator and Internet Explorer tend to err on the side of caution when you use the "auto" option—they both put in a scroll bar if there's a character anywhere near. If you absolutely don't want a scroll bar for your two lines of copyright information in the bottom frame, specify the height of the frame in pixels and set the SCROLLING attribute to "no".

By default, all frames can be resized by the viewer. To do this, you just position your cursor on the border of a frame (the cursor will become a double-headed arrow) and drag the frame until it's a new size. This is a very user-friendly feature to leave in, if possible. However, some frames are pointless to resize (the two lines of copyright information, for example). To prohibit resizing, you use the NORESIZE attribute in the <FRAME> tag.

Here's the code for a frame that disables both resizing and the scroll bar:

```
<FRAME SRC="copyrite.htm" NAME="copyrite" SCROLLING="no" NORESIZE>
```

Frame Borders   All frames have borders by default. Because frames share common borders, you must use the FRAMEBORDER="no" attribute and value in the <FRAME> tag for both frames to turn off the borders between them. Until recently, only Internet Explorer allowed borderless frames, but Navigator 4.0 has incorporated this feature. This can be a very effective design, although borderless frames that have scroll bars can be distracting. Figure 8.6 shows a sample frame-based Web page mixing borders and open frames; notice that the bottom frame is not resizeable.

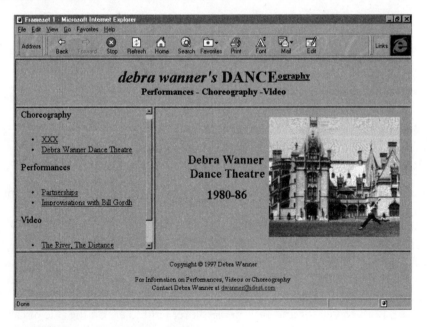

Figure 8.6: A Web page that uses frames

As with the enhanced <TABLE> tag, when using frames you can control the color of frame borders. The BORDERCOLOR attribute for the <FRAME> tag takes either a hexadecimal triplet in the form of "#rrggbb" or one of the color names noted in Chapter 2.

LINK TARGETS

To get a hyperlink to appear in a specific frame, you must "target" that frame. You do this by using the TARGET attribute of the anchor tag, <A>, and referencing the frame's name as assigned by the NAME attribute of the <FRAME> tag. Let's build on the previous example to see how this works.

Suppose that, in the middle row, the left column acts as a table of contents and the right column contains each chapter as it is called. In this case, the file midleft.html would contain a series of anchor tags all with the same target:

```
<A HREF="chap1.html" TARGET="midright">Chapter 1</A>
<A HREF="chap2.html" TARGET="midright">Chapter 2</A>
<A HREF="chap3.html" TARGET="midright">Chapter 3</A>
```

TARGET can be used relatively as well as specifically. You can use the following values in any HTML frame:

- ▸ **_blank** Loads the link into a new browser window
- ▸ **_parent** Loads the link over the frame that spawned the current frame
- ▸ **_self** Loads the link in the originating frame, overwriting the frame
- ▸ **_top** Loads the link in the uppermost level of a series of frames

Note the special underscore character (_) that starts each of these relative values. The _self target can lead to a phenomenon known as recursive frames, which has the potential to crash any browser.

Recursive Frames   Have you ever held a mirror up to a mirror and seen all the hundreds of similar reflections getting smaller and smaller on to infinity? That's basically the concept behind recursive frames, and, as you can imagine, computers don't handle doing anything until infinity very well.

You specify a frame as its own target when you set the TARGET attribute to "_self". This works well for many situations where you want to completely update a list. The problem comes from linking that target to a URL that contains that frame's own frameset.

As an example, let's take the same four-frame layout used earlier and insert this HTML code for the middle-right frame:

```
<HTML>
<HEAD>
<TITLE>midright</TITLE>
</HEAD>
```

```
<BODY>
<H1>Middle Row, Right Column</H1>
<!--The following line causes the recursion."-->
<A HREF="main.htm" target="_self">Recursive</A>
</BODY>
</HTML>
```

This will put one link in the frame, which will call "main.htm," the earlier code that sets up the framesets and frames. Because we have made the TARGET this same frame with the "_self" value, a mini-version of the entire frameset will appear in the one frame! Moreover, the link within that frameset is still active, and clicking on it causes yet another version of the full frameset to appear in the even smaller frame. Figure 8.7 shows what a 3rd generation recursion looks like.

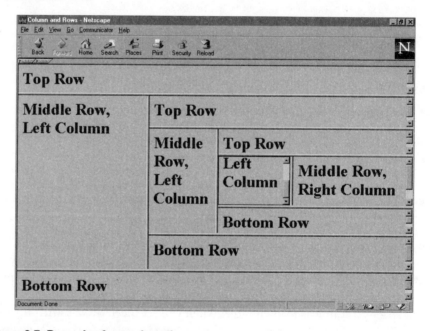

Figure 8.7: Recursive frames in action

Although this is an extreme example, you must be careful not to include a link to any frame that contains your frameset. If you do, you run the risk of crashing most browsers.

THE <NOFRAMES> ALTERNATIVE

There is one last tag to remember when using frames: <NOFRAMES>. This is a container tag whose content will be shown to browsers that cannot render frames. You place it after the closing </FRAMESET> tag, like this:

```
<FRAMESET ROWS="25%,50%,25%">
<FRAME SRC="top.html" NAME="top">
<FRAME SRC="middle.html" NAME="middle">
<FRAME SRC="bottom.html" NAME="bottom">
</FRAMESET>
<NOFRAMES>
<!--Anything in here is visible to browsers that can not read frames -->
</NOFRAMES>
```

Typically, you would put a link to a nonframe version of your Web page within the <NOFRAME> </NOFRAME> tags. Keep in mind that there are still a lot of "frame-challenged" browsers, and proper use of this tag will keep your audience as wide as possible.

CASCADING STYLE SHEETS

Content and style struggle for dominance in an HTML document. Too much emphasis on style and the point gets lost; too little attention to design and the content is dry and less communicative. Cascading Style Sheets can ease the conflict by separating content and style. A separate style sheet (a concept borrowed from desktop publishing) allows designers a finer degree of control over layout, permits global changes over thousands of documents simultaneously, and maintains the flexibility of presentation that HTML founders stressed.

Cascading Style Sheets were originally developed by the World Wide Web Consortium to address the concerns of designers and prevent the fight over the implementation of a host of single-purpose HTML extensions, such as FONT. Currently, Cascading Style Sheets 1 (CSS1) is supported by Microsoft's Internet Explorer 3.0 and Netscape Navigator 4.0. There is a draft proposal for CSS2, which Internet Explorer already supports through an ActiveX control; many of its features will be covered in the Dynamic HTML section later in this chapter. Finally, Netscape has introduced a variation on CSS1, JavaScript Style Sheets. This section focuses on the primary implementation of Cascading Style Sheets, CSS1.

RULES OF STYLE

A style sheet is a collection of rules. "Color all H2 headings blue" is one rule; "indent all paragraphs ? inch" is another. A style sheet can include just one rule or a hundred. Your rules can affect only one character or hundreds of documents. The rules give Cascading Style Sheets that power and flexibility.

Selectors and Declarations   A CSS1 rule is made up of a selector (what is affected) and a declaration (the effect). You use curly braces (the { and } characters) to enclose the declaration. Within the declaration, you specify the property that is to be altered and its new value, separated by a colon.

The examples "color all H2 headings blue" and "indent all paragraphs ½ inch," when translated into CSS1 syntax, become

```
H2 {color:blue}
P {text-indent:0.5in}
```

CSS1 includes over 50 properties, covering fonts, text, color, and boxes. Appendix B lists many of them, and the full specification is at www.w3.org/pub/WWW/TR/REC-CSS1. The language of desktop publishing is heavily used, so you'll see references to point sizes, em dashes, and other typographic terms.

The <STYLE> Element   How do you integrate a style rule into your HTML document? With <STYLE>, of course. You can use STYLE as both a tag and an attribute. Typically, STYLE is used as a tag.

Because the <STYLE></STYLE> tags affect the entire document, you put them in the <HEAD> section after the title. As an acknowledgement to the rapid growth and development of HTML, you must use the TYPE attribute to declare which type of style you are using. CSS1 is known as TYPE="text/css". Here are the two previous rules, in HTML code:

```
<HTML>
<HEAD>
<TITLE>CSS Example</TITLE>
<STYLE TYPE="text/css">
H2 {color:blue}
P {text-indent:0.5in}
</STYLE>
</HEAD>
<BODY>
<H2>I'm so blue!</H2>
<P>Oh, yeah? Well, I'm indented a half an inch! What do think about that, you big
cry baby?</P>
</BODY>
</HTML>
```

The result, shown in Figure 8.8, has a blue H2 heading and an indented paragraph. Any H2 headings or paragraphs in the document would have these styles.

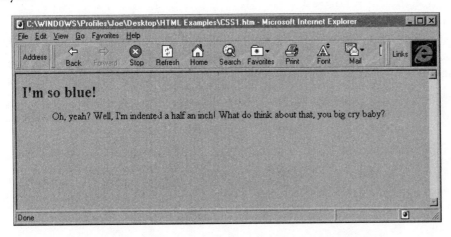

Figure 8.8: Heading and paragraph formatted with Cascading Style Sheet

Grouping and Inheritance   Although you could list all the selectors and declarations individually, one of the driving forces behind Cascading Style Sheets is the desire to save time. To that end, two helpful concepts have been incorporated into CSS1: grouping and inheritance. Grouping allows the style sheet designer to combine selectors when they have common declarations and declarations when they have common selectors. Inheritance carries imposed styles from one group to another.

Grouping   You can group selectors just by separating them with commas. This means that the following four lines of code:

```
H1 {font-family:Arial}
H2 {font-family:Arial}
H3 {font-family:Arial}
H4 {font-family:Arial}
```

can be reproduced with just one line of code:

```
H1, H2, H3, H4 {font-family:Arial}
```

Moreover, you're not limited to selectors of one type—you can mix headings, paragraphs, and even logical style tags like <STRONG>.

```
<H2>, <P>, <EM> {color:green}
```

Similarly, you can group declarations by using semicolons as dividers. The syntax for changing a range of options for one (or more) selectors looks like this:

```
H1 {font-family: Arial; font-weight: Bold; font-size: 18pt}
```

Inheritance   Like grouping, inheritance allows you to address more than one HTML element. However, the inheritance is not explicitly stated. One way that properties can be inherited by a tag is if that tag is contained within a style sheet defined element. Here's an example:

```
<HEAD>
<TITLE>CSS Example</TITLE>
<STYLE TYPE="text/css">
H2 {color:blue}
</STYLE>
</HEAD>
<BODY>
<H2>I'm still <I>very</I> blue!</H2>
</BODY>
</HTML>
```

Using the Font-Family Property

A variation of the grouping technique is used when addressing the font-family property. Because you cannot be sure what fonts are on the client's machine, it is best to list alternatives. You can do this with a comma-separated list of values, such as this one:

```
H1 {font-family: Arial, Helvetica, Geneva, sans-serif}
```

These are listed in order of preference: If Arial is not on the machine, try Helvetica; no Helvetica, try Geneva; and so on. The last choice, sans-serif, is the generic font family name. The other generic choices are

- ▶ **serif** (for example, Times)
- ▶ **cursive** (for example, Zapf-Chancery)
- ▶ **fantasy** (for example, Western)
- ▶ **monospace** (for instance, Courier)

When font names contain spaces, such as "Bookman Old Style," you should enclose them within quotes when including them in an options list.

The <I> (italic) element inherits the style of the H2 tag because of its position within the H2 tag. To override this inheritance, you would have to declare a different style for the <I> tag, as in this code excerpt:

```
<STYLE TYPE="text/css">
H2 {color:blue}
I {color:red}
</STYLE>
```

The other way CSS inheritance works is through the parent-child relationships of elements within an HTML document. A good example is the unordered list <UL> element. The <UL> tag is considered to be the parent of each of the list items <LI>. Because of inheritance, if you set the <UL> tag to a particular style, each of the <LI> elements will have the same style.

This gives you an easy way to alter all the tags on a visible page. Because everything on the screen has <BODY> as the parent, you can set an entire page to a different font with one command:

```
Body {font-family: Arial}
```

Again, you can override inheritance by declaring a different style for a more specific element, such as the <BLOCKQUOTE> tag.

EXPANDING SELECTORS

So far you've seen how tags can be used as the selectors in CSS1 rules. To make style sheets more flexible, a method of identifying document-specific groups as a selector was developed. These groups are known as classes, pseudo-classes, and pseudo-elements.

Classes Classes are user-defined groups—and the user, in this case, is you, the Web designer. You can specify almost any portion of your HTML document to be a member of a particular class. You add the CLASS attribute to any HTML block element to tie it to a specific group. For example, suppose you have one or more contract-like paragraphs in the body of your page. To identify a paragraph as belonging to a new class called "legal" you are creating, assign the CLASS attribute, like this:

```
<P CLASS="legal">
Before clicking on the "accept" button, carefully read the terms and conditions
of this agreement. By clicking on the "accept" button, you are consenting to be
bound by and are becoming a party to this agreement. If you do not agree to all
of the terms of this agreement, click the "do not accept" button.</P>
```

You can apply styles to all "legal" paragraphs in your document with the following style declaration:

```
<STYLE NOTATION="CSS">
  P.legal {font-family: serif,
           font-style: small-caps,
           align: justify}
</STYLE>
```

You can use class names as selectors just as you use HTML element names. Notice the use of the period to indicate that the "legal" is a subgroup (or member) of the <P> tag. This is similar to the object-oriented programming syntax you saw in connection with JavaScript.

You can also use class names in a more general manner—without binding them to a certain tag. To do this, just declare the class name as a selector by itself with a leading period, like this: ".farout". In the following HTML, all of the content between the starting and ending <DIV> tags will be rendered in a green and unusual font—"fantasy" is one of the generic font families like serif and sans-serif—and aligned to the right margin. There's an exception for level 3 headings and unordered lists, which will be aligned left and rendered white. As you can see in Figure 8.9, that which is not explicitly altered—here, the font family—stays in effect.

```
<HTML>
<HEAD>
<TITLE>CSSta</TITLE>
<STYLE TYPE="text/css">
  .farout {font-family: fantasy; color: green; text-align: right}
  H3, UL {text-align: left; color:white}
</STYLE>
</HEAD>
<BODY>
<DIV CLASS="farout">
<!-- GOING WILD FOR THIS SECTION OF THE PAGE -->
<H1>It's Wacky Time!</H1>
<P>Choose from the following items - on the other side of the page.</P>
<H3>The Left Bank</H3>
<UL>
<LI>The Left Hand of God</LI>
<LI>Left in the Lurch</LI>
<LI>Left to their Own Devices!</LI>
</UL>
</DIV>
</BODY>
</HTML>
```

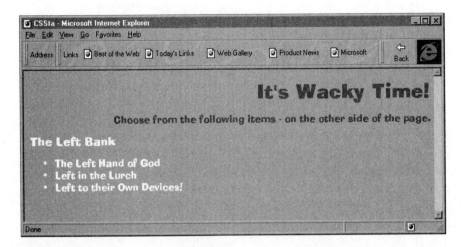

Figure 8.9: Having fun with classes

Pseudo-Classes and Pseudo-Elements Pseudo-classes and pseudo-ele-ments are intended to offer a finer degree of control over your document than classes. Both are abstractions based on HTML tag behavior rather than HTML tags. Before you get too concerned about what this all means, note that neither of these two categories has widespread browser support: Only Internet Ex-plorer can handle pseudo-classes. Caveat Programmer.

The only defined pseudo-class is one for the anchor tag's link attributes. Be-cause this is a behavior of a tag rather than a tag itself, it is dealt with as a pseudo-class. The link states, LINK, VLINK, and ALINK, correspond to the "link," "visited," and "active" key words as used in the following style sheet syntax:

```
<STYLE TYPE="text/css">
A:link {color:green}
A:visited {color:red}
A:active {color:brown}
</STYLE>
```

This pseudo-class structure is the only one supported by Internet Explorer; Navigator does not support it at all.

Pseudo-elements work with HTML block elements in a "virtual" manner—that is, as they are defined on the fly. There are two such pseudo-elements in the current CSS1 specification: first-letter and first-line. Neither pseudo-ele-ment is currently supported by any popular browser, which is too bad, because the possibilities are enticing. You could use the first-letter pseudo-element to make a drop-cap of the first letter of a stylized block element; similarly, you could use the first-line pseudo-element to automatically indent the first line of a paragraph—or negatively indent it, forming a hanging indent.

CASCADING AREAS

Why are they called *Cascading* Style Sheets and not just Style Sheets? Picture a gentle stream going over a ledge. If you put another ledge in its path, the water still flows, it is simply diverted. You can continue to put ledges in the stream's way and each time the water takes a slightly modified course. All of the ledges in turn influence the water's direction, but the ledge closest to the final destination has the most effect. This is analogous to Cascading Style Sheets: You can have more than one, and the most specific—the one closest to the destination—has the most control.

Inline Styles   The inline style command qualifies as the closest style and thus, the one with the final say-so. An inline style uses the STYLE attribute, not the <STYLE> tag. As the name suggests, you use it inline with the other elements. This example uses it within a paragraph tag, although you can use it with most elements:

```
<P STYLE="font-family:Arial"> We just switched fonts for this one paragraph</P>
```

This will override any other style that you may have set earlier for the <P> tag.

Linking and Importing External Style Sheets   You've already seen how you can use the <STYLE> tag in the head of an HTML document to affect the entire page. But what if you want to "stylize" your entire Web site? You could cut-and-paste the <STYLE>...</STYLE> section on each page—but there's an easier way. In fact, there are two easier ways: linking and importing.

To tie your HTML document to a completely separate style sheet, you use the <LINK> tag. Within the LINK tag, you need to define the relationship with the REL attribute by setting it to "stylesheet" and identify the type as "text/css". Finally, you need to give the hypertext reference or URL for the file. The file itself is a text file with the style rules listed. Here's the code for linking an external style sheet to your document:

```
<HTML>
<HEAD>
    <TITLE>Your Title Here</TITLE>
<LINK REL=STYLESHEET TYPE="text/css" HREF="http://www.stylecenter.com/offbeat1">
</HEAD>
<BODY>
<!-- Body copy here -->
```

```
</BODY>
</HTML>
```

Notice that you didn't have to use the <STYLE> tags to attach this style sheet to the HTML document. However, you could have, and any declarations made in there would have overridden any conflicting rules in the linked style sheet. Remember, the rules closest to the documents have the final say.

In addition to linking style sheets to the HTML document, you can import them. This gives you the potential to import multiple style sheets to govern different areas of the document. This import property would work well in corporate intranets where you have an overall style sheet linked from the company as well as divisional and even departmental style sheets—each with their own particular styles to append. As with LINK, you specify the URL, only this time you actually refer to it as a "url". Here's what the code for a fictional intranet might look like:

```
<HTML>
<HEAD>
    <TITLE>Your Title Here</TITLE>
<LINK REL=STYLESHEET TYPE="text/css" HREF="http://www.company.com/mainstyle.css">
<STYLE TYPE="text/css">
@import url(http://www.company.com/div1/style.css)
@import url(http://www.company.com/div1/dept1/style.css)
</STYLE>
</HEAD>
<BODY>
<!-- Body copy here -->
</BODY>
</HTML>
```

This action will merge the three style sheets, with the departmental rules taking precedence over the company or divisional rules.

Cascading Style Sheets are a valuable but evolving addition to HTML. At this writing, the CSS2 specification is in the "working draft" stage at the World Wide Web Consortium. Some of these proposals have been incorporated into the new Dynamic HTML commands in the latest versions of Netscape Navigator and Internet Explorer, and are covered later in this chapter.

DYNAMIC HTML

Dynamic means changing—and change is coming to HTML. Both of the latest versions of Netscape Navigator and Microsoft Internet Explorer are supporting variations of this next level in Web programming. Dynamic HTML (D-HTML) promises to bring a finer degree of screen layout control, snappier interactive response, an entry into layered documents, advanced multimedia features, and enhanced database connectivity.

Par for the course of HTML development, the implementations of D-HTML from Microsoft and Netscape differ, although the results are similar. Microsoft's core approach follows a working draft from the W3C, adding ActiveX ingredients to achieve some of the more dynamic effects. Netscape has specified new tags to achieve the same result and increased the degree of JavaScript control. It's too early to tell which protocol will prove the more robust, but it's certain that the change indicated by D-HTML's arrival is here to stay.

LAYERING

Perhaps the most exciting development in Dynamic HTML—and surely the most visible—is the addition of layering. Layering not only increases the graphic possibilities, it also enhances potential interactivity.

There are three main interlocking components to layering: positioning, depth control, and visibility. You'll learn about each one via Netscape Navigator's new <LAYER> tag. Internet Explorer also supports layering to a similar degree, but uses the style sheet method for integrating into HTML.

Absolute Positioning   HTML designers have been crying out for the ability to position elements anywhere on the page without have to insert carriage returns or other spacers. The new <LAYER> tag from Netscape can handle that chore and more.

LAYER is a container element and everything that is contained between the opening and closing tags is controlled by the attributes. Layers can be nested and, as in Cascading Style Sheets, the attributes closest to the element have the most impact. The positioning attributes of the LAYER tag include

- ▶ **TOP** The "y" position relative to the top of the browser or the parent layer
- ▶ **LEFT** The "x" position relative to the left edge of the browser or the parent layer
- ▶ **CLIP** A rectangle that specifies the portion of the layer to be drawn

Let's start with a simple blue box and place it on the screen. Notice that LAYER also takes a NAME attribute so that it can be identified and controlled later.

```
<HTML>
<HEAD>
```

```
<TITLE>Layers 101</TITLE>
</HEAD>
<BODY>
<LAYER NAME="bluebox" BGCOLOR="aqua" LEFT=50 TOP=50 CLIP=500,300>
</LAYER>
</BODY>
</HTML>
```

Next you'll nest several layers to populate this blue box.

```
<HTML>
<HEAD>
<TITLE>Layers 101</TITLE>
</HEAD>
<BODY>
<LAYER NAME="bluebox" BGCOLOR="aqua" LEFT=50 TOP=50 CLIP=500,300>
     <LAYER TOP=10 LEFT=50 NAME="shark1">
     <IMG SRC="shark.gif">
     </LAYER>
     <LAYER TOP=100 LEFT=150 NAME="turtle">
     <IMG SRC="turtle.gif">
     <IMG SRC="yikes.gif">
     </LAYER>
     <LAYER TOP=200 LEFT=400 NAME="shark2">
     <IMG SRC="shark.gif">
     </LAYER>
</LAYER>
</BODY>
</HTML>
```

As you can see in Figure 8.10, this simple blue box has become a metaphor for modern society. Well, okay, maybe not. But you have added inner layers that are relative to the outer layer. If you alter the TOP and LEFT attributes of the "blue box" layer, all the other layers nested within will move accordingly. Moreover, because JavaScript can individually address and alter any of the named elements—meaning any and all of the layers—you could program an interactive net game of "Avoid the Sharks."

It's snazzy, but it's only part of what layers can do. In the next section, you'll explore the added dimension that the <LAYER> tag offers.

Almost-3D HTML   Implicit in the word "layers" is the idea that one lays on top of another. Netscape's <LAYER> tag lets you control the apparent depth of objects on the screen. One layer can be on top of another which, in turn, is on top of a third. Although this is a significant development by itself, what makes this Dynamic HTML is that you can control the depth of layers.

Figure 8.10: Turtle, shark, and aquarium layers

The attributes for controlling depth in the <LAYER> tag are ABOVE, BE-LOW, and Z-INDEX. These three attributes specify the "stacking order," or "Z-order," of layers. In describing three-dimensional space on a two-dimensional medium like a screen or paper, the Z axis indicates how near or far an object is, just as the X axis describes its horizontal position and the Y axis, the vertical. The Z-INDEX attribute is a positive integer; layers with a higher Z-INDEX attribute are stacked on top of those with a lower Z-INDEX value.

As an example, let's take our poor turtle and put one shark behind him and one on top of him. Here's the revised code with Z-INDEX attributes included:

```
<HTML>
<HEAD>
<TITLE>Layers 102</TITLE>
</HEAD>
<BODY>
<LAYER NAME="bluebox" BGCOLOR="aqua" LEFT=50 TOP=50 CLIP=500,300>
    <LAYER TOP=150 LEFT=100 NAME="shark1" Z-INDEX=1>
    <IMG SRC="shark.gif">
    </LAYER>
    <LAYER TOP=90 LEFT=170 NAME="turtle" Z-INDEX=2>
```

```
    <IMG SRC="turtle.gif">
    <IMG SRC="yikes.gif">
    </LAYER>
    <LAYER TOP=100 LEFT=300 NAME="shark2" Z-INDEX=3>
    <IMG SRC="shark.gif">
    </LAYER></LAYER>
</BODY>
</HTML>
```

The TOP and LEFT attributes were adjusted in each layer to achieve the overlapping visible in Figure 8.11.

Figure 8.11: Turtle layer between two shark layers

Figure 8.12 shows a less frivolous example from Netscape's site where the overlapping layers are a series of tabbed items. Clicking on a tab brings that item to the front—thanks to a little JavaScript programming.

Visibility Control   <LAYER>'s final major attribute is VISIBILITY. Each layer can be shown or hidden individually, again under JavaScript control. The three values that the VISIBILITY attribute accepts are "show", "hide", and "inherit". The first two are self-explanatory; "inherit", the default value, indicates that a layer's visibility is the same as that of the parent's layer. If you have a

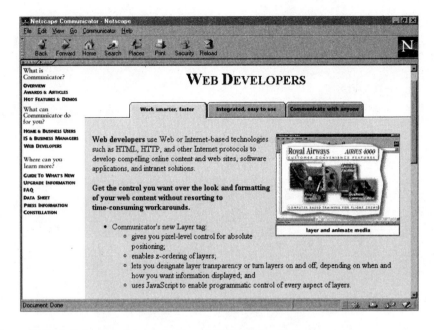

Figure 8.12: A Netscape demonstration of layer technology

layer hidden on the screen and nest other objects within it, by default these, too, will be hidden. With JavaScript, you can set the hidden object's VISIBILITY attribute to "show" and the object will appear.

From a practical standpoint, this opens up the door for such things as context-sensitive help as well as animation. You could hide help balloons and Tool-Tips on the screen where they would appear when a user's mouse passed over an item (JavaScript has an onMouseOver() event handler). Because the basis for all animation is page-flipping, you could stack a series of frames at the same TOP and LEFT coordinates and "show" each one in succession. When combined with the Z-INDEX attribute, animated characters could literally leap off the screen.

All in all, Netscape's implementation of the <LAYER> tag (and Microsoft's use of the CSS extension) opens up numerous doors for the Web designer. It is too early to tell what, if any, adverse side effects such as increased downloading time might occur. Only time—and the Web designer's imagination—will tell.

DYNAMIC CONTENT
Microsoft is just about to release version 4.0 of Internet Explorer. One of key enhancements being touted for this new version is Dynamic HTML. In addition

to offering layering control, Internet Explorer promises to bring a full range of dynamic content to the table. Dynamic content means a responsive, interactive HTML document—one that stays interactive even when downloaded. Some of the areas that Internet Explorer's Dynamic HTML affects include tables, forms, and multimedia support.

Dynamic Content   Under Microsoft's Dynamic HTML, Web page designers can alter the content of an HTML page on the fly, modifying text or inserting and removing elements on a page. Using a series of CSS-related scripts, Internet Explorer can modify the document completely at runtime. For example, a script can scan the elements of a page and, using dynamic content, insert a table of contents at the beginning of the page. Furthermore, the table of contents can be made live, using links to bookmarks.

Unlike JavaScript, which restricts content changes to when the HTML document loads into the browser, Internet Explorer can enable the changes at any time, even after the entire document has been loaded. Here are some examples of how you can build interactive documents using Dynamic HTML:

- ▶ **Dynamic expansion**. With Dynamic HTML, search results pages can be enabled to provide a detailed synopsis of any listing when the mouse is passed over it.

- ▶ **Text effects**. Hyperlinks or other text elements can change style based on mouse or keyboard actions. The font of a hyperlink could grow—or the audio score could get louder—as a mouse pointer approaches.

- ▶ **Table manipulation**. Tabular data such as price lists and search results can be sorted, filtered, and viewed using the built-in local database engine.

The last example represents a very important area the Dynamic HTML under Internet Explorer has expanded upon. Microsoft refers to this area as "Data Awareness."

Data Awareness   Many HTML pages are based on data, either from databases or files. Dynamic HTML incorporates several new features to integrate data with HTML. Microsoft Internet Explorer 4.0 includes the following data awareness features:

- ▶ **Automatic table generation**. Dynamic HTML can automatically create a table row for each record in a data source, by linking a table to that data source.

▸ **Dynamic table expansion**. Unlike conventional server-generated tables, the table can be viewed while it's still being rendered.

▸ **Dynamic regeneration.** User-defined sorting and filtering operations can be run without accessing the server.

▸ **Binding data to HTML elements.** Data from the current record is displayed as part of the HTML in the document.

▸ **Dynamic forms.** Forms can be created with Dynamic HTML and appropriate ActiveX controls that allow easy data entry and storing either to an separate database or to the Web-related database.

Data aware pages are made possible by a data source control on each page. A data source control is an invisible ActiveX control that knows how to communicate with a database. Dynamic HTML includes data source controls to access comma-delimited data in files, SQL data in Microsoft SQL Server, and other open database connectivity (ODBC) sources, and Java database connectivity (JDBC) data sources. Java applet and ActiveX control developers can implement additional data source controls to communicate with other data sources.

Dynamic HTML's data awareness promises to provide a rich set of options for manipulating and inputting data efficiently. The implications for all Web designers are significant, but perhaps more so for those involved with intranets. A good place to keep up to date with Microsoft's implementation of Dynamic HTML is their SiteBuilder network at www.microsoft.com/sitebuilder. Although these claims are promising, I can't verify them until the release of Internet Explorer 4.0. In other words, I don't know how it tastes, but it sure smells good.

COUGAR: THE NEXT HTML VERSION

What's next for the standard version of HTML? The W3 Consortium is already working on the next implementation. Code name: Cougar. Specs under discussion include

▸ The ability to include advanced scripting through the <SCRIPT> tag

▸ Improvements to forms, including nested forms, field labels, and a new database record entry mechanism

▶ Standardization of frames, with extensions allowing designers to offer different layouts for the same document depending on the medium (whether it be a desktop, palmtop, hard copy, or a speech-based browser)

▶ Enhanced math capabilities via plug-ins and "meta-math," a proposal for an extensible notation for math

▶ Increased use of the <META> and <LINK> tags to enable better navigation and search capabilities

▶ A general solution for embedding objects in an HTML document that respond to a variety of different events

Enhancements to the Internet infrastructure are also underway with the development of HTTP/1.1. Studies indicate a speedup of Web communication by as much as a factor of 80. Check http://www.w3.org/pub/www/Protocols/HTTP/Performance/Pipeline.html for the latest information.

Tutorials

- Creating a Home Page

- Creating a Guest Book: A Form Application

- A Small Business Web Site

- Converting an Existing Document to HTML

- Automating HTML with Templates

This chapter contains five "walk throughs" that illustrate how to create Web pages using the HTML elements and techniques described in this book. First, we make a simple personal home page. Next, we create a guest book page with an interactive form. Then we develop Web pages for a small business using imagemaps and frames. Next up is the conversion of a word processing document into a hypertext work—including a version using style sheets. Finally, we describe how to automate your HTML with templates. These exercises cover much of what's involved in building a Web site. The HTML used is basic enough to produce excellent results over a wide range of HTML 3.2 browsers.

CREATING A HOME PAGE

A home page is the hypertext document that introduces a Web site, and is intended as its primary starting point. Your personal home page is the starting point for a hypertext work about you. Because you create a home page from scratch, it's best to use a top-down approach, starting with a simple outline like this:

1 Your name

2 A welcome message

3 Information about you

4 A statement of your goals

5 Current activities/announcements

6 Related information

7 Signature, address, time stamps

You needn't follow this outline exactly, but this is the information readers generally expect to see in a home page. The information under each category in the preceding numbered list will be summary in nature; the details will be in other, hyperlinked pages.

MAKING AN HTML TEMPLATE FILE

Before we begin editing the HTML files, we need somewhere to put them. We need to create a new directory for these files. This directory will be the local, working copy of the Web site. Place a text file containing an HTML template in this new directory. A template file is one that has the basic HTML tags set up for the <HTML>, <HEAD>, and <BODY> elements. Here's a sample template file:

```
<!DOCTYPE HTML PUBLIC "-//W3C//DTD HTML 3.2//EN">
<HTML>
<HEAD>
<TITLE>  </TITLE>

</HEAD>
<BODY>

</BODY>
</HTML>
```

We like to leave some white space where the missing elements—that is, a title, body text, and so on—should go as a reminder not to leave anything out.

This file should have an obvious filename such as template.html and should be saved as a read-only document so that it's not accidentally overwritten. (All HTML documents should have filenames that have the extension .html unless the files will reside on a system that only allows three-character extensions, in which case they should have the extension .htm.) Make sure it's saved as a plain text file instead of in your word processor's normal format.

THE FIRST DRAFT

Next we'll take a copy of the template file and fill in the <TITLE> and <BODY> sections based on the earlier outline. For this example home page, we used the seventeenth-century astronomer Johannes Kepler. For the content, we used as a reference Arthur Koestler's book *The Sleepwalkers:*

```
<HTML>
<!-- Kepler's Home Page, created 1 August, AD 1610 -->
<HEAD>
<TITLE>Kepler's Home Page</TITLE>
</HEAD>
<BODY>
<H1>Johannes Kepler</H1>
<EM>Welcome to my Homepage!</EM>
<HR>
<H2>Who am I</H2>
<H2>What is this Document</H2>
<H2>Current Activities</H2>
<H2>Related Information</H2>
<HR>
<ADDRESS>
Johannes Kepler &lt;kepler@astronova.com&gt;<BR>
Last updated: September 7, 1610
</ADDRESS>
</BODY>
</HTML>
```

Edit and save this file in your WWW directory as homepage.html. Opening this file in a browser results in a display similar to the one shown in Figure 9.1.

Filling in the Details   The next step is filling in paragraphs of narrative text under each heading. We'll put in the hypertext links in a later stage, when the page and its content are more stable. Under the first two headings, just a couple of plain paragraphs will do. "Current Activities" will be a list of items and descriptions, so a definition list will be used. Under "Related Information" will be an unordered list of other World Wide Web and Internet sites. The HTML should now look something like this:

```
<HTML>
<!-- Kepler's Home Page, created 1 August, AD 1610 -->
<HEAD>
<TITLE>Johannes Kepler's Home Page</TITLE>
</HEAD>
<BODY>
<H1>Johannes Kepler</H1>
<EM>Welcome to my Home page!</EM>
<HR>
<H2>Who am I</H2>
<P>I am an Author and Astronomer; servant and successor to the great Tycho Brahe.
```

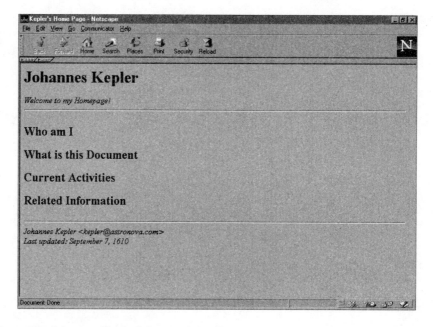

Figure 9.1: Johannes Kepler's home page—first draft

```
Currently employed as Imperial Mathematician to his highness, Emperor Rudolph
II.</P>
<H2>What is this Document</H2>
<P>This is my home page on the World Wide Web with which I endeavor to provide
the World with the latest and most important news from the frontiers of
Astronomy.</P>
<H2>Current Activities</H2>
<P>Much has happened the past few months.
 Here are some of the highlights.</P>
<DL>
<DT><H3><CITE>A New Astronomy</CITE></H3></DT>
<DD>Based A PHYSICS OF THE SKY derived from
Investigations of the MOTIONS OF THE STAR MARS Founded on
Observations of the noble Tycho Brahe. The mystery of planetary
motion has been solved, revealing The Creator's grand design.
<P>
After 8 hard years of work, my opus is finally in print.
You can order <CITE>Astro Nova</CITE> here. If all goes well,
I'll have a hypertext version available shortly
</DD>
<DT><H3>Jupiter has Moons! Saturn has Ears!</H3></DT>
<DD>Galileo's astonishing new discoveries resulting from his
```

```
investigations of the heavenly bodies as described in his
booklet, <CITE>Messenger from the Stars</CITE>.</DD>
<DT><H3>The Telescope</H3></DT>
<DD>Everybody is talking about what may be the most important
invention of our age. Thanks to the generosity of our noble
patron, the Duke of Bavaria, we now have access to one of these
amazing devices. Read our draft report on Jupiter's four
wandering satellites.</DD>
</DL>
<H2>Related Information</H2>
<UL>
<LI>The Tycho Brahe Memorial Page
<LI>Welcome to Prague
<LI>Galileo's World of Wonders
<LI>Yahoo's Astronomy Index
</UL>
<HR>
<P>This page, dear reader, is <EM>Under Construction</EM> so please be patient.
Your comments and suggestions are welcome. Please send them to the address
below.</P>
<HR>
<ADDRESS>
Johannes Kepler &lt;kepler@astronova.com&gt;<BR>
Last updated: September 7, 1610
</ADDRESS>
</BODY>
</HTML>
```

Figure 9.2 shows what this code looks like when viewed through a browser.

Adding Graphics   Okay so far. Let's add an image to the welcome message.
There are many ways to get a picture onto your computer—scanner, digital
camera, or Photo CD, to name a few—and the image file formats differ from
one operating system to the next. Digitized images must be converted into the
GIF format before they can be used inline on a page. (Some, but not all, browsers also accept inline JPEG images.) There are utilities (many shareware or
freeware) that you can use to convert images from one format to another. See
Appendix C for the details.

The image tag will go before the emphasis style tag. It could just as well be
inside of the emphasis tags, because images cannot be styled.

```
<H1>Johannes Kepler</H1>
<IMG SRC="images/kepler.gif">
<EM>Welcome to my Homepage!</EM>
<HR>
```

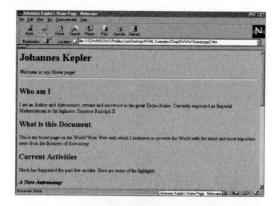

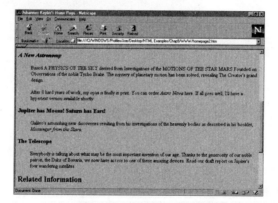

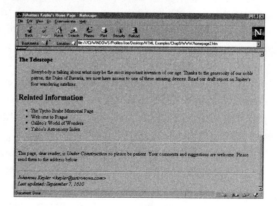

Figure 9.2: Johannes Kepler's home page—second draft

The carriage return after the image tag will force a blank space between the image and the text. This looks better than having the image right up against the text. This is okay, but let's go a step further and force the text to flow around the image by adding the ALIGN attribute to the image tag. We'll incorporate the level 1 heading and use the HSPACE attribute for better positioning.

```
<IMG SRC="images/kepler.gif" ALIGN=left HSPACE=16>
<H1>Johannes Kepler</H1>
<EM>Welcome to my Homepage!</EM>
<HR CLEAR>
```

There are other alternatives. Experiment with the placement of text and images until you find something that suits you.

Linking the Page   By now we should have a good idea where links might go. In the preceding example, we'll add links to the Tycho Brahe and Galileo home pages as well as to the sites listed under the "Related Information" heading. (Rudolph II, unconvinced of the Web's importance, didn't have a home page. He was forced to abdicate the following year.) We'll also add links to pages on *A New Astronomy* and the Telescope. These links will use relative addressing because they refer to pages in this Web site. See the listing that follows.

When you work on your home page, try to incorporate the text that anchors hypertext links into the natural flow of the paragraph's prose. Avoid using "Click here" for anchors. If a program scans your page, recording each anchor URL and its associated anchor text, "Click here" doesn't provide any useful information about the document it points to. Besides, you can pretty well assume that the readers know what is and what is not a link by the time they get to your page.

THE FINAL DRAFT

Here's the HTML for the final version of Johannes Kepler's home page. We've added small star images as bullets to the level 2 headings, fattened up the horizontal rules, and indented the text paragraphs by enclosing the main part of the page in a definition list. The page is shown in Figure 9.3.

```
<HTML>
<!-- Kepler's Home Page, created 1 August, AD 1610 -->
<HEAD>
<TITLE>Johannes Kepler's Home Page</TITLE>
</HEAD>
<BODY>
<IMG SRC="images/kepler.gif" ALIGN=left HSPACE=16>
<H1>Johannes Kepler</H1>
```

```
<EM>Welcome to my Homepage!</EM>
<BR CLEAR=left>
<HR SIZE=4>
<DL>
<DT><H2><IMG SRC="images/redstar.gif"> Who am I</H2></DT>
<DD>I am an Author and Astronomer; servant and successor to the great Tycho
Brahe. Currently employed as Imperial Mathematician to his highness, Emperor
Rudolph II.
</DD>
<DT><H2><IMG SRC="images/redstar.gif"> What is this Document</H2></DT>
<DD>This is my homepage on the
<A HREF="http://www.w3.org/">World Wide Web</A>
with which I endeavor to provide the World with the latest and most important
news from the frontiers of Astronomy.
</DD>
<DT><H2><IMG SRC="images/redstar.gif"> Current Activities</H2></DT>
<DD>Much has happened the past few months.
 Here are some of the highlights.
<DL>
<DT><H3>
<A HREF="newastro.html"><CITE>A New Astronomy</CITE></A>
</H3></DT>
<DD>Based A PHYSICS OF THE SKY derived from
Investigations of the MOTIONS OF THE STAR MARS Founded on
Observations of the noble Tycho Brahe. The mystery of planetary
motion has been solved, finally revealing The Creator's grand
design.
<P>
After 8 hard years of work, my opus is finally in print.
You can <A HREF="order.html">order it here</A>.
If all goes well, I'll have a hypertext version of it shortly
</DD>
<DT><H3>Jupiter has Moons! Saturn has Ears!</H3></DT>
<DD>Galileo's astonishing new discoveries resulting from his
investigations of the heavenly bodies as described in his
booklet, <CITE>Messenger from the Stars</CITE>.</DD>
<DT><H3><A HREF="telescope.html">The Telescope</A></H3></DT>
<DD>Everybody is talking about what may be the most important
invention of our age. Thanks to the generosity of our noble
patron, the Duke of Bavaria, we now have access to one of these
amazing devices. Read our <A HREF="jupiter.html">draft report
on Jupiter's four wandering satellites</A>.</DD>
</DL>
</DD>
<DT><H2><IMG SRC="images/redstar.gif"> Related Information</H2></DT>
<DD><UL>
<LI><A HREF="http://www.nada.kth.se/~fred/tycho.html">
```

```
The Tycho Brahe Memorial Page</A>
<LI><A HREF="http://turnpike.net/metro/muselik/prague.html">
Welcome to Prague</A>
<LI><A HREF="http://www-groups.dcs.st-
and.ac.uk/~history/Mathematicians/Galileo.html">
Galileo's World of Wonders</A>
<LI><A HREF="http://www.yahoo.com/Science/Astronomy/">
Yahoo's Astronomy Index</A>
</UL>
</DD>
</DL>
<HR SIZE=2>
<P><IMG SRC="images/workman.gif"> This page, dear reader, is <EM>Under
Construction</EM> so please be patient. Your comments and suggestions are
welcome. Please send them to the address below.</P>
<HR SIZE=4>
<ADDRESS>
Johannes Kepler
&lt;<A HREF="mailto:kepler@nova.com">jkepler@astronova.com</A>&gt;<BR>
Last updated: September 7, 1610
</ADDRESS>
</BODY>
</HTML>
```

CREATING A GUEST BOOK: A FORM APPLICATION

The World Wide Web is a client-server environment, and that means interactivity. The simplest way to interact with your readers through a Web page is with a form that electronically mails readers' input back to you. This method is a one-shot deal. Your server sends the form to the reader, who fills in information and sends it off to you. Other, more interactive methods of exchanging information with your readers require a CGI script—a computer program running on the server. This tutorial will cover both methods.

The form application developed here is a simple guest book page that lets visitors inform you of their visits to your Web site. The information is sent back to you via e-mail messages from which you extract information to be added to a visitors' page. In the second part of this tutorial, you'll use a CGI script to process the information in real time.

The form asks the reader for his or her name, e-mail address, location, and home page URL. The reader can rate the Web site and leave a comment. Submit and Reset buttons appear at the bottom of the page. Figures illustrate each step.

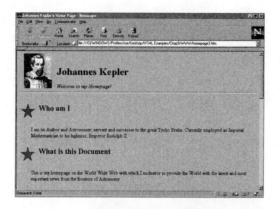

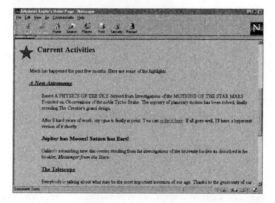

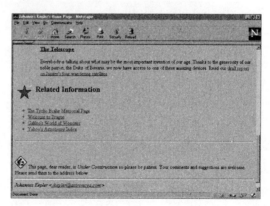

Figure 9.3: Johannes Kepler's home page—final draft

BUILDING THE CODE

First, we'll sketch out an outline of the code and use comments as placeholders for the actual form fields. Here's the basic code for the page as rendered in Figure 9.4:

```
<HTML>
<!-- Guest Book from "HTML 3.2 Manual of Style"  -->
<!-- Larry Aronson              -->
<HEAD>
<TITLE>Guest Book</TITLE>
</HEAD>
<BODY>
<H1>Guest Book</H1>
<!-- WELCOME MESSAGE -->
<HR SIZE=4>

<FORM METHOD=POST ACTION="mailto:yew@yerplace.com">
<H3>About You</H3>
<!-- FIELDS FOR name, email, location, url -->
<HR>
<H3>Your Opinion</H3>
<!-- RADIO BUTTON SET OF CHOICES -->
<HR>
<H3>Comments</H3>
<!-- TEXTAREA FOR COMMENTS -->
<HR>
<!-- SUBMIT AND RESET BUTTONS -->
</FORM>

<!-- ADDRESS AND EXIT LINKS -->
</BODY>
</HTML>
```

The beginning FORM tag,

```
<FORM METHOD=POST ACTION="mailto:yew@yerplace.com">
```

is placed just after the welcome message. It could go just after the <BODY> tag; it makes no difference, as long as it appears before the tags defining the form's input objects. The ACTION attribute specifies that the contents of the form should be e-mailed to the fictitious address, yew@yerplace.com.

Filling in the Form   The first section, *About You,* will have four sets of prompts and input fields, one set per line. Each input field will be 40 characters wide (most browsers will let the reader enter more characters than the fixed width of the field). The fields will have obvious names such as "Your Name."

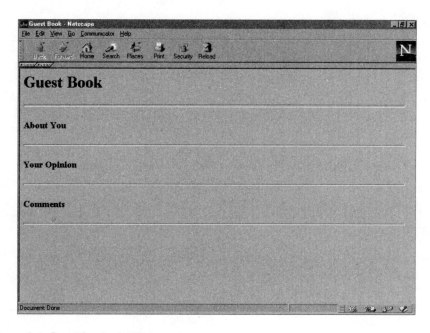

Figure 9.4: Guest book—basic layout

```
<H3>About You</H3>
<!-- FIELDS FOR name, email, location, url -->
<P>Your Name: <INPUT TYPE="text" NAME="nam" SIZE=40><BR>
Email Address: <INPUT TYPE="text" NAME="addr" SIZE=40><BR>
Location: <INPUT TYPE="text" NAME="loc" SIZE=40><BR>
Home Page URL: <INPUT TYPE="text" NAME="url" SIZE=40></P>
<HR>
```

Figure 9.5 shows how these fields would appear in a typical browser.

Aligning Form Fields Wouldn't it be nice if the prompts and input fields could be aligned vertically? Well, we can do that by putting the prompts and input fields in a four-row-by-two-column table, like so:

```
<H3>About You</H3>
<!-- FIELDS FOR name, email, location, url -->
<TABLE>
<TR><TD>Your Name:</TD>
    <TD><INPUT TYPE="text" NAME="nam" SIZE=40></TD></TR><BR>
<TR><TD>E-mail Address:</TD>
    <TD><INPUT TYPE="text" NAME="addr" SIZE=40></TD></TR><BR>
<TR><TD>State or Country:</TD>
```

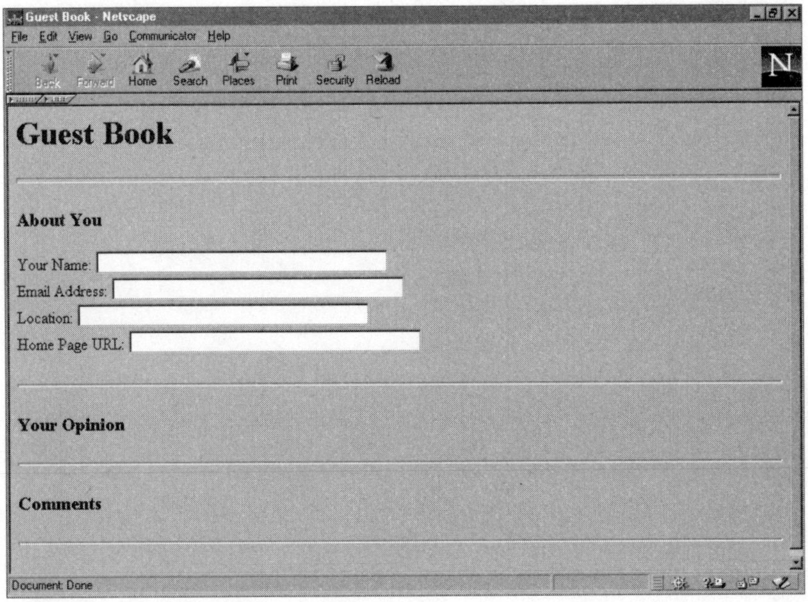

Figure 9.5: The guest book input fields

```
    <TD><INPUT TYPE="text" NAME="loc" SIZE=40></TD></TR><BR>
<TR><TD>Home Page URL:</TD>
    <TD><INPUT TYPE="text" NAME="url" SIZE=40></TD></TR><BR>
</TABLE>
<HR>
```

Take a look at the difference, as seen in Figure 9.6.

The default table attributes do just fine here, illustrating the power of tables to organize content. Note that we've dropped the paragraph tags but kept the line break tags, <BR>, just in case someone out there has a browser that supports forms but not tables.

Including Radio Buttons   The radio buttons in the next section are straightforward. We will bind them into a set by giving each the same name, "choice." The VALUE attributes are given numeric values from 1 to 4 so that, when the reader clicks on the submit button, one of these numbers will be returned, depending on which radio button is selected. For example, if the reader selects the radio button labeled "Just OK," the form will return "choice=2."

```
<H3>Your Opinion</H3>
<!-- RADIO BUTTON SET OF CHOICES -->
```

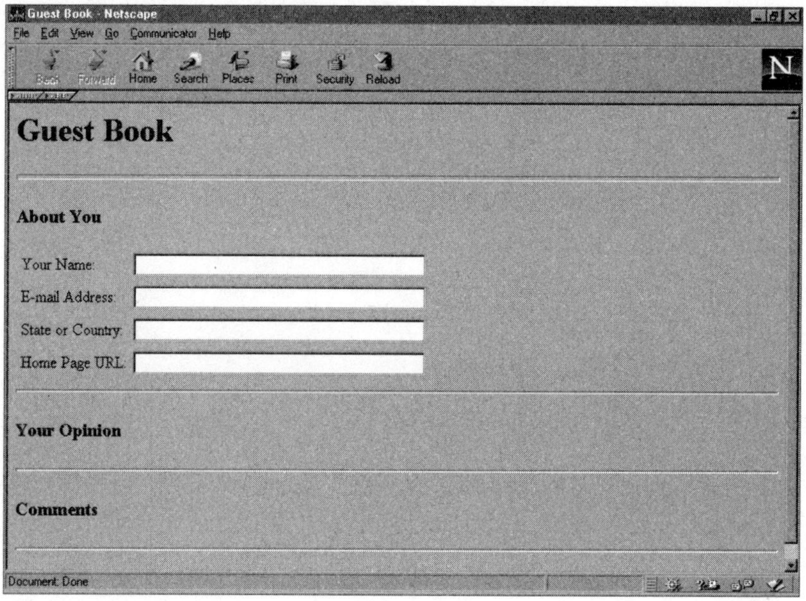

Figure 9.6: Guest book fields in a table format

```
<P><INPUT TYPE="radio" NAME="choice" VALUE=4> Hotlist Pick!<BR>
   <INPUT TYPE="radio" NAME="choice" VALUE=3 CHECKED> Very Good<BR>
   <INPUT TYPE="radio" NAME="choice" VALUE=2> Just OK<BR>
   <INPUT TYPE="radio" NAME="choice" VALUE=1> Trash</P>
<HR>
```

As you can see in Figure 9.7, the CHECKED attribute set in the "Very Good" INPUT field preselects that radio button.

Adding a Comments Field   The comments field is the easiest. We'll encourage readers by providing a large 12-row-by 60-character field.

```
<TEXTAREA NAME="comment" ROWS=12 COLS=60></TEXTAREA>
```

Be aware that the preceding is not the same as

```
<TEXTAREA NAME="comment" ROWS=12 COLS=60></TEXTAREA>
```

which initializes the input field with a single blank space because a carriage return separates <TEXTAREA> and </TEXTAREA>. The difference between no input, single blank input, and all blank input is one of those things that give programmers headaches. When you get your response from the mailer, the field will not be listed if there has been no input.

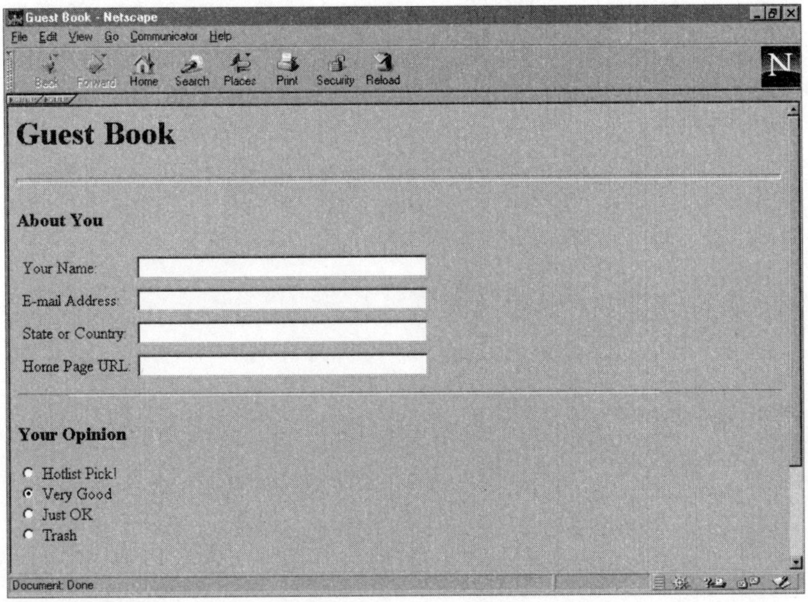

Figure 9.7: Guest book with radio buttons

Interactive Buttons   Finally, we add Submit and Reset buttons. It's a good idea to explicitly provide the button labels using the VALUE attribute.

```
<!-- SUBMIT AND RESET BUTTONS -->
<P>Click one:
<INPUT TYPE="submit" VALUE="Send It">
<INPUT TYPE="reset" VALUE="Forget It"></P>
```

Full Code Listing—First Draft   With a bit of narrative text to guide the reader along, here's the complete contents of the file, guestbook.html. Figure 9.8 shows this file rendered by a typical browser.

```
<HTML>
<!-- Guest Book from "HTML 3.2 Manual of Style"  -->
<!-- Larry Aronson          -->
<HEAD>
<TITLE>Guest Book</TITLE>
</HEAD>
<H1>Guest Book</H1>
<!-- WELCOME MESSAGE -->
Hi, Welcome to my <STRONG>Guest Book</STRONG>.
<P>Here you can leave information to let me know of your visit to my Web site.
```

```
Check the <A HREF="visitors.html">visitor's page</A> in a day or two for your
info.</P>
<HR SIZE=4>
<FORM METHOD=POST ACTION="mailto:yeruserid@yerplace.com">
<H3>About You</H3>
<!-- FIELDS FOR name, email, location, url -->
<TABLE>
<TR><TD>Your Name:</TD>
<TD><INPUT TYPE="text" NAME="nam" SIZE="40"></TD></TR><BR>
<TR><TD>E-mail Address:</TD>
<TD><INPUT TYPE="text" NAME="addr" SIZE="40"></TD></TR><BR>
<TR><TD>Location:</TD>
<TD><INPUT TYPE="text" NAME="loc" SIZE="40"></TD></TR><BR>
<TR><TD>Home Page URL:</TD>
<TD><INPUT TYPE="text" NAME="url" SIZE="40"></TD></TR><BR>
</TABLE>
<HR>
<H3>Your Opinion</H3>
<!-- RADIO BUTTON SET OF CHOICES -->
<P>Please let me know what you think of my Web site.</P>
<P><INPUT TYPE="radio" NAME="choice" VALUE=4> Hotlist Pick!<BR>
<INPUT TYPE="radio" NAME="choice" VALUE=3 CHECKED> Very Good<BR>
<INPUT TYPE="radio" NAME="choice" VALUE=2> Just OK<BR>
<INPUT TYPE="radio" NAME="choice" VALUE=1> Trash</P>
<HR>
<H3>Comments</H3>
<!-- TEXTAREA FOR COMMENTS -->
<H4>Anything else you care to add? Use the input area below.</H4>
<TEXTAREA NAME="comment" ROWS=12 COLS=60></TEXTAREA>
<HR>
<!-- SUBMIT AND RESET BUTTONS -->
<P>Click one:<INPUT TYPE="submit" VALUE="Send It">
<INPUT TYPE="reset" VALUE="Forget It"></P>
<H5>Thanks for your input.</H5>
</FORM>
<!-- ADDRESS AND EXIT LINKS -->
<H4><A HREF="homepage.html">
<IMG SRC="images/lefthand.gif" BORDER=0>
Return to my Homepage</A></H4>
<HR>
<ADDRESS>LA - 95/10/10<ADDRESS>
</BODY>
</HTML>
```

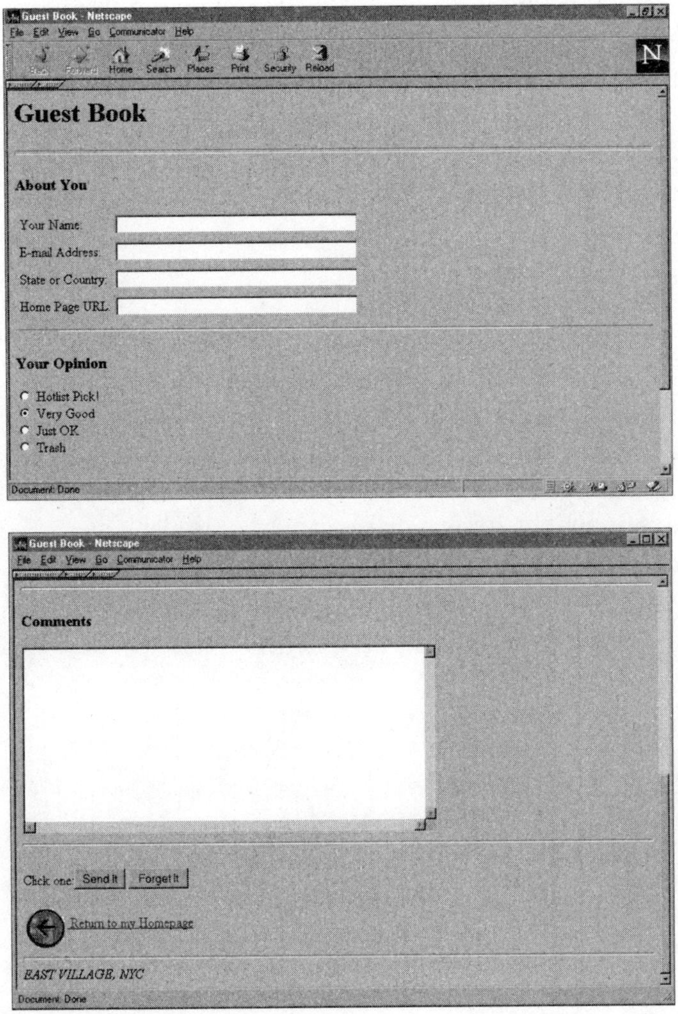

Figure 9.8: Guest book—completed first draft

ENHANCING WITH GRAPHICS

This guest book is serviceable but a bit plain. Next you'll spruce it up a little, and in the process you'll learn a few of the graphic tricks that Web designers use.

First you'll add a background image to bring the whole page together. One of the problems with forms is that they often tend to break up a page into separate sections. Using a background image helps to unify the page.

The GIF image in Figure 9.9 provides a great background because it makes your guest book look like a notebook! As with all backgrounds, the image is tiled (that is, repeated) by the browser until it fills the page.

Figure 9.9: Background image for guest book

To set this image as the background, we use the BACKGROUND attribute for the BODY tag, like this:

```
<BODY BACKGROUND="spiral2.gif">
```

As you can see in Figure 9.10, the graphic looks nice, but it causes some problems. The image of the spiral notebook overlaps (or, rather, "underlaps") some of the text and the conflict makes the text unreadable.

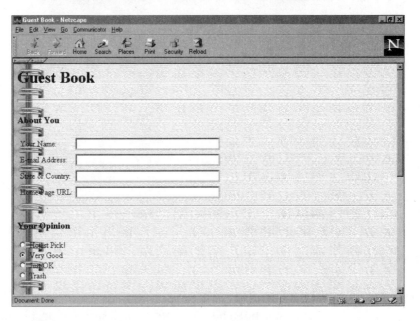

Figure 9.10: Guest book with overlapping background

Troubleshooting Background-Foreground Conflicts   What to do? Centering the various elements is a good choice because, no matter the size of the browser, the images will be off the conflicting part of the background. We can center some of the elements (such as the headings) with no further modification; however, other parts will look more awkward when centered. For example, even if they're centered, the horizontal rules will run into the spiral border on the left; the solution here is to reduce the width of the rule. Use the WIDTH attribute of the <HR> tag to set the size to three-quarters of the screen:

```
<HR WIDTH=75% ALIGN="center">
```

Aligning with Tables   The INPUT fields of the form require a different solution. Remember how we put the "About You" form fields in a table to keep them all neat and tidy? Web designers often take advantage of the table feature's ALIGN attribute. We can align the entire table to the center, just as if it were a single element like a heading. We'll group the radio buttons into a table 1 cell wide and 4 cells high. We can also put the TEXTAREA field into a single-cell table. In either case, all the table needs to align to the center is

```
<TABLE ALIGN="center">
```

Figure 9.11 shows the changes made to the revised guest book.

Another Alignment Option   To align the final portion of the guest book—the submit and reset buttons—we need to use a different solution. We could put them in a table also, but that would form a space separating the two buttons, and we want them next to each other. If we set the <P> tag to ALIGN="center", only the text "Click one:" will obey; the two buttons will stay left-aligned. Another option is to use the <DIV></DIV> tag pair.

Remember, the <DIV> tag stands for "division"; we can control the alignment of anything within that division with the ALIGN attribute. This is how to frame the code using the <DIV> element:

```
<DIV ALIGN="center">
<P>Click one:<INPUT TYPE="submit" VALUE="Send It">
<INPUT TYPE="reset" VALUE="Forget It"></P>
</DIV>
```

Incorporating Inline Graphics   The final bit of clean-up comes with the graphic and anchor at the bottom of the page that returns the user to the home page. We like to take advantage of HTML's ability to mix graphics and text on the same line. As you can see in Figure 9.12, the word "Return" has been cut and the arrow image has taken its place. What makes this work is the

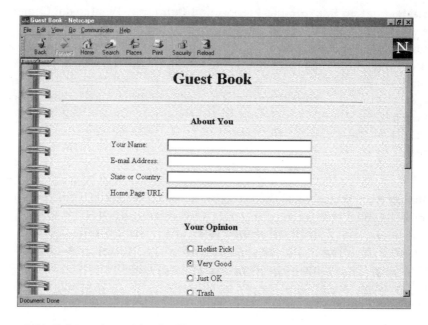

Figure 9.11: Enhanced guest book—First half

ALIGN="middle" attribute in the <IMG> tag. Here ALIGN does not refer to the image's position on the page, but rather the alignment of the text following the image. Setting ALIGN to "middle" makes the text that follows come in the middle of the graphic.

Complete Code—Guest Book 2.0   Here, then, is the complete, revised code for the second draft of the guest book, with enhanced graphics.

```
<HTML>
<!-- Guest Book from "HTML 3.2 Manual of Style"  -->
<!-- Larry Aronson          -->
<!-- Joseph Lowery          -->
<HEAD>
<TITLE>Guest Book</TITLE>
</HEAD>
<BODY BACKGROUND="spiral2.gif">
<H1 ALIGN="center">Guest Book</H1>
<!-- WELCOME MESSAGE -->
<HR WIDTH=80% ALIGN="center">
<FORM METHOD=POST ACTION="mailto:yew@yerplace.com">
<H3 ALIGN="center">About You</H3>
<TABLE ALIGN="center">
```

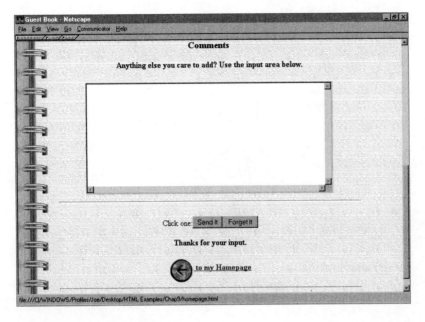

Figure 9.12: Inline graphics and text

```
<TR><TD>Your Name:</TD>
    <TD><INPUT TYPE="text" NAME="nam" SIZE=40></TD></TR>
<TR><TD>E-mail Address:</TD>
    <TD><INPUT TYPE="text" NAME="addr" SIZE=40></TD></TR>
<TR><TD>State or Country:</TD>
    <TD><INPUT TYPE="text" NAME="loc" SIZE=40></TD></TR>
<TR><TD>Home Page URL:</TD>
    <TD><INPUT TYPE="text" NAME="url" SIZE=40></TD></TR>
</TABLE>
<HR WIDTH=80% ALIGN="center">
<H3 ALIGN="center">Your Opinion</H3>
<!-- RADIO BUTTON SET OF CHOICES -->
<TABLE ALIGN="center">
<TR><TD>
<INPUT TYPE="radio" NAME="choice" VALUE=4> Hotlist Pick!
</TD><TR>
<TR><TD>
    <INPUT TYPE="radio" NAME="choice" VALUE=3 CHECKED> Very Good<BR>
</TD><TR>
<TR><TD>
    <INPUT TYPE="radio" NAME="choice" VALUE=2> Just OK<BR>
</TD><TR>
```

```
<TR><TD>
  <INPUT TYPE="radio" NAME="choice" VALUE=1> Trash</P>
</TD><TR>
</TABLE>
<HR WIDTH=80% ALIGN="center">
<H3 ALIGN="center">Comments</H3>
<!-- TEXTAREA FOR COMMENTS -->
<H4 ALIGN="center">Anything else you care to add? Use the input area below.</H4>
<TABLE ALIGN="center"><TR><TD>
<TEXTAREA NAME="comment" ROWS=12 COLS=60></TEXTAREA>
</TD></TR></TABLE>
<HR WIDTH=80% ALIGN="center">
<!-- SUBMIT AND RESET BUTTONS -->
<DIV ALIGN="center">
<P>Click one:<INPUT TYPE="submit" VALUE="Send It"><INPUT TYPE="reset"
VALUE="Forget It"></P>
</DIV>
<H4 ALIGN="center">Thanks for your input.</H4>
</FORM>
<!-- ADDRESS AND EXIT LINKS -->
<H4 ALIGN="center"><A HREF="homepage.html">
<IMG SRC="left.gif" BORDER=0 ALIGN="middle"> to my Homepage</A>
<HR WIDTH=80% ALIGN="center">
<ADDRESS ALIGN="center">EAST VILLAGE, NYC<ADDRESS>
</BODY>
</HTML>
```

HANDLING FORM RESPONSES

Suppose our net.friend, Johannes, visited our guest book and filled in the fields. Clicking on the Submit button, he would have sent an e-mail message to yew@yerplace.com with the body of that message containing:

```
nam=Johannes+Kepler&addr=jkepler@astronova.com&loc=Prague&url=http%3A%2F%2Fwww.ast
ronova.com%2F%7Ejkepler%2Fhomepage.html&choice=3&comment= Looking!Good%21
```

If you put up a guest page and start getting more than one of these messages a day, you'll want a program to do all the work of converting the message to a more readable format for you. You can download a number of CGI scripts that, installed on your server, can do the hard work of parsing this input. As long as you set it up correctly, you can use the CGI script covered in Chapter 7, FormMail, no matter what fields are on your form. It's a PERL script that can be installed on most Web servers. It parses the input, e-mails it to a recipient, and then serves a reply page of your choice back to the reader. FormMail requires that fields with specific names be sent to it. This can be done with "hidden" input fields.

To use FormMail (assuming the webmaster installed it on the server in the cgi-bin directory) in the guest book, replace the <FORM> tag with:

```
<FORM METHOD=POST ACTION="http://www.yerplace.com/cgi-bin/mailform.pl">
```

Then insert the following fields to supply the required information. These input fields will be hidden; they don't appear anywhere on the Web page and the tags can be placed anywhere within the <FORM></FORM> tags. We recommend grouping them together near the top of the FORM declaration for easy reference.

You can use a lot of variables with FormMail. The only required one is "recipient"—you should set this value to the e-mail address you want the form responses to go to. Here's how the code would look using our fictitious e-mail address:

```
<INPUT TYPE="hidden" NAME="recipient" VALUE="yew@yerplace.com">
```

Next we want to include a subject line for the e-mailed response. Most e-mail programs will not send mail without a subject. FormMail uses a standard subject ("Submission: WWW Form Submission"), which is a tad redundant. In addition, if you use FormMail for more than one form, all of your responses will have the same subject heading. Personalizing each form subject heading makes it easier to keep them all straight. Here's an example:

```
<INPUT TYPE="hidden" NAME="subject" VALUE="GuestBook Visitor">
```

Requiring and Sorting Fields   The "required" and "sort" fields also ease your form response chores. The "required" field allows you to specify any of the fields on your form that must be filled out. The "sort" field lets you specify the order of the fields on the response e-mail. Both use the names specified in each of the <INPUT> tags to reference the fields.

The syntax for the "required" field is

```
<INPUT TYPE="hidden" name="required" value="field1,field2,etc.">
```

where the names in your form are substituted for the "field1,field2,etc." line. The guest book form has the fields "nam", "addr", "loc", "url", "choice", and "comment". Suppose we want to require the visitor's name, e-mail address, and radio button selection. To achieve this, use the following code:

```
<INPUT TYPE="hidden" name="required" value="nam,addr,choice">
```

If one or more of these fields are empty when the user clicks on the Submit button, the FormMail CGI script generates an HTML page on the fly, listing the uncompleted fields. The user must return to the form by pressing the browser's Back button to fill out the missing fields.

Unless you specify the sort order of the fields, they will be returned to you in the order in which they appear in HTML code. FormMail lets you permit this, sort the fields in alphabetical order, or specify the order you want the fields to appear in. To get your responses in A-to-Z order, use the following code:

```
<INPUT TYPE="hidden" name="sort" value="alphabetic">
```

In the example this would return the responses in the order "addr", "choice", "comment", "loc", "nam", and "url".

Most often you'll want to specify the sort order for your fields. Suppose that we wanted to have our response form put the radio button choice at the top of the listing, followed by the "About You" information fields and comment. Here's how that code would look:

```
<INPUT TYPE="hidden" name="sort" value="order:choice,nam,addr,loc,url,comment">
```

Note the key word "order:" that starts the value text string.

You can place all the code for the FormMail choices right after the <FORM> tag. Here's the code fragment:

```
<FORM METHOD=POST ACTION="http://www.yoursite.com/cgi-bin/formmail.pl">
<INPUT TYPE="hidden" NAME="recipient" VALUE="yew@yerplace.com">
<INPUT TYPE="hidden" NAME="subject" VALUE="GuestBook Visitor">
<INPUT TYPE="hidden" name="required" value="nam,addr,choice">
<INPUT TYPE="hidden" name="sort" value="order:choice,nam,addr,loc,url,comment">
<!-- Balance of form goes here-->
</FORM>
```

A SMALL BUSINESS WEB SITE

This tutorial describes how to build two pages of a small business Web site. The first page is once again a home page; however, this home page uses a graphics-intensive layout and incorporates an imagemap as a navigational tool. Then we build one of the site's primary pages, which uses frames to present the wide range of information.

USING CLIENT-SIDE IMAGEMAPS

The site we will build is for a bar called "d.b.a." in New York City that specializes in first-class beers and liquors from around the world. The bar itself has a very understated style that welcomes a range of customers; the Web site should reflect this warmth and openness.

Making the graphic is the first step in developing a imagemap. It should be an unambiguous image that clearly handles the navigational chores, and fits in with the nature of the site. Because there is no common user interface to the

Web, each new visitor to the Web site will have to quickly understand what the site is about and what the choices are.

Building the Initial Graphics   The initial graphics consist of several scanned images—the bar matchbook and several bottlecaps. The matchbook is left as is—incorporating existing marketing elements saves time and links the everyday business of the company to the Web—but the bottlecaps are altered in a paint program. As you can see in Figure 9.13, raised lettering was added to the bottlecaps that correspond to each of the main Web site sections: Menu, Info, and Stuff.

Figure 9.13: The initial graphic for an imagemap

We worked on the image in pieces in Adobe Photoshop. First, we scanned the matchbook in as a JPEG file and chose it as the primary image. Second, we also scanned sample bottlecaps to keep the look similar. We added coloring and the lettering for the bottlecaps. We tilted each element to a different angle and placed it on a larger canvas. We added the three-dimensional shadows to the whole picture to unify the elements.

At this point, the JPEG file was weighing in at a hefty 1.1 megabytes. (As a general rule, you should keep your images about 30 to 50 kilobytes per page; this ensures a fairly swift download.) We converted the file from a JPEG file consisting of 16 million possible colors to a GIF file of 256 colors; this reduced the file size to a much more workable 40K. The file conversion was handled by the Export to GIF feature of Adobe Photoshop.

During that conversion, two switches were turned "on"—the first saves the file as an interlaced one, and the second makes the background color transparent. Remember that an interlaced GIF "develops" like a photograph on screen. This is far more interesting for the visitor to watch than a blank screen loading in the background. Using an interlaced GIF is an especially good option if the graphic is toward the upper end of the acceptable range and will take a while to load.

Integrating a Background The transparency option makes graphics appear to float above any background. In the example, the bar's marble countertops were replicated with a small image of marble set to be the background in the <BODY> tag. Figure 9.14 shows the marble by itself.

Figure 9.14: Marble background tiled by the browser

In this case, saving the image as a JPEG file yielded a smaller file size than saving it as a GIF. Be sure to try both methods to find your best case.

Combining the foreground and background images is very simple. Remember, set the background attribute in the <BODY> tag. Then use the <IMG> tag to lay on the matchbook and bottle caps. Here's the initial code:

```
<HTML>
<HEAD>
<TITLE>d.b.a.</TITLE>
</HEAD>
<BODY BACKGROUND="marble2a.jpg">
<DIV ALIGN="center">
<IMG SRC="/combo2b.gif" BORDER="0">
```

```
</DIV>
</BODY>
</HTML>
```

Notice that the BORDER attribute is set to 0 to make sure that no border surrounds the foreground image and destroys the illusion of a free-floating nonrectangular graphic.

Using an Imagemap Tool   An imagemap is based on a range of pixel coordinates within a graphic. An imagemap tool is used to gather those coordinates and put them in the right HTML format. Many of the full-featured Web site creation tools like FrontPage, PageMill, and BackStage Designer have built-in imagemap programs. There are also numerous freeware and shareware programs that do an excellent job. The example will use Map This!, a freeware program published by TuCows Software (www.tucows.com).

Using Map This!, or any imagemapping tool, takes just four straightforward steps:

1 Open your graphic file.

2 Outline each element to be mapped.

3 Assign a URL to each element.

4 Generate the HTML code and save the file.

Map This! uses a series of familiar drawing tools—the oval, rectangle, and polygon—to handle the outlining phase of the project. In the example, the oval tool lets us quickly outline each of the bottlecaps. Figure 9.15 shows the "Menu" bottlecap ready to be mapped.

The outline in Map This! toggles between a hatched see-through and a solid design. The hatched see-through appearance indicates that outline is selected and can be deleted or modified.

Now we can either draw other circles to cover the other bottlecaps or, because all the caps are the same size, we can copy and paste to duplicate the circles. The arrow tool lets us move and resize the circles to fit properly over the graphic.

For odd-shaped objects, use the polygon tool for outlining. We used the polygon tool to outline the irregularly shaped matchbook. Start by clicking on one edge and then clicking on each point around the figure; the outline is completed, it fills in. Figure 9.16 shows all of the elements outlined and the matchbook selected.

Figure 9.15: A mapped image in Map This!

Figure 9.16: All of the elements mapped

You can assign the URLs to the maps one at a time or after you have out-lined all the elements to be mapped. In Map This!, you can either double-click on the outline or click on the Pencil toolbar button to edit the associated URL. This brings up a dialog box with information about the object—its coordi-nates in the picture and its size—and several text boxes to fill out. The only one that is required is the first, the URL. This is where you would put the hy-pertext reference value—in other words, where you want the Web browser to jump to when this button is chosen. The second (optional) line allows you to name a frame target, as described later in this section. The third line lets you put in a comment, which will go into the ALT attribute of the imagemap. Fig-ure 9.17 shows this dialog box filled out for our site.

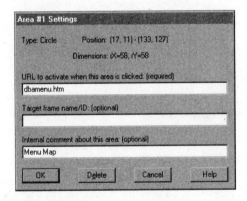

Figure 9.17: Setting a imagemap's URL

After you have assigned URLs for all the elements in your imagemap, there is one more dialog box to be filled in: the general file settings. First, the entire map (which consists of each of the individually mapped elements) must be named so that it can be called in the HTML code. Second, in addition to as-signing each element a URL, it is a good idea to assign a default URL to the rest of the picture. If the user clicks outside of any defined area, the browser will jump to this default URL. Typically, the same page you are on is the de-fault URL. When you use an imagemap and the browser's pointer passes over a mapped element, its URL appears in the browser window. By assigning the de-fault URL to the same page, you indicate the page until a mapped element is touched. Figure 9.18 shows a completed general file settings for our example.

At the bottom of the settings dialog box are three radio buttons for the "Map file format." We chose CSIM, which stands for client-side imagemap. The other choices, NCSA (National Center for Supercomputing Applications)

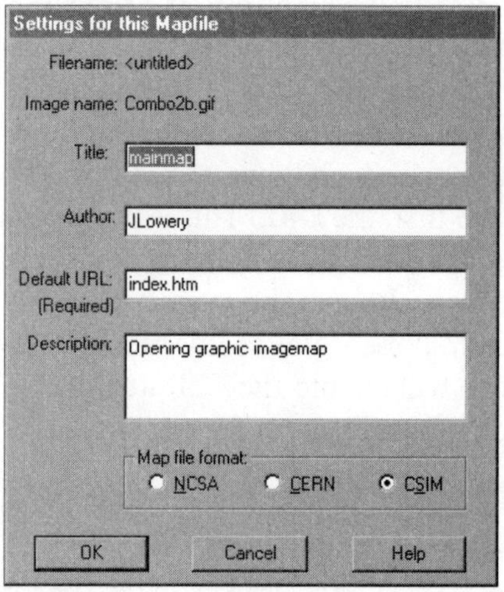

Figure 9.18: The general imagemap file settings

and CERN (the European Laboratory for Particle Physics, birthplace of the Web) are formats used for server-side imagemaps.

Integrating an Imagemap into HTML   The final step in using Map This! to create an imagemap is to save the file. The easiest way to integrate the client-side imagemap information is to save the file as an HTML file. This creates code that can be easily cut and pasted into the main document or—if you are just starting—serve as the basis for a beginning HTML page. Here's the code generated from Map This! for our settings:

```
<BODY>
<MAP NAME="mainmap">
<!-- #$-:Image Map file created by Map THIS! -->
<!-- #$-:Map THIS! free image map editor by Todd C. Wilson -->
<!-- #$-:Please do not edit lines starting with "#$" -->
<!-- #$VERSION:1.30 -->
<!-- #$DESCRIPTION:Opening graphic imagemap -->
<!-- #$AUTHOR:JLowery -->
<!-- #$DATE:Sat Apr 05 18:03:19 1997 -->
<!-- #$PATH:C:\dba\ -->
<!-- #$GIF:Combo2b.gif -->
<AREA SHAPE=CIRCLE COORDS="75,69,58" HREF="dbamenu.htm" ALT="Menu Map">
<AREA SHAPE=POLY COORDS="279,15,263,20,231,164,221,226,428,272,477,60,279,15"
HREF="dbageneral" ALT="Matchbook">
<AREA SHAPE=CIRCLE COORDS="132,203,58" HREF="dbainfo" ALT="Info button">
```

```
<AREA SHAPE=CIRCLE COORDS="546,236,58" HREF="dbastuff.htm" ALT="Stuff button">
<AREA SHAPE=default HREF="index.htm">
</MAP></BODY>
```

Notice how the map information is found within the <BODY> tags. The comments (the lines starting with ("<!--") retain information about the source of your imagemap. The NAME in the <MAP> tag ("mainmap" in the example) is referenced in the USEMAP attribute of the <IMG> tag to bind the imagemap information to the graphic:

```
<IMG SRC="/combo2b.gif" BORDER="0" USEMAP="#mainmap">
```

The hash sign ("#") indicates that this name can be found within this document. Presently, no browsers support external client-side imagemaps, but this is used to be consistent with other HTML code.

Finishing the Imagemap   We'll finish off with a heading welcoming our visitors to the site and some text navigation links. Why include text links after going to all that trouble to do an imagemap? Although the Web may seem like a graphics-intensive medium most of the time, some browsers (such as linemode browsers) don't use graphics at all and all browsers have the capacity to "turn-off" the images. If traffic is particularly heavy on the Web, access times can increase tremendously and some people opt to turn off the images temporarily so that they can get the information they want as quickly as possible. It is strongly advised that you provide text alternatives for your graphic URL links.

Here's the final code for our small business home page. It shows the full integration of the imagemap code generated by our utility into the standard HTML code; Figure 9.19 shows the results you'll see if you access the actual Web site at www.drinkgoodstuff.com.

```
<HTML>
<HEAD>
<TITLE>d.b.a.</TITLE>
</HEAD><BODY>
<IMG SRC="/combo2b.gif" BORDER="0" USEMAP="#mainmap">
<MAP NAME="mainmap">
<!-- #$-:Image Map file created by Map THIS! -->
<!-- #$-:Map THIS! free image map editor by Todd C. Wilson -->
<!-- #$-:Please do not edit lines starting with "#$" -->
<!-- #$VERSION:1.30 -->
<!-- #$DESCRIPTION:Opening graphic imagemap -->
<!-- #$AUTHOR:JLowery -->
<!-- #$DATE:Sat Apr 05 18:03:19 1997 -->
<!-- #$PATH:C:\dba\ -->
<!-- #$GIF:Combo2b.gif -->
```

```
<AREA SHAPE=CIRCLE COORDS="75,69,58" HREF="dbamenu.htm" ALT="Menu Map">
<AREA SHAPE=POLY COORDS="279,15,263,20,231,164,221,226,428,272,477,60,279,15"
HREF="dbageneral" ALT="Matchbook">
<AREA SHAPE=CIRCLE COORDS="132,203,58" HREF="dbainfo" ALT="Info button">
<AREA SHAPE=CIRCLE COORDS="546,236,58" HREF="dbastuff.htm" ALT="Stuff button">
<AREA SHAPE=default HREF="index.htm">
</MAP>
<HR>
<H1>
<FONT COLOR="#FF0000">
Welcome to the d.b.a. website.
</FONT>
</H1>
</CENTER>
<CENTER>| <A HREF="dbamenu.htm">Menu</A> | <A HREF="dbainfo.htm">Info</A> | <A
HREF="dbastuff.HTM">Stuff</A> |
<HR>
</CENTER>
</BODY>
</HTML>
```

Figure 9.19: The completed imagemap results on the Web

INCORPORATING FRAMES

For the next stage of our small business Web site, we will build a page using frames. Remember that frames are independent Web page divisions that can load separate HTML documents. The Menu section of our example Web site is a perfect candidate for frames because there are several categories, each of which could call its own page that would load into the main frame. This process would allow the primary navigation tools to stay always accessible in one of the frames. Our final frame will keep the establishment's contact information on screen at all times. We start by outlining the frameset.

Developing the Frameset   It always helps to sketch out a proposed Web site, especially when working with frames. Because the coding for the frameset can be difficult to master, it's best to have a pretty clear idea of your goal before beginning to code.

There are two basic approaches to deciding how the frames should divide the Web page. The first approach starts with the largest frame. How much proportional screen room does it need to do the job? Most likely, it will be in the 50 to 80 percent range—under 50 percent and it's probably not getting enough emphasis, over 80 percent and there's no room for anything else. Remember that the largest frame will contain the bulk of the information, so it will most likely have a scroll bar on one side, which takes up a bit more of your screen.

The second approach to placing the frames is to look at what frame, if any, has to be a certain width. Most often your navigational panel has small GIFs acting as links. You want these GIFs to appear in their full size without scroll bars being invoked; after all, the whole purpose of using frames for navigation is to have one panel always available with all of your primary links visible. Aside from setting the width with the <FRAMESET> tag, turn off the scroll bars by setting SCROLLING="no" in the navigation frame.

Next consider the primary frame's position. Perhaps because "Page 1" is almost always on the right in our culture, the right-hand side of a page tends to weigh in with a little more importance. For whatever reason, the navigation frame is generally placed on the left side of the screen and the major data frame is on the right. Keep in mind that these are guidelines, not rules—and breaking "rules" can lead to more exciting design.

Finally, ask yourself (or your client) if there is any information besides the navigational buttons that should remain on screen at all times. This would indicate another smaller nonscrolling frame at either the top or the bottom of the page. Common uses for such a frame are copyright information, contact information for companies or stores, or—in a sign of these merchandising times—advertisements that stay on the screen while the content scrolls.

For our example, we are going to divide the page into three frames: one column on the left to hold the navigational buttons, one main area on the right and top for the changing content, and one thin row along the bottom to keep the company's name and address as well as links to other areas of the Web site always visible. The following code will outline our frames as depicted in Figure 9.20.

```
<html>
<head>
<TITLE>Frame Setup</TITLE>
</HEAD>
<frameset cols="125,*">
<FRAME SRC="dummy.htm" NAME="left">
<FRAMESET ROWS="80%,*">
    <FRAME SRC="dummy.htm" NAME="main">
<FRAME SRC="dummy.htm" NAME="bottom">
</frameset>
</frameset>
</html>
```

The dummy.htm files are template HTML documents with no content that are included in the <FRAME> tag so that the browser will draw the borders of the frames.

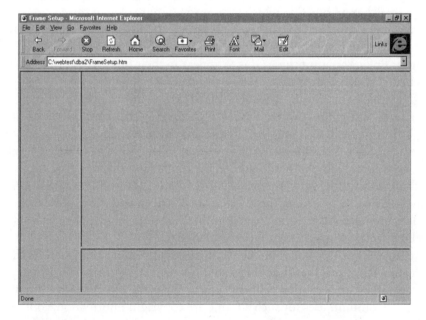

Figure 9.20: Initial frame layout

Filling in the Frames   Because the left-hand frame acts as our main control panel, let's start filling in our frameset there. Remember that each frame is its own HTML document, so we'll open our HTML template and insert the elements.

After an opening H3 heading ("What's On Tap and On the Shelf"), we will use four different but similar icons as our navigation buttons. One of the design elements of the bar itself is the use of blackboards to keep track of the constantly updating taps and liquors. This imagery is appropriated and, using a "Chalk" font, four separate images are created and stored as GIF files.

For each of the four icons, in addition to specifying an image SRC attribute, we must also declare where this URL should appear. We do this by adding the TARGET attribute to each <IMG> tag. In the example, the primary frame where we want the information to appear is named "main"—this was declared in the initial frameset. Finally, to maintain continuity from the home page, we've added the marble background to the frame. There's no additional download time here, because the image is already cached by the browser. Here's the code for the left-side frame; the result is shown in Figure 9.21.

```
<HTML>
<HEAD>
<TITLE>Left Frame in d.b.a. - Menu</TITLE>
</HEAD>
<BODY BACKGROUND="marble2a.jpg">
<H2 ALIGN="center"><FONT COLOR="white"> What's On Tap and On the Shelf.</F></H2>
<P ALIGN="center">
<A HREF="regdraft.htm" TARGET="main"><IMG SRC="draft2.GIF" ALT="Draught Beers"
BORDER="0" WIDTH="75" HEIGHT="64"></A>
<A HREF="handpump.htm" TARGET="main"><IMG SRC="hand2.GIF" ALT="Handdrawn Ales"
BORDER="0" width="75" HEIGHT="64"></A>
<A HREF="beerbotl.htm" TARGET="main"><IMG SRC="bottle2.GIF" ALT="Bottled Beer"
BORDER="0" WIDTH="75" HEIGHT="64"></A>
<A HREF="liquors.htm" TARGET="main"><IMG SRC="liquor2.GIF" ALT="Liquors and
Wines" BORDER="0" WIDTH="75" HEIGHT="64"></A></P>
</body>
</HTML>
```

Combining Tables and Frames   The contents of the main frame is, of course, dependent on whatever button is selected in the left frame. All of the menu options lead to pages that describe what's available in each category. Because of the database-like nature of these listings, each page uses tables extensively. Let's look at one example in code and then discuss each section. Figure 9.22 illustrates the code that appears here:

```
<HTML>
<HEAD>
```

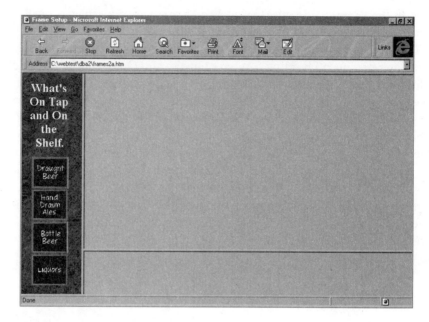

Figure 9.21: The left frame in place

```
   <TITLE>d.b.a. - ON TAP</TITLE>
</HEAD>
<BODY BGCOLOR="white">
<H2><IMG SRC="glass.gif" HEIGHT=164 WIDTH=98 ALIGN="middle"><IMG SRC="glass.gif"
HEIGHT=164 WIDTH=98 ALIGN="middle"><IMG SRC="glass.gif" HEIGHT=164 WIDTH=98
ALIGN="middle"><IMG SRC="glass.gif" HEIGHT=164 WIDTH=98 ALIGN="middle">Regular
Draught </H2>
<P>
<HR></P>
<H3 ALIGN=CENTER>Updated Sunday, March 30, 1997</H3>
<P>
<HR></P>
<!-- Table starts here -->
<TABLE CELLSPACING=0 WIDTH=624 ALIGN="center">
<!-- Header Row starts here -->
<TR>
<TD VALIGN=MIDDLE><BR>
<B>Brand</B></TD>
<TD VALIGN=MIDDLE>
<CENTER><P><B>Date <BR>
Tapped </B></P></CENTER>
</TD>
```

```
<TD VALIGN=MIDDLE>
<CENTER><P><BR>
<B>  Mug  </B></P></CENTER>
</TD>
<TD VALIGN=MIDDLE>
<CENTER><P><B>  U.S. <BR>
 Pint</B></P></CENTER>
</TD>
<TD VALIGN=MIDDLE>
<CENTER><P><B>Imperial<BR>
Pint</B></P></CENTER>
</TD>
<TD VALIGN=MIDDLE>
<CENTER><P><B>Wine <BR>
Glass</B></P></CENTER>
</TD>
</TR>
<!-- Header Row ends; Data starts here -->
<TR><TD VALIGN=MIDDLE COLSPAN=6><CENTER><P><HR></P></CENTER></TD></TR>
<TR>
<TD VALIGN=MIDDLE><B>Anchor Foghorn</B></TD>
<TD VALIGN=MIDDLE ALIGN=CENTER><B>3/28</B></TD>
<TD VALIGN=MIDDLE ALIGN=CENTER><B>$ 3.50</B></TD>
<TD VALIGN=MIDDLE ALIGN=CENTER><B>$ 5.00</B></TD>
<TD VALIGN=MIDDLE ALIGN=CENTER><B>$ 6.00</B></TD>
<TD VALIGN=MIDDLE ALIGN=CENTER><B></B></TD>
</TR>
<!-- Many more beers in same format follow -->
<TR><TD colspan=6><HR></TD></TR>
</TABLE>
</BODY>
</HTML>
```

First, we repeat the same GIF file four times. Repeating an image is a classic design technique and it works well on the Web, if you don't overdo it. Notice that each of the images has its alignment set to "middle", which lines up all the images in a row and sets up the text to fall in the center of the image.

Following the "Updated" line, the table that will contain most of the data is started. Some cells in the header row are in one line ("Mugs") and some take up two lines ("Imperial Pint"). When combining cells with a varying number of lines in a single row, use the <BR> tag as demonstrated. Single lines will take two line breaks, one after another, to line up with the other two-line cells.

Navigating Out of the Frame   The final frame consists of a single line of text and two navigational buttons. The difference here is that these buttons will

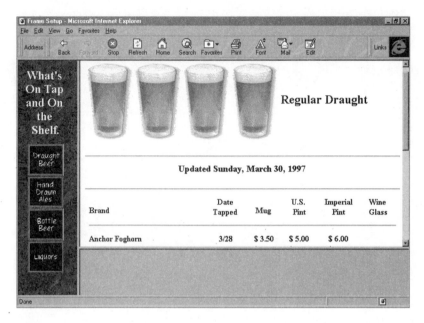

Figure 9.22: A main frame in place

take us out of the frame and onto other areas of the Web site. Here's the code for the bottom frame:

```
<HTML>
<HEAD>
<TITLE>Bottom Frame in d.b.a. Menu</TITLE>
</HFAD>
<BODY BACKGROUND="marble2a.jpg">
<H3 ALIGN="center">
<A HREF="dbainfo.htm" TARGET="_top"><IMG SRC="info2.gif" ALIGN="middle"
BORDER=0></A>
<FONT COLOR="white"> d.b.a. -  41 1st Avenue, New York, NY </FONT>
<A HREF="dbastuff.htm"><IMG SRC="stuff2.gif" ALIGN="middle" BORDER=0></A>
</H3>
</BODY>
</HTML>
```

The key difference here is in the anchor tags for each of the two buttons. The TARGET attribute is set to "_top"; this is one of the reserved words that was covered in the section on Frames in Chapter 8. "_top" refers to the upper-most level of the frameset and has the effect of replacing the entire frameset with whatever is linked. This could, of course, be a regular HTML file or another frameset.

Final Frameset Code   There are only a couple of clean-up items remaining to finish the frameset. We want the left and bottom frames to remain stationary and so we turn off the SCROLLING attribute in each <FRAME> tag. Most browsers allow the user to resize frames by dragging their borders. That option doesn't make sense for this situation, so let's turn that off for all three frames by including the NORESIZE attribute in each FRAME tag.

Finally, we include the <NOFRAME></NOFRAME> pair for users whose browsers can't handle frames. In the example, we issue a brief apology and, more importantly, give readers another way to access the information. Ideally, you should provide an alternate link path for nonframe browsers on the home page. However, even if you do that, you should also take advantage of the <NOFRAMES> tags, because it is entirely possible that a visitor will not enter through your home page "front door."

Here's the final code for the Menu frameset; Figure 9.23 shows the resulting page.

```
<html>
<head>
<TITLE>d.b.a. - Menu</TITLE>
</HEAD>
<frameset cols="125,*">
    <FRAME src="frleft.htm" NAME="left" SCROLLING="no" NORESIZE>
<FRAMESET ROWS="80%,*">
    <FRAME SRC="frmiddle.htm" NAME="main" NORESIZE>
    <noframes>
    <body>
<H3>Sorry, but you really need a Frame-enabled browser to view this site.</H3>
<P ALIGN="center">
| <A HREF="index.htm">Main</a> | <A HREF="dbainfo.htm">Info</A> | <A
HREF="dbastuff.htm">Stuff</A> | </P>
</body>
</noframes>
<FRAME SRC="frbottom.htm" NAME="bottom" NORESIZE SCROLLING="no">
</frameset>
</frameset>
</html>
```

CONVERTING AN EXISTING DOCUMENT TO HTML

Unlike creating a home page, converting an existing document to hypertext is best approached from the bottom up. Suppose you have a user's guide for some aspect of your business. It could even be a guide to using the Internet.

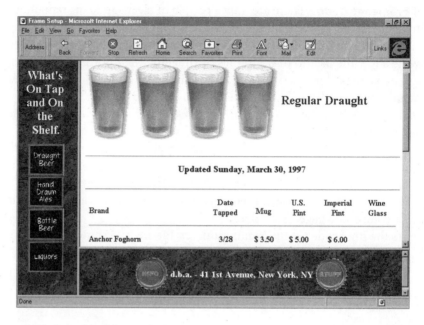

Figure 9.23: Completed frame design

Let's assume that the document exists in the normal format of a word processing program such as Microsoft Word.

THE BOTTOM-UP APPROACH

Working from the bottom up, you'll create a series of versions of the guide, each a refinement of the previous one. When the conversion is complete, you'll have a full hypertext version consisting of linked files, a single formatted version suitable for printing, a text-only version for readers with nongraphical browsers, and the original version in a format suitable for downloading. On top of all this, you'll create a home page for the guide that describes the work and has links to the various versions and to related works, as well as authorship and status information for the guide.

Preliminary Conversions   The first step is to create an ASCII text version of the guide. The file needs a bit of preparation before it's saved, however. Start with a copy of the Microsoft Word file and substitute character entities for the markup characters. That is, globally change

   & to &
   < to <
   > to >

and replace any "curly" quotes (', "") with the straight ASCII versions (", ""). You should also replace any special characters from the ISO Latin-1 character set with their character entities at this point.

Next, delete any unnecessary horizontal tabs like those used for paragraph indentation. You can decide later what to do with other tab marks; whether to use preformatted text, HTML tab stops, or table markup to re-create the original structure. Remove any headers and footers from the guide, because you have no control over how many lines a browser will display per page or screen, and page numbering is not important in hypertext works.

Create a new directory for the project—let's call it a guide. It can be a subdirectory of a Web site or whatever is appropriate to the relation of this work to your other hypertext works. Save a copy of the file in either "Text only" or "Text with line breaks" format. Put it in the guide directory and give it a filename with the .txt extension. This is the file you will make available to readers with linemode browsers.

Go back to the original guide in your word processor's normal format. You can create the downloadable version from this file by compressing or encoding it. Compressing compacts the file by removing excess space; encoding creates a seven-bit portable version of the file, allowing it to be moved and stored as a text file on any kind of operating system. This process is often referred to as "uuencoding." (You have to decompress or decode files to use them again.) There are many sources for uuencoding and decoding programs as well as compression programs such as StuffIt from Aladdin Software or PKZip from PKware. One good overall source for such utilities for all platforms is http://www.cweb.net/~christer/compression-utilities.html.

From the original document, capture any illustrations and figures in the text. Convert these to GIF or JPEG format and save them in a subdirectory of the guide called images. Use a file-naming convention that preserves the image's location—for example, guide03-f04.gif—for the fourth figure in Chapter 3 of the guide. The leading zeros in the filename will ensure proper sorting in a directory listing if you have more than nine items.

Converting to HTML   Edit the text-only version, make notations in the text where the illustrations and figures were, and resave this file. Now, also save a copy of the file with the extension .html if you are using a Macintosh or .htm if you are using a Windows-based machine.

At the beginning of this new file, create an HTML head section with the main title enclosed within title tags, followed by the starting tag for the body section, followed by the main title again as a level 1 heading. Place the matching end tags at the end of the file. The code should look something like this:

```
<HTML>
<!-- guide.html, a hypertext guide to the Internet -->
<!-- Converted from MS Word file: INT_GUIDE        -->
<!-- J. Kepler, October 29, 1609.                  -->
<HEAD>
<TITLE>Internet Guide</TITLE>
</HEAD>
<BODY>
<H1>Internet Guide</H1>
<!-- rest of the file -->
</BODY>
</HTML>
```

Next, starting from the beginning of the file, work your way through, placing line breaks (<BR>) and paragraph tags (<P></P>) where needed and enclosing headings in heading tags. Work with a printed copy of the original as a guide, but don't try to match specific font sizes with different heading levels. Use headings logically—level 2 for the major divisions of the guide, level 3 for the next level, and so on. As you go through the file, enclose any styled text with appropriate tags—<EM></EM> for text that should be emphasized, <STRONG></STRONG> for strongly emphasized text, <QUOTE-BLOCK></QUOTEBLOCK> and <CITE></CITE> for quoted text and titles, and so forth. Try to avoid using the style tags <B></B>, <U></U>, and <I></I> unless that style is explicitly referred to within the text.

Look for places in the text where HTML lists or tables can structure information. Likewise, identify and mark up footnotes and sidenotes with <FN></FN> and <NOTE></NOTE> tags. When you've completed this pass, the first draft of the HTML version of the guide is finished. Save this file.

Testing Your Work   It's time to load your work into a browser and see what it looks like. Print it and show it around. The next step is to go through the file adding internal anchors and links and inserting image and figure tags for any illustrations and figures appearing in the original text. Make the text of each of the major headings a named anchor with the ID or NAME attribute. Use the heading's index from the table of contents as the name, for example:

```
<H3 ID="G32">3.2 Gopher</H3>
```

In the table of contents, create a link to each of these headings:

```
<LI><A HREF="#G32">3.2 Gopher</A>
```

If there are references to other documents on your network or references to resources on the Internet, create links to them as well. An incorrect URL will not crash the system; if you put a wrong one in by mistake, you can repair these bad links when you have the correct information.

When you are finished with this process, you'll have the long hypertext version of the guide. This version will be more suitable for printing than your final version, but will still be fine for online browsing (although it may take some time for the entire file to load over a slow line). Take some time to clean up and test this version, using different browsers if possible. If the original guide had a glossary, an index, or a quick reference section, now is the time to decide how to implement these features.

Linking to Other Pages   When the long version is fairly stable, decide how to divide it into separate files. Having a hypertext work in a series of linked files—rather than one giant file—has several advantages. The individual files load faster and the reader can have more than one section of the work displayed at the same time. Ideally, no single part of the guide should be more than a dozen screens' worth of information. The exception to this is very long list structures, which should go into separate files for easier maintenance. The table of contents will go into the guide's home page. If a section of the guide is long and has many subsections, consider creating a mini-home page for that section with its own, linked mini-table of contents.

Each file has to begin and end with the <HTML> tags defining the head and body of the page. Copy the title of the work as a whole and make it a level 1 heading that's the very first element of the page body of each file so your readers know what they're reading. Put a horizontal rule under the level 1 heading and you have a page header. Here is what the beginning of the Chapter 3 page might look like:

```
<HTML>
<!-- guide - 3.html, Chapter 3 of Internet Guide     -->
<!-- Converted from MS Word file: INT_GUIDE        -->
<!-- J. Kepler, Nov. 4, 1609.                       -->
<HEAD>
<TITLE>Internet Guide, Chap. 3</TITLE>
</HEAD>
<BODY>
<H1>Internet Guide</H1>
<HR>
<H2 ID="G30">Chapter 3 - Clients</H2>
A nice introductory paragraph should go here.
<H3>Contents</H3>
<OL>
```

```
<LI><A HREF="#G31">ftp</A>
<LI><A HREF="#G32">Gopher</A>
<LI><A HREF="#G33">...</A>
</OL>
<H3 ID="G31">3.1 ftp</H3>
```

Any links to anchors that are now in different files must be updated to include the filename of the destination. Links in other files to anchors in this file will also have to be updated. The home page for the entire guide will contain the table of contents, the introduction, the guide's authorship information (make your name a link to your personal home page), and links to related works.

A nice touch is to add a set of navigational buttons to the bottom of each page in the guide. This next bit of HTML, at the end of the file for Chapter 3, creates a set of four text buttons that link to other files of the guide. The last link, [CONTENTS], goes to an anchor named ToC on the guide's home page, the file GuideHome.html. You can also use small icons for these buttons. Following the buttons is a link back to the authorship information on the guide's home page.

```
<HR>
<A HREF="guidehome.html">[TOP]</A>
<A HREF="guide - 2.html">[PREVIOUS]</A>
<A HREF="guide - 4.html">[NEXT]</A>
<A HREF="guidehome.html#ToC">[CONTENTS]</A>
<ADDRESS>
<A HREF="guidehome.html#author">JK</A> -- Nov. 4, 1609
</ADDRESS>
```

Figure 9.24 shows what the Chapter 3 title page (minus a lot of the middle) might look like.

USING STYLE SHEETS

As you learned in Chapter 8, Cascading Style Sheets give you a lot of control over HTML documents. They can also enable you to integrate existing documents into the general look-and-feel of a Web site without reformatting each one individually. Remember, so far no browser has completely implemented CSS1 specifications; Internet Explorer has taken the lead, but its version 3.0 is still not a full implementation. Nonetheless, the potential is so great that the technique is worth exploring. Let's use a somewhat absurd example to illustrate some powerful concepts.

Document Preparation   The document we're importing into our Web site is in standard recipe format: a general overview, the tools needed, the ingredients,

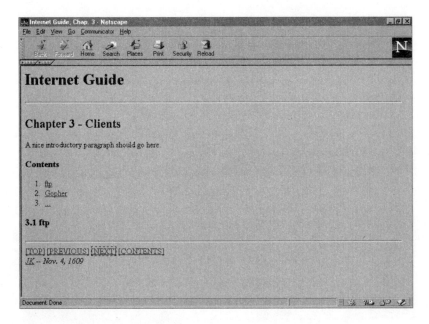

Figure 9.24: Title page for a converted chapter

and a step-by-step procedure. Although our example is taken from William Shakespeare's *Macbeth,* it could just as easily be any other text. Figure 9.25 shows the text when it first arrives.

As with the previous conversion, the first step involves cleaning up the text to translate any characters reserved for HTML to their equivalent character entities. In this example, only the quote character is changed to """.

Next, open your HTML template as before and begin to mark up your text. Make the very top heading an <H1> heading and each of the subheadings <H2>. Each paragraph should begin with a <P> and end with a </P>. The list of ingredients is treated as an unordered list and the step-by-step instructions are an ordered, numbered list.

The preliminary HTML file will look like the one in Figure 9.26. Please note that some of the ingredients have been temporarily removed to show the balance of the document in one screen. We'll put them back (with a bit of a twist!) a little later.

Building the Style Sheet Rules   All the CSS rules go within the <STYLE> tag. (At some later point, external style sheets—files completely separate from your HTML document—will probably be fully supported by the various

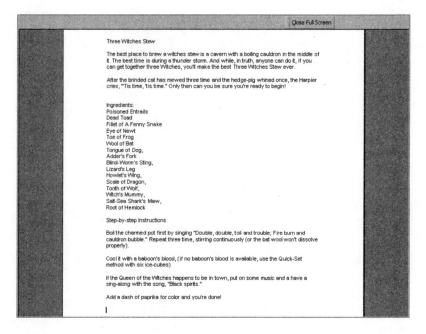

Figure 9.25: The raw data for the style sheet

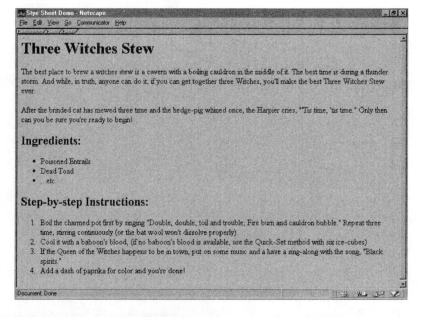

Figure 9.26: Pre-style sheet HTML file

browsers but for now this is the only alternative.) Let's start by making our headings distinctive:

```
H1 {font-family: artistik, fantasy; text-align:center; color:red}
H2 {font-family: artistik, fantasy; text-align:left; color:blue}
```

Remember that CSS rules are made up of selectors and declarations. Here the selectors are the two headings and the declarations are contained within the curly brackets following. The font-family property will use a specific font, "artistik," if it is on the system; otherwise, it will use the generic "fantasy" font. The relative sizes are retained, but the alignment and color are changed for both headings.

Relative and Absolute Measurements Now let's alter the paragraphs a bit. You can set the "text-size" and "text-indent" property to either a relative or an absolute value. The relative values used are ones familiar to typographers and desktop publishing designers: ems, x-height, and pixels. An "em" is equal to the height of the font; the x-height is, oddly enough, the height of the letter "x" and is abbreviated "ex"; and pixels ("px") are relative to the user's screen resolution. Absolute values include millimeters (abbreviated "mm"), centimeters ("cm"), inches ("in"), points ("pt"), and picas ("pc").

If we wanted to increase the font size to 14 points and indent all of our paragraphs 1/2 em, we would use the following code:

```
P {font-size: 18pt; text-indent: 2em} /* Indent is then 36pt */
```

(The slash-star characters are the separators for CSS comments; the <STYLE> tag ignores anything between "/*" and "*/".) As the comment indicates, and as you can see in Figure 9.27, the em indent is relative to the size of the font.

Style Sheet List Options To alter the elements in an ordered or unordered list, style sheets use the inheritance concept. Rather than change the individual <LI> tags, the <UL> or <OL> tags are the designated selectors in the CSS rules. Because all of the <LI> tags are contained within either the <UL></UL> or <OL></OL> pair, the list elements inherit any property set for the unordered or ordered list elements. Here's how it would work in our example:

```
UL {font-style: italic;font-weight:bold}
OL {font-family: arial,sans-serif}
```

Figure 9.28 shows the changes.

Style Sheet Deviations Keep in mind that your documents don't have to pull all their characteristics from style sheets. You can specify other tags that

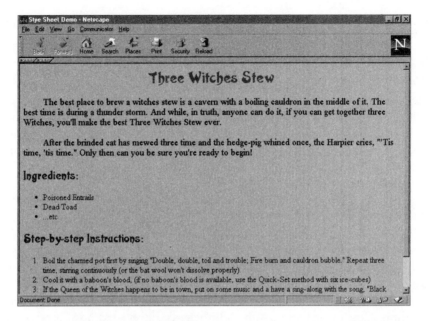

Figure 9.27: First style sheet changes

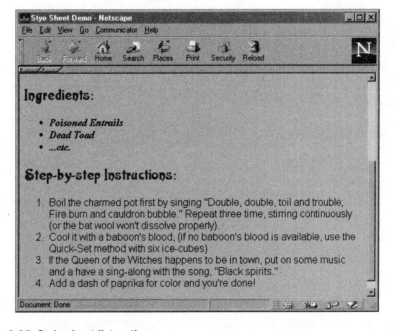

Figure 9.28: Style sheet list options

will override style sheet guidelines. For example, Netscape has implemented a <MULTICOL> tag that allows its browser to display lists in multiple columns. This would be ideal for our ingredient list, which has a large number of short items. The question is how to take advantage of Netscape's capabilities and still be compatible with other browsers.

The key is placement. Instead of eliminating the unordered list tag altogether, simply put the new <MULTICOL></MULTICOL> tag pair within the <UL></UL> pair. <MULTICOL> takes three attributes: COLS, the number of columns; WIDTH, the overall width of the entire list; and GUTTER, the size of the margin between each column. Here's what our new code excerpt would look like; Figure 9.29 shows the results.

```
<H2>Ingredients:</H2>
<UL>
<MULTICOL COLS=3 WIDTH=80% GUTTER=20>
    <LI>Poisoned Entrails</LI>
    <LI>Dead Toad</LI>
    <LI>Fillet of A Fenny Snake</LI>
    <LI>Eye of Newt</LI>
    <LI>Toe of Frog</LI>
    <LI>Wool of Bat</LI>
    <LI>Tongue of Dog</LI>
    <LI>Adder's Fork</LI>
    <LI>Blind-Worm's Sting</LI>
    <LI>Lizard's Leg</LI>
    <LI>Howlet's Wing</LI>
    <LI>Scale of Dragon</LI>
    <LI>Tooth of Wolf</LI>
    <LI>Witch's Mummy</LI>
    <LI>Salt-Sea Shark's Maw</LI>
    <LI>Root of Hemlock</LI>
</MULTICOL>
</UL>
```

AUTOMATING HTML WITH TEMPLATES

HTML templates can both speed up production and give an overall continuity to a Web site. A Web site template provides the bare bones code for a Web site, which you can add to, plugging in new values to make each page unique in content but united in design. Think of templates as cookie-cutters; you can quickly make a lot of cookies the same basic size and shape, but they can all taste different depending on how you flavor them.

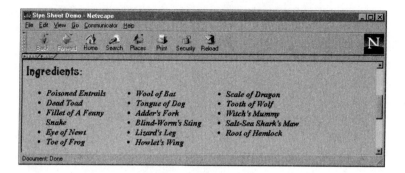

Figure 9.29: The <MULTICOL> tag within a style sheet

We'll look at three ways to create work with templates, from the simplest (and slowest) to the most complex (and fastest). First, we extract our templates by hand by using text editors and cutting and pasting. Next, we use one of the easiest to use Web page development tools out today, Netscape Composer. Finally, we look at a technique derived from mail-merging practices. But first, before we make any copies using a template, we have to build one.

CONSTRUCTING A TEMPLATE

The easiest and most productive way to make a template is to build the first page that would be derived from this template. In other words, build a sample Web page and make that into the template. Here's how it works.

For this project, we'll look at a Web site created for a research firm that specializes in publishing newsletters and reports for the managed health care industry. They put out a number of different publications with similar characteristics: They all have individual logos, each can be described in a paragraph, they are all available by subscription, all can represent themselves with a series of headlines or chapter titles, and they are all interconnected to each other and to an order-form page. Figure 9.30 shows the overall design as it exists in a complete form.

Deconstructing the Template   Now let's deconstruct our finished page to make a template. Working from the top-down, the first element to change will be the logo. The best strategy is to replace the GIF file in the <IMG> tag with a simple "PLACE LOGO HERE" placeholder notation. Leave all the other elements exactly at they appear in your previous HTML file, but save this file as template.html (or .htm). If you temporarily set the BORDER attribute to 1 or 2 and don't change the HEIGHT and WIDTH attributes, the browser will continue to draw the surrounding box, but not the graphic.

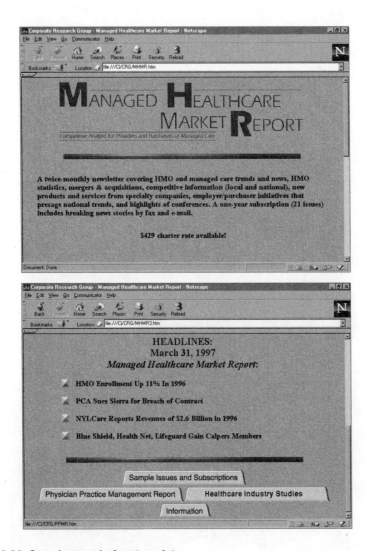

Figure 9.30: Sample page before template

Next we'll do the same thing for the description below the logo. Because this is in a table, here, too, we can set BORDER=1 and see the outline of our temporary text. Here is the code; Figure 9.31 shows the resulting template image.

```
<HTML>
<HEAD>
  <TITLE>NEW TITLE HERE</TITLE>
</HEAD>
```

```
<BODY BACKGROUND="bluebackground.jpg">
<CENTER><IMG SRC="PLACE LOGO HERE" WIDTH=600 HEIGHT=145 BORDER=1></CENTER>
<CENTER><IMG SRC="3Drainbowbar.gif" HEIGHT=12 WIDTH=576></CENTER>

<TABLE CELLSPACING=10 WIDTH="100%" BORDER=1>
<TR>
<TD ALIGN=left>
</TD>
<TD ALIGN=left>
<H3>MARKETING DESCRIPTION</H3>
</TD>
</TR>
<TR>
<TD ALIGN=left>
</TD>
<TD ALIGN=center>
<H3>PUT SUBSCRIPTION RATE HERE</H3>
</TD>
<TD ALIGN=left>
</TD>
</TR>
</TABLE>

<CENTER><IMG SRC="3Drainbowbar.gif" HEIGHT=12 WIDTH=576> </CENTER>
```

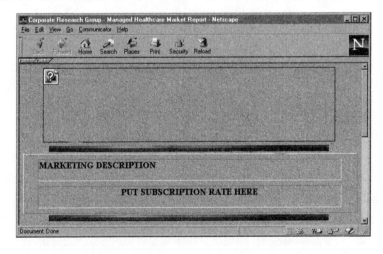

Figure 9.31: Top half of the template

The bottom half of the template starts out simply, but then gets a little tricky. The "headlines" are all contained in a separate rows in a table and so each one will be replaced with a "Headline" placeholder. Be sure to put generic text wherever something more specific will go, such as the date of a more recent update. The only other elements on the page that will change as part of our template are the navigational buttons.

Most templates include navigational buttons that will not change on every page. In this example, the Order and Info buttons stay the same while the middle report-specific buttons change. You must include placeholding text for the HREF attribute in the anchor tags as well as the <IMG> tag. Once again, it's helpful if the BORDER attribute is turned on as a reminder. Here's the code for the bottom half of the template. Figure 9.32 shows what it looks like in a browser.

```
<CENTER>
<TABLE CELLSPACING=0 CELLPADDING=0 WIDTH="600" BORDER=1>
<TR>
<TD COLSPAN=2 ALIGN=center>
<H2>
HEADLINES:<BR>
AS OF THIS DATE<BR>
<I>NAME OF PUBLICATION</I></H2>
</TD>
</TR>
<TR>
<TD VALIGN=top><IMG SRC="blueblock.gif" HEIGHT=18 WIDTH=18> 
</TD>

<TD VALIGN=TOP>
<H4><FONT SIZE=+1>HEADLINE</FONT><BR>
</TD>
</TR>
<TR>
<TD VALIGN=top><IMG SRC="blueblock.gif" HEIGHT=18 WIDTH=18> 

<TD VALIGN=top>
<H4>
<FONT SIZE=+1>HEADLINE</FONT></H4>
</TD>
</TR>
<TR>
<TD VALIGN=top><IMG SRC="blueblock.gif" HEIGHT=18 WIDTH=18> 
</TD>

<TD VALIGN=top>
<H4>
<FONT SIZE=+1>HEADLINE</FONT></H4>
```

```
</TD>
</TR>

<TR>
<TD VALIGN=top><IMG SRC="blueblock.gif" HEIGHT=18 WIDTH=18> 
</TD>

<TD VALIGN=top>
<H4>
<FONT SIZE=+1>HEADLINE</FONT></H4>
</TD>
</TR>
</TABLE></CENTER>
<BR>
<CENTER><IMG SRC="3Drainbowbar.gif" HEIGHT=12 WIDTH=576></CENTER>
<BR>
<CENTER>
<A HREF="ORDER.htm"><IMG SRC="ORDERtab.gif" ALT="Sample Issues and Subscriptions"
BORDER=0 HEIGHT=35 WIDTH=305></A><BR>
<A HREF="????.htm"><IMG SRC="BUTTON.gif" BORDER=1 HEIGHT=35 WIDTH=355></A>
<A HREF="????.htm"><IMG SRC="BUTTON.gif" BORDER=1 HEIGHT=35 WIDTH=355></A>
<A HREF="index.htm"><IMG SRC="INFOtab.gif" ALT="Main Information" BORDER=0
HEIGHT=32 WIDTH=128></A>
</CENTER>

</BODY>
</HTML>
```

Using the Template   After template.html is saved one more time, the file is ready to be used. The "by-hand" approach means that you open your template.html file in your favorite text editor and immediately use the Save As feature to save it as a new document. This preserves your template file and gets you set up to begin plugging in the values.

From this point, it is a simple matter to "fill in the blanks." Wherever placeholder text was inserted (for example, "YOUR LOGO HERE"), the new information—whether an image file name, marketing description, or URL—is placed. Then the code should be tested to make sure that all the new elements are in and none of the placeholding text remains. There will be a little bit of "house-cleaning" to take care of as well—turning off BORDER attributes that were left on to mark boundaries and adjusting the WIDTH and HEIGHT attributes of the previous images to match the new ones.

For areas such as table rows that need to have straight text replaced, it is best to use your computer's copy and paste features. For example, to replace the headlines in our example, one of the new headlines is highlighted and copied

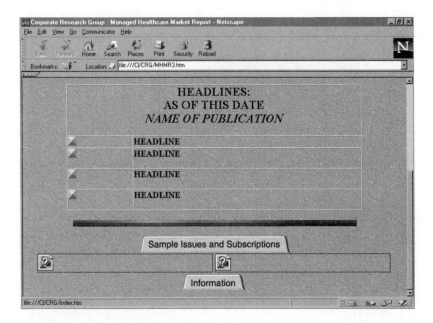

Figure 9.32: Bottom half of the template

in a text processor. We then switch to our fresh template and paste in the headline in the appropriate place. Avoid retyping wherever possible; besides saving time, this makes it far less likely that typos will creep in.

TEMPLATES WITH TOOLS

At this stage of HTML development, there are a lot of terrific tools to assist in Web site layout and design. Appendix C includes a full, but by no means complete, list of HTML WYSIWYG editors. WYSIWIG stands for "what you see is what you get," and it makes filling in templates very fast and easy. Let's look at one tool, Composer from Netscape, that simplifies template production.

Composer is one of the suite of programs that come under the Netscape Communicator umbrella. As such, it integrates nicely with the Navigator 4.0 browser; this allows for easy testing and adjusting, and a relatively gentle learning curve.

Replacing Images and Text   You can replace images by double-clicking on the existing template placeholder. This brings up the Image Properties dialog box. Here you can set not only the new filename for the image, but also the alignment, size, alternative text, and border. When it comes time to replace the navigational buttons, you use a separate tab on the same dialog box to specify the links. Figure 9.33 shows a partially filled in Image Properties dialog box.

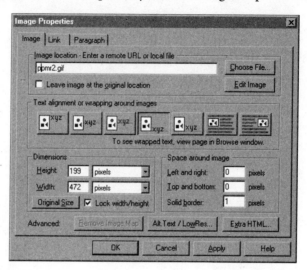

Figure 9.33: Setting an image's properties in Netscape Composer

The text can be filled in with the copy-and-paste technique described earlier. After you've copied the text to the computer's Clipboard (a special memory location that allows applications to share data), highlight the placeholding text and paste in your new information. Most programs will automatically replace the old text with the new; in a few programs, you will have to delete the old text manually.

As mentioned, the navigational links are a subset of the image properties. Double-clicking on the placeholding button image will bring up the image properties box; click on the Links tab at the top. Fill in the new URL in the "Link to:" area or click on the Browse button to find it with the help of a directory utility. Even if you remember the name, you should use the Browse button—again, it cuts down on typing and potential typos. If you are working with frames, this is also where you would specify the target for your URL. Figure 9.34 shows the Link tab of the Image Properties dialog box.

A New Page Although this is an extremely fast and easy way to fill out your templates, sometimes you do have to "tweak" the code. Composer and all other HTML WYSIWIG editors produce standard HTML code that can be viewed and altered in a text editor. Don't spend a lot of time trying to get just

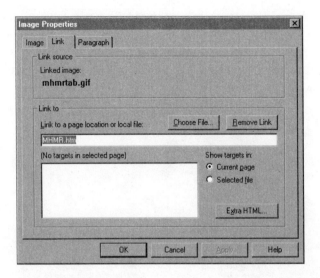

Figure 9.34: Linking with image properties

the right effect in a your HTML editor when it will take you a few seconds to adjust the code manually. Although WYSIWIG editors have improved greatly over the last year, the truth is that HTML development is moving too quickly for the programs to keep up. No editor available can handle all of standard HTML much less some of the more exotic enhancements.

A recent trend has been to include an Add HTML button on all property dialog boxes so that you can "roll your own" from within the program. This is a nice amenity, but you still have to know your HTML code inside and out to get the most functionality. The other addition you'll notice is that all the editors put their own stamp on the code in the HEAD section by using a <META> tag or two. Here's what Composer inserted in our newly generated file:

```
<META HTTP-EQUIV="Content-Type" CONTENT="text/html; charset=iso-8859-1">
<META NAME="GENERATOR" CONTENT="Mozilla/4.0b2 (Win95; I) [Netscape]">
```

The first line is intended to help servers read your code by identifying the MIME type ("text/html") and the character set used (standard Latin 1). The second line is a bit of interior marketing—"Mozilla" is the old name for Navigator. This information could conceivably be used by a indexing "spider" to find out the number of HTML pages created by each program—if you leave the code line in, which you are under no obligation to do.

Here's a final look at our newly generated Web page. As you can see by comparing Figure 9.35 with the original page in Figure 9.30, there is an overall similarity to the pages, but each maintains its individuality with logos and content.

If you want to learn one technique for generating a lot of Web pages, really quickly, check out the next section on merging templates.

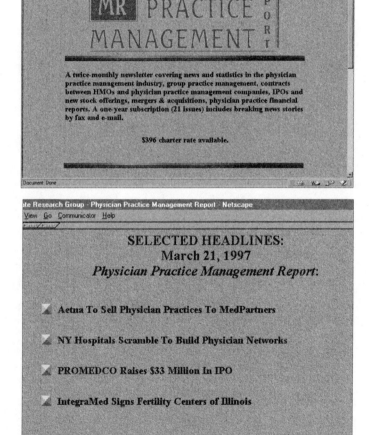

Figure 9.35: Completed Web page from template

MERGING TEMPLATES

Here's a method that takes advantage of the "t" in HTML: text. Because all HTML files are text files, we can use the power of modern word processors to automate the production of Web pages from templates. This is done through the facility normally reserved for mail merges—the system that makes those fabulous form letters and marvelous mailing labels. Our example will use Microsoft Word and the template file we built by hand earlier in this section.

Mail Merge Technology   All mail merge procedures work in basically the same way. Two documents are first created: one is a form (whether a form letter or a mailing label form) that provides the template (aha!) for our final product, and the other is the data that provides the changing content for our final product. The final product is the merged result of the other two documents. The key is in placing what are often referred to as "merge codes" in the HTML form.

Microsoft Word uses a Mail Merge Helper that clearly defines each step necessary for a successful merge. First, open (or create) the main document, the form. In our case, we'll open our template.html file, which has all of our placeholding text in the areas we want to change. Word 97 can open HTML documents like a browser, but in this case we want to open it as text.

Second, we open (or create) the data document that will hold all the various information to flow into our template. In our case, we will be creating the data document and filling in each of the fields as we go. The word "field" comes from the realm of databases; you can also think of fields as "categories." All the data for one Web page will be contained on one "record"—another database term. Each section that we marked with placeholding text such as "PLACE LOGO HERE" becomes a field; in that case, it would be the "logo" field. Microsoft Word makes it easy because it presents us with a dialog box for setting up our fields.

The fields are set up by initially removing the preset fields—these have names like "FirstName", "LastName", and "Address" and are used for a regular mail merge. Next we add our field names: "LOGO", "BLURB", "RATE", "HEADLINE_1", and so on. If you forget to set up a field you can always put it in later. When this section is completed, you'll need to save the data file; give it an obvious name like "MergeData".

Click on OK again, and you will be presented with another dialog box with the field names you just set up on one side and blank boxes on the other. Fill in the data for each field in the empty boxes next to the field names. Again, the easiest way to do this is by using the copy and paste feature of your word processor and text editor. Make sure that you paste in only the text and none of the code or extra punctuation such as quote marks. Figure 9.36 shows the first completed record.

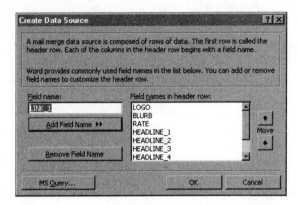

Figure 9.36: Filling in the data for a template merge

Now if you had a lot of Web pages to generate you could enter all of your data here, one record at a time. Each record would have a complete set of fields necessary to fill out our main HTML document. Let's go back to our main document and complete its setup.

Microsoft Word puts a new toolbar up on the screen to handle mail, and other, merges. The first button on that toolbar is labeled Insert Merge Field. When you click on this button, a list of the fields that were previously entered appears, as shown in Figure 9.37.

Now the process entails finding all our placeholding text and replacing it with the merge fields. This means that "PLACE LOGO HERE" would be re-placed by <<LOGO>>. The double angle brackets surrounding the field name indicate to Word that this is a merge field. After we've replaced the first three fields, our HTML code looks like this:

```
<HTML>
<HEAD>
    <TITLE><<TITLE>></TITLE>
</HEAD>
<BODY BACKGROUND="bluebackground.jpg"><CENTER><IMG SRC="«LOGO»" BORDER=1
HEIGHT=145 WIDTH=600><BR><BR></CENTER>
<CENTER><IMG SRC="3Drainbowbar.gif" HEIGHT=12 WIDTH=576><BR>
<BR></CENTER>

<TABLE BORDER CELLSPACING=10 WIDTH="100%" >
<TR>
```

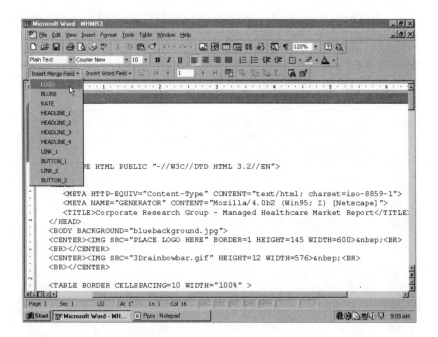

Figure 9.37: The merge list in Word

```
<TD ALIGN="left">
</TD>

<TD ALIGN="left">
<H3>«BLURB»</H3>
</TD>
</TR>
<TD ALIGN="center">
<H3>«BLURB»</H3>
</TD>
</TR>
```

Can you find the merge fields <<LOGO>>, <<BLURB>>, and <<RATE>> in the preceding code?

To add more records—and so more Web pages capable of being merged—click on the Edit Data Source toolbar button. This will bring back the form that the data was first entered on. Clicking on Add New will bring up a blank record to be completed. If you click on View Source in this dialog box, you will be taken to another view of the data—in table format. All of your fields are listed across the top row (the header row) and each record is contained in one row. Any additions, corrections, or deletions made to this table will be incorporated into your form and data.

Merging into HTML   Word has a great preview facility that lets you view the merged data in place. Figure 9.38 shows the code as merged in Word as well as the Merge toolbar.

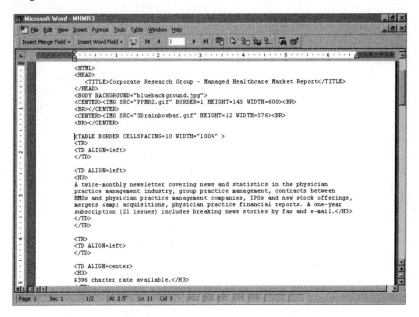

Figure 9.38: The merged Web page in Word

Now we're ready to complete the merge. Because of the nature of the mail merge, you can merge all or part of your records at one time to either a new document or to a printer. For our purposes, it is best to merge one record at a time to a new document. HTML documents can easily be more than a single page long in code; merging more than one record at a time would involve cutting and pasting each new Web page to a separate document and then saving it. When you save your newly merged HTML document, be sure to save it as a text file with an .htm or .html extension so any browser can read it properly.

This merging technique works very well in intranet situations where there are a lot of similar documents to be produced in a short time. Moreover, once the system is established, Web page updates (such as our headlines described earlier) can be handled by someone who is fluent in mail merging but doesn't speak HTML.

HTML Examples

Example 1—An Extended Personal Home Page

Example 2—A Tutorial Page

Example 3—A Small Organization's Home Page

Example 4—A Large Organization's Home Page

Example 5—A Page of Internet Resources

Example 6—Inside an Extranet

Chapter

10

This chapter consists of a number of examples of World Wide Web pages. Each example includes a presentation and discussion of the HTML source for the example Web page followed by a reproduction of the page. The examples were chosen with variety in mind to let you know what you can do with HTML and your information. Not all of the pages represent the best HTML use. That's fine. This is the work of busy people, motivated by the desire to make their information public with tools that are still evolving. We'll point out instances of poor (in our opinion) HTML use here and there, and we hope the authors won't think we're being judgmental. We've written a zillion lines of code over the years and would hate to have anyone judge our work on such a small sample.

These example pages—like many on the Web—are continually evolving. What are presented here are snapshots of pages at a particular point in time. We're providing the URLs of the example pages with no guarantee that they will continue to be valid, and certainly no guarantee that the pages seen on the Web at those addresses will be the same as those presented here. If they are, you'll probably see improvements.

EXAMPLE 1—AN EXTENDED PERSONAL HOME PAGE

This example is the work of Gary Welz. When the first edition of this book was published, Gary's home page was at http://found.cs.nyu.edu/found.a/ CAT/misc/welz/. Going there today will generate an "Error 404," which is server talk for "no such animal." Gary's Web site has grown considerably and now even his resumé has an introductory home page. In this example, we'll actually look at two pages of HTML. The first is Gary's new home page and the second is a revision of his resumé. Seeing how the pages relate to each other emphasizes one of the truths about the Web: It's always changing.

His opening page (www.scitv.com/welz/) is brief and informative, with links to all the major areas of interest, one of which is the resumé. I like this page because Gary has worked on many interesting Web projects, all of which are linked to this page.

The page begins with a <BODY> tag setting the background color to white (#FFFFFF) followed by a recent photo of Gary. The image is embedded in the level 1 heading; the ALIGN="middle" attribute aligns the middle of the image with the rest of the heading text.

Next is a series of categories and links. Gary uses nested unordered lists and lets the browser do all the formatting. Remember that nesting refers to the practice of putting one tag inside another similar tag, like this:

```
<UL>
    <LI>This is a one level
 <UL>
            <li>And here is the next</LI>
        </UL>
    </LI>
</UL>
```

The browser will automatically alter the type of bullet for each level—usually starting with a solid disc, followed by an open circle, and then a square—although the exact order of this is browser-dependent.

Gary's Web pages are a testament to the forgivingness of browsers. His code is based on earlier version of HTML where neither the <LI> or <P> elements were container type tags, so you won't find a closing </LI> or </P> anywhere in this code. But it still works. Of course, there is no guarantee that the code won't break on a future release of a browser that is more strictly HTML compliant. Figure 10.1 shows the browser's view of the following code:

```
<HTML>

<HEAD>
<TITLE>Gary Welz</TITLE>
</HEAD>


<BODY BGcolor="FFFFFF">
```

EXAMPLE 1—AN EXTENDED PERSONAL HOME PAGE **269**

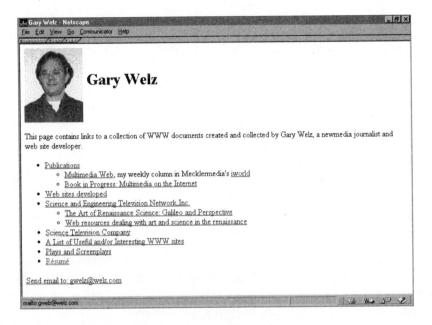

Figure 10.1: Gary Welz's introductory home page

```
<H1><IMG ALIGN ="middle" SRC=gwelz.gif> Gary Welz</H1><P>

This page contains links to a collection of WWW documents created and collected
by Gary Welz, a newmedia journalist and web site developer.<P>

<UL>
<LI><A HREF="pubs/index.html">Publications</A>
<UL>
<LI><A HREF="http://netday.iworld.com/devforum/">Multimedia Web</A>, my weekly
column in Mecklermedia's <A HREF="http://www.iworld.com/">iworld</A>
<LI><A HREF="http://www.scitv.com/welz/internetmm/">Book in Progress:  Multimedia
on the Internet</A>
</UL>
<LI><A HREF=websites.html>Web sites developed</A>
<LI><A HREF=http://www.setn.org>Science and
Engineering Television Network,Inc.</A>
<UL>
<LI><A HREF=http://www.setn.org/pubs/index.html>The Art of Renaissance Science:
Galileo and Perspective</A>
<LI><A HREF=http://www.setn.org/pubs/arsresources.html>Web resources dealing with
art and science in the renaissance</A>
</UL>
<LI><A HREF=http://www.scitv.com/>Science Television Company</A>
```

```
<LI><A HREF=sites.html>A List of Useful and/or Interesting WWW sites</A>
<LI><A HREF=plays/index.html>Plays and Screenplays</A>
<LI><A HREF=welzresume.html>R&eacute;sum&eacute;</A>
</UL>
<P>
<HR>
<P>

<A HREF="mailto:gwelz@welz.com">Send email to:  gwelz@welz.com</A><BR>
<P>

</BODY>
</HTML>
```

The final anchor tag on this opening page is a special hyperlink called a *mailto.* The code,

```
<A HREF="mailto:gwelz@welz.com">Send email to:  gwelz@welz.com</A>
```

will call up an e-mail form similar to the one in Figure 10.2. Notice that the address line is already filled in and, although you can't see it, your e-mail address will be included so that your e-mail can be easily replied to.

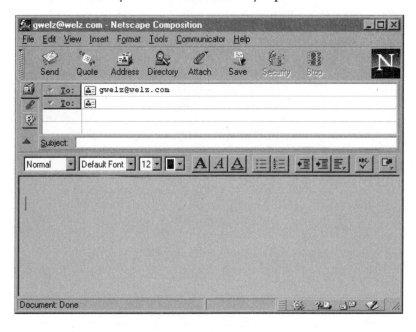

Figure 10.2: A e-mail form called from a mailto link

Example 1—An Extended Personal Home Page   **271**

The HTML source in this example is a combination of resumé and work summary and can be found at www.scitv.com/welz/welzresume.html.

The resumé page also begins with a <BODY> tag setting the background color to white (#FFFFFF), which this time is followed by a earlier black-and-white image of Gary. This grayscale image loads quickly on a slow connection (a good idea). The same level 1 heading is placed using the ALIGN="middle" attribute. Following that are three short address elements providing Gary's postal and electronic mail addresses. These address elements could easily have been coded as a single address block with two-line break tags, for example

```
<address>165 Bennett Ave #4-M<br>
New York, NY 10040<br>
email: gwelz@weltz.com</address>
```

The remainder of the page is a series of short sections, each introduced by a level 3 heading. There are really no major divisions of this page and that is reflected in the lack of any level 1 or 2 headings. There's a lot of information on this page neatly organized by unordered lists and short narrative paragraphs. Other than setting the background color, this page uses no HTML 3.2 features and should display uniformly over the widest range of browsers.

I have only a handful of overall suggestions for this HTML code: First, the author should have used citation tags (<CITE></CITE>) around the name of publications in the text instead of italic tags (<I></I>). Second, although it is not critical, the single <P> tag is often used to add "carriage returns" when a <P></P> pair is preferred. Finally, if the length of the page increased any more, I would consider adding some in-page navigational aids, such as a link to each of the headings and to the top of the page.

The following code is the complete HTML for Gary's resumé and work-summary page. Like all the code in this chapter, it is reproduced verbatim, with all style conventions (such as lowercase for tags) intact.

```
<html>
<head>
   <title>Gary Welz: Resume</title>
</head>
<body bgcolor="#FFFFFF">

<h1><img src="gary2.gif" border=0 align=center> Gary
Welz</h1>

<address>165 Bennett Ave #4-M</address>

<address>New York, NY 10040</address>
```

```
<address>(212) 569-8079</address>

<address>email: gwelz@welz.com</address>

<P>

<h3>Recent Activity:</h3>

<p>For the past two years I have been an Internet consultant and new media
journalist. My clients have included <A HREF="http://www.ibm.com/">IBM</A>, the
<A HREF="http://www.nypl.org/">New York Public Library</A>, the <A
HREF="http://www.acm.org/">Association for Computing Machinery</A> and <A
HREF="http://www.viacomnewmedia.com/">Viacom New Media</A>.  I've published
articles in such publications as <A
HREF="http://www.iworld.com/"><i>iworld</i></A>, <A
HREF="http://www.iw.com/"><i>Internet World</i></A> and the ACM's <A
HREF="http://www.acm.org/interactions/"><i>Interactions</i></A>.
</p>

<h3>Education:</h3>

<ul>
<li>1976 B.A. Philosophy &amp; Mathematics, Bedford College, University of
London, London, England. </li>

<li>1977 M. Sc. Mathematics, Bedford College, University of London, London,
England. </li>
</ul>

<h3>Teaching:</h3>

<ul>
<li>1995 Taught staff of the <A HREF="http://www.nypl.org/">New York Public
Library</A> how to gather information on the Internet and author documents in
Hypertext Markup Language. </li>

<li>1994 Instructor at the <A HREF="http://www.cuny.edu/">CUNY Computer
Center</A>, teaching faculty and staff how to gather information on the Internet
and author documents in Hypertext Markup Language. </li>

<li>1982-1994 Adjunct Lecturer in Mathematics at <A
HREF="http://www.jjay.cuny.edu/">John Jay College</A>, and <A
HREF="http://www.lehman.cuny.edu/">Herbert H. Lehman College</A> of the <A
HREF="http://www.cuny.edu/">City University of New York</A>.</li>
</ul>
```

Example 1—An Extended Personal Home Page **273**

```
<h3>Internet Sites Developed or Worked On</h3>

<ul>

<li><a href="http://www.summit96.ibm.com/">The 1996 Education Summit</a>, a site
created for and with staff of the IBM Corporate home page. </li>

<li><a href="http://www.epicurious.com/">Epicurious</a>, a publication
of Conde' Nast New Media </li>

<li><a href="http://www.nypl.org/research/sibl/index.html">Science, Industry
and Business Library Home Page</a> SIBL is a division of the New York Public
Library. </li>

<li><a href="http://math240.lehman.cuny.edu/art/">Breaking Out (of the Virtual
Closet)</a>, a WWW art project designed for artist Douglas Davis at the Lehman
College Art Gallery. </li>

<li><a href="http://www.setn.org/pubs/">The Art of Renaissance Science: Galileo
and Perspective</a>, a hypermedia essay created with Prof. Joseph W. Dauben of
the CUNY Computer Center as a protype WWW journal article.
</li>
<li><a href="http://www.acm.org/pubs/">Association for Computing Machinery
Publications</a>, electronic versions of their publications for computer
scientists.</li>

<li><a href="http://www.setn.org">Science and Engineering Television Network</a>
, a not-for-profit organization dedicated to promoting the use of television as a
medium for scientific communication.</li>

<li><a href="http://www.scitv.com/">Science Television Company</a> , a company
that produces and distributes videotapes for scientists.</li>

<li><a href="http://www.scitv.com/welz/">My WWW home page</a> </li>
</ul>
```

Note the .shtml extensions in some of the following anchor hypertext references. Remember that these refer to HTML files that incorporate server-side includes (covered in Chapter 8). Not only is the form interesting, but the content is very informative, particularly in regard to Web-related multimedia.

```
<h3>Internet Media Related Publications:</h3>

<H4><a href="http://netday.iworld.com/devforum/multimweb.html">Multimedia
Web</A>, a weekly column in Mecklermedia's <a
ref="http://www.iworld.com/">iworld</a></H4>
<ul>
```

```
<li><a
href="http://netday.iworld.com/devforum/multimedia/mw961204.shtml">12.04.96
Microsoft Plays the Endgame</a>
<li><a
href="http://netday.iworld.com/devforum/multimedia/mw961127.shtml">11.27.96 User
Interfaces and Network Computing</a>
<li><a
href="http://netday.iworld.com/devforum/multimedia/mw961120.shtml">11.20.96
Developments in Online Virtual Environments</a>
<li><a
href="http://netday.iworld.com/devforum/multimedia/mw961113.shtml">11.13.96
Multiplayer Games and Network Computing</A>
<li><a
href="http://netday.iworld.com/devforum/multimedia/mw961106.shtml">11.06.96
Interactive Objects</A>
<li><a
href="http://netday.iworld.com/devforum/multimedia/mw961030.shtml">10.30.96 The
Real Time Streaming Protocol</A>
<li><a
href="http://netday.iworld.com/devforum/multimedia/mw961016.shtml">10.16.96
Streaming Media</A>
<li><a
href="http://netday.iworld.com/devforum/multimedia/mw961009.shtml">10.09.96
OLiVR</A>
<li><a
href="http://netday.iworld.com/devforum/multimedia/mw961002.shtml">10.02.96
OnlineTV</A>

<li><a
href="http://netday.iworld.com/devforum/multimedia/mw960925.shtml">09.25.96
Internet Video Product Comparison</a>
<li><a
href="http://netday.iworld.com/devforum/multimedia/mw960918.shtml">09.18.96
Apple Rocks With Webcast</a>
<li><a
href="http://netday.iworld.com/devforum/multimedia/mw960904.shtml">09.04.96
Innovators Part IV:  Your Personal Network (YPN)</a>
<li><a
href="http://netday.iworld.com/devforum/multimedia/mw960828.shtml">08.28.96
Innovators part III:  Netcast</a>
<li><a
href="http://netday.iworld.com/devforum/multimedia/mw960821.shtml">08.21.96
Electronic Investing Part II:  An Electronic Investment Strategy</a>
<li><a
href="http://netday.iworld.com/devforum/multimedia/mw960814.shtml">08.14.96
Electronic Investing I: A New Investing Environment</a>
<li><a
```

Example 1—An Extended Personal Home Page **275**

```
href="http://netday.iworld.com/devforum/multimedia/mw960807.shtml">08.07.96
Innovators II:  EarthWeb</a>
<li><a
href="http://netday.iworld.com/devforum/multimedia/mw960731.shtml">07.31.96
Internet Advertising V:  Buying Advertising</a>
<li><a
href="http://netday.iworld.com/devforum/multimedia/mw960724.shtml">07.24.96 Web
Advertising IV:  DoubleClick, Inc.</a>
<li><a
href="http://netday.iworld.com/devforum/multimedia/mw960717.shtml">07.17.96
Innovators I:  KPE</a>
<li><a
href="http://netday.iworld.com/devforum/multimedia/mw960710.shtml">07.10.96
Internet Advertising III:  Selling Advertising</a>
<li><A HREF="http://netday.iworld.com/devforum/multimedia/mw960703.html">07.03.96
Internet Advertising II:  Will it Work</A>
<li><A HREF="http://netday.iworld.com/devforum/multimedia/mw960626.html">06.26.96
Internet Advertising I:  The Role of the Agency</A>
<li><A HREF="http://netday.iworld.com/devforum/multimedia/mw960619.html">06.19.96
Multiuser Virtual Environments IV:  Collaborative Network Tools</A>
<li><A HREF="http://netday.iworld.com/devforum/multimedia/mw960612.html">06.12.96
Multiuser Virtual Environments III:  Virtual Warfare</A>
<li><A HREF="http://netday.iworld.com/devforum/multimedia/mw960605.html">06.05.96
Multiuser Virtual Environments II:  The Palace</A>
<li><A HREF="http://netday.iworld.com/devforum/multimedia/mw960529.html">05.29.96
Multiuser Virtual Environments I:  Worlds, Inc.</A>
<li><A HREF="http://netday.iworld.com/devforum/multimedia/mw960522.html">05.22.96
New Paradigms of Publishing: Part II - Dynamic Documents</A>
<li><A HREF="http://netday.iworld.com/devforum/multimedia/mw960515.html">05.15.96
New Paradigms of Publishing: Part I--What is Content?</A>
<li><A HREF="http://netday.iworld.com/devforum/multimedia/mw960508.html">05.08.96
Net Video: VDOLive</A>
<li><A HREF="http://netday.iworld.com/devforum/multimedia/mw960501.html">05.01.96
Net Video: Xing StreamWorks</A>
<li><A HREF="http://netday.iworld.com/devforum/multimedia/mw960424.html">04.24.96
Net Video: CU-SeeMe</A>
<li><A HREF="http://netday.iworld.com/devforum/multimedia/mw960417.html">04.17.96
Streaming Audio</A>
<li><A HREF="http://netday.iworld.com/devforum/multimedia/mw960410.html">04.10.96
When Should You Use Java Instead of Shockwave?</A>
</ul>
</li>
</ul>

<H4>Mecklermedia's <a href="http://www.iw.com/">Internet World</a></H4>
<ul>
<li><a href="http://www.scitv.com/welz/pubs/iwmultimedia.html">Net Multimedia
```

```
Comes of Age</A>, to appear in <i>Internet World</i>, February 1997. </li>
<li><a href="http://www.iw.com/1996/12/vrml.html">VRML Evolution</A>, <i>Internet
World</i>, December 1996. </li>
<li><a href="http://www.iw.com/1996/07/adgame.html">The Ad Game</A>, <i>Internet
World</i>, July 1996. </li>
<li><a href="http://www.internetworld.com/1996/01/welz.html">Personal
Bests</a>,<i> Internet World</i>, January 1996. </li>

<li><a href="http://www.internetworld.com/1995/11/vrml.html">VRML in
Action</a>,<i> Internet World</i>, November 1995. </li>

<li><a href="http://pubs.iworld.com/iw-online/1995/06/feat36.htm">New
Deals</a>,<i>Internet World</i>, July 1995. </li>

<li><a href="http://www.internetworld.com/1995/05/feat48.htm">Cyber Spiels:
A tour of web ads online &amp; Career Connections: Job seeking on the net</a>,
<i>Internet World</i>, May 1995. </li>

<li><a href="http://www.internetworld.com/1995/03/feat30.htm">New Dimensions:
a Multimedia Revolution is Unfolding on the Net</a>, <i>Internet World</i>,
March 1995 </li>
</ul>

<H4>Discovery Publishing Group's <a href="http://landru.unx.com/DD/advisor/">The
X Advisor</A></H4>
<ul>
<li><a href="http://landru.unx.com/DD/advisor/docs/dec95/dec95.gwelz1.shtml">Video
and Television on the Net </a><i>The X Advisor</i>, December1995. </li>

<li><a
href="http://landru.unx.com/DD/advisor/docs/nov95/nov95.gwelz1.shtml">Virtual
Reality on the Internet</a> <i>The X Advisor</i>, November 1995. </li>

<li><a href="http://landru.unx.com/DD/advisor/docs/oct95/oct95.gwelz.shtml">Audio
and Radio on the Net</a> <i>The X Advisor</i>, October 1995.
</li>

<li><a
href="http://landru.unx.com/DD/advisor/docs/sep95/sep95.gwelz.shtml">Internet
Telephony</a> <i>The X Advisor</i>, September 1995.
</li>

<li><a href="http://landru.unx.com/DD/advisor/docs/aug95/aug95.gwelz.shtml">Phase
Transition: The Online Medium Comes of Age</a> <i>The X Advisor</i>, August
1995. </li>

<li><a href="http://landru.unx.com/DD/advisor/docs/jul95/welz.genome0.shtml">Is
```

Example 1—An Extended Personal Home Page   **277**

a Genome Like a Computer Program?</a>, <i>The X Advisor</i>, July 1995.
</li>

<li><a
href="http://landru.unx.com/DD/advisor/docs/jun95/jun95.gwelz.shtml">Zooming
Through Information Space on Pad++</a>, <i>The X Advisor</i>, June 1995.
</li>
</ul>

<h4>Conference Papers</h4>
<ul>
<li><a
href="http://www.ncsa.uiuc.edu/SDG/IT94/Proceedings/ComEc/welz/welzwwwconf.html">T
he Media Business on the WWW</a>, 2nd International WWW Conference, October
1994. </li>

<li><a href="http://www.scitv.com/welz/pubs/internettv.html">Television
on the Internet - Scientific Publishing in a New Medium</a>, Proceedings
of the 7th Conference and General Assembly of the International Federation
of Science Editors, July 1993. </li>
</ul>

<H4>Other Publications</H4>
<ul>
<li><a href="http://www.crispzine.com/contents/currents/radio.html">Radio
on the Net</a> in <a href="http://www.crispzine.com/">Crisp</A>, an new
electronic magazine. </li>

<li>A World Wide Web Publishing Primer, <A
HREF="http://www.sigs.com/publications/txjr/"><I>The X Journal</I></A>, June
1995</li>

<li><a href="http://www.scitv.com/welz/pubs/welz_vr.html">Through the Electronic
Veil: Acting and Interacting in Virtual Worlds</a>,
Net Editors, internetMCI, April 28, 1995. </li>

<li><a href="http://www.scitv.com/welz/pubs/interact.html">Hypermedia,
Multimedia and Television on the Internet: Some of the best tools in life
are free</a>, ACM <i>Interactions</i>, July 1994 </li>
</ul>

<H4>A book in progress</H4>
<ul>
<li><a href="http://www.scitv.com/welz/internetmm/">Multimedia on the
Internet</a>. </li>
</ul>

```
<P>
<P>
<HR>
<P>

</body>
</html>
```

Figure 10.3 shows how the Web page generated by this HTML code looks displayed with Netscape. Oh, one more criticism, which I illustrate with the old saying "It's a long cow that has no tail": This page needs an ending; something to balance the visual weight of the image and heading that began the page, and to provide a final focus for its content. Adding some additional navigational buttons—either for this same page or to back to his intro page—would work.

EXAMPLE 2—A TUTORIAL PAGE

I was surfing my publisher's pages when I found this wonderful tutorial on how to create a home page. There are dozens of pages on the Web that try to explain how to put together Web pages. This is the best one I've seen. It's written by Anna Smith of *ComputerLife UK* magazine and I'm pleased to be able to include it here. It's especially good for those of you who have bought this book (or maybe it was given to you) but who don't really want to read it. The page's URL is now at www.cariboo.bc.ca/daad/lmanual/html/fig7-2.htm. I've edited the HTML only for length, removing the last three sections.

The <BODY> tag includes a BACKGROUND attribute pointing to an image to be used as the background pattern. It's a very nice lightened graphic based on the logo image, *ComputerLife*, at the top of the page, in pink and purple. The URL for the GIF file references it from the root directory of the server. The background graphic is up a couple directory levels from the HTML page's location, so it's a lot cleaner to address it from the root. If this page is later archived at a different level of the server, the link will still work.

The first element on the page is *ComputerLife*'s logo image. The image tag prespecifies the size of the image for better performance. If you check the very end of the code, you will see that the logo is repeated, but without the HEIGHT and WIDTH attributes; this allows the logo to be displayed at its original size—slightly larger than the version shown at the top. The VSPACE and HSPACE attributes are not needed here. They only apply when text flow is specified by giving the ALIGN attribute a value of "right" or "left". This image tag and the one at the end of the page include an ALT attribute providing

Example 2—A Tutorial Page **279**

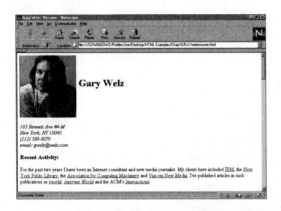

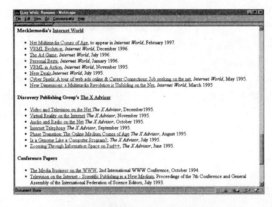

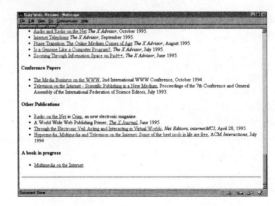

Figure 10.3: An online resumé

descriptions of the images for readers who don't have their browsers set to automatically load images. Including the ALT attribute is a good habit; it has the added advantage of documenting the image tags in your HTML source.

This Web work is nicely designed. It was *built* from a magazine article rather than *converted* from one. After the *ComputerLife* logo is a level 1 heading with the title of the page followed by a short, clear introduction and a table of contents implemented as an unordered list. The introduction and the contents are given a little punch by enclosing them in font tags specifying that a font size one larger than normal should be used to render these elements. The links in the table of contents are all to anchors within this same page. Although this work could have been implemented as several Web pages—one per section—there really isn't a good reason to do the extra work. Because images are used sparingly, it loads fast enough on slow connections and has the advantage of printing in one piece.

After the contents is a more formal introductory section of three paragraphs separated from other page elements with horizontal rules. Another technique in writing a page like this would be to enclose the three-paragraph section in division tags with a class attribute, for example, <DIV CLASS="intro"> ... </DIV>, to do something interesting with it later using Cascading Style Sheets.

Here is the code for the tutorial Web page, minus one section of repetitive code edited out for length.

```
<HTML>
<HEAD>
<TITLE>
Computer Life UK gets you online
</TITLE>
<!--Computer Life Issue 2 Web Pages May 1995-->
</HEAD>

<BODY BACKGROUND="/~clifeuk/graphics/clbg1.jpg">
<IMG WIDTH="166" HEIGHT="38" VSPACE="0" HSPACE="0"
SRC="/~clifeuk/graphics/cluklog2.gif" ALT="Computer Life UK logo">
<H1>Create your own home pages</H1>
<FONT SIZE="+1">
Become at one with the Internet by setting up your own World Wide Web pages. We
show you how. <EM>by Anna Smith</EM>
<UL>
<LI><A HREF="#step1">Step 1</A> Design a template
<LI><A HREF="#step2">Step 2</A> Add the <A HREF="#words">words,</A> <A
HREF="#pics">pictures,</A> and <A HREF="#links">links</A>
<LI><A HREF="#pub">Publish your page</A>
<LI><A HREF="#more">You want more!?</A>
```

Example 2—A Tutorial Page **281**

```
<LI><A HREF="#tricks">Party Tricks</A>
<LI><A HREF="#donts">Don't do this.. at all</A>
<LI><A HREF="#acalert">Acronym Alert</A>
</UL>
</FONT>

<HR>
Writing your own home pages will give you 15 minutes of fame and stardom -
and a healthy respect for the annoying problems that can crop up when
you create them. We'll walk you through the basics of how to create a
text file that will turn into an HTML file when viewed using a browser
such as Netscape.

<P>
Ever wondered why some Web pages have those embarrassing line breaks or
why not every page is full of graphics? Well, Web pages, written in the
text-based browser language known as HTML, can be more than a little
tricky to get just right. However, there is a variety of new shareware
and commercial packages on the market which make it easier. We've
included two software programs on the CD-ROM:
<A HREF="http://pringle.mta.ca/~peterc/">HTMLed</A> and
<A HREF="http://www.microsoft.com/pages/deskapps/word/ia/default.htm">Microsoft
Word 6.0's Internet Assistant.</A>

<P>
Braver souls can write HTML pages using any text editor (including
Windows Notepad) and by saving it as a TXT file, just as long as you
follow certain basic guidelines. Although the more sophisticated
programs automate the process, it's helpful to understand the basics of
HTML design when you set out to create your own pages.
<HR>
```

The rest of the content of the page is divided into sections, each beginning with a level 2 heading. Each heading is given a name with an anchor tag, which is referenced in the table of contents at the top of the page. The ID attribute could also be used, added to the heading tag, but, when this page was written in mid-1995, not many browsers supported this attribute; the NAME attribute is preferred because it gives an easier to track reference. Anna has used the <STRONG></STRONG> tag pair to strongly emphasize all HTML code to distinguish it from the narrative text. To display the markup characters &, <, and >, she is using character entities providing the ASCII index of these characters—for example, < for the less than sign and > for the greater than sign. She also could have used the character name entities &#lt; (less than) and &#gt; (greater than).

```
<H2><A NAME="step1">Step 1: Design a template</A></H2>
There are certain tags (instructions to a hypertext browser) that you must
include in your Web page. It's easiest to put these in first as the bones of your
template. To begin, open a file using one of the packages we've included on the
CD-ROM or a basic text editor and save the file with an HTM extension. Then add
the following text.
<P>
<STRONG>&#60;HTML&#62;</STRONG><BR>
The very first tag. This tells the browser that a hypertext page is coming up. If
the tag's not there, the browser will display anything that follows as plain
text, including all other tags.
<P>
<STRONG>&#60;HEAD&#62;</STRONG><BR>
The head of a hypertext page contains information about it: its title and any
version/ownership info.
<P>
<STRONG>&#60;TITLE&#62;</STRONG><BR>
The title of your page as browsers will see it. The TITLE element always sits
between the <STRONG>&#60;HEAD&#62;</STRONG> and <STRONG>&#60;/HEAD&#62;</STRONG>
tags and must be plain text only.
<P>
<STRONG>&#60;/TITLE&#62;</STRONG><BR>
Closes the title part of the page.
<P>
<STRONG>&#60;!--Your comment here--&#62;</STRONG><BR>
Comment tags. Put the date here, for example. Comments aren't shown on screen.
<P>
<STRONG>&#60;/HEAD&#62;</STRONG><BR>
Closes the head part of your page. Now you can go on to the fun bit!
<P>
<STRONG>&#60;BODY&#62;</STRONG><BR>
The start tag of the area where you put text, pictures, sound files, and pointers
to other interesting parts of the Web. Be bold, be smart, be creative!
Presentation is crucial, so make your pages a pleasure for others to read.
<P>
<STRONG>&#60;HR&#62;</STRONG><BR>
This optional tag displays a horizontal rule across the page. Use it as a visual
cue that this is the end of the page. Put your e-mail address under the rule.
<P>
<STRONG>&#60;/BODY&#62;</STRONG><BR>
Closes the body area.
<P>
<STRONG>&#60;/HTML&#62;</STRONG><BR>
```

Example 2—A Tutorial Page   **283**

The very last tag. It closes your hypertext page.
<HR>
<H2><A NAME="step2">Step 2: Add the words, pictures and links</A></H2>
<STRONG><A NAME="words">Headings</A></STRONG>
It's considered good hypertext practice to make the first element after the opening <BODY> tag a heading, announcing what your page is about.
<P>
There are six levels of heading, the first of which produces large, bold lettering, with space above and below. Experiment with your HTML editor and various browsers to see what they look like. The tag for a level one heading looks like this:
<P>
<STRONG><H1></STRONG>
<H1>This is a first level heading</H1>
<STRONG></H1></STRONG>
<P>
I've tagged the sentence "This is a first level heading" so you can see what a level one heading looks like on your browser.
<P>
<STRONG>Text</STRONG>
Any text that is not enclosed within tags is shown on screen as plain text. All HTML documents must be saved as plain ASCII files. Browsers recognise nothing but word-breaks--they won't see the line and paragraph breaks generated by your word processor. You must specify exactly where you want each paragraph to break. Line width changes according to the size of the window your reader has chosen on her browser.
<P>
Be kind to your readers and keep paragraphs short--a huge block of unbroken text is off-putting.
<P>
To break a line, type
<STRONG>
</STRONG>
The next line starts immediately below.
<P>
For a paragraph break, type
<STRONG><P></STRONG>
<P>
This inserts a space between the lines.
<P>
You may want to emphasise a line or a word. There are two basic attribute tags. The first is <P>
<STRONG><STRONG></STRONG>
<STRONG>Usually makes your text look bold.</STRONG>
<STRONG></STRONG></STRONG>
<P>
And the other is <P>
<STRONG><EM></STRONG>

```
<EM>Short for "emphasised". Usually makes your text look italic.</EM><BR>
<STRONG>&#60;/EM&#62;</STRONG>
<HR>
<H2><A NAME="pics">Pictures</A></H2>
Pictures should be in GIF or JPEG formats. There are programs available for
downloading which will convert PC graphics into whichever of these two you
prefer. JPEGs tend to compress smaller than GIFs (especially with large images),
but use a "lossy" algorithm that degrades image quality. Best thing to do is
experiment and see how your graphics look in your browser.
<P>
The HTML tag for inserting a picture is:
<P>
<STRONG>&#60;IMG SRC=yourpic.gif ALT="Picture of a whatever"&#62;</STRONG>
<P>
Obviously replace <STRONG>'yourpic.gif'</STRONG> with the actual name of your
graphics file. The ALT tag displays text which describes your picture. It is a
courtesy for the benefit of text-only browser users.
<HR>
<H2><A NAME="links">Linking to other Web pages</A></H2>
If your home page is all about "Star Trek," for example, you'll want to tell
other fans where more ST goodies can be found. You do this with what HTML calls
an "anchor"--it's the blue underlined text that you click on to do something or
go somewhere. Graphics can be anchors too. This is the tag you use:
<P>
<STRONG>&#60;A
HREF="http://www.somewhere.co.uk/brilliant_startrek_site.html"&#62;</STRONG><BR>
Click here for a brilliant Star Trek site!<BR>
<STRONG>&#60;/A&#62;</STRONG>
<P>
The text between the double quotes is the URL of the Web page you want people to
visit. You can also link to FTP sites and newsgroups. Because URLs are case-
sensitive, be careful to type them correctly--some use all lower-case letters,
some include capital letters. You can also use them to link to additional pages
that you create, giving your home page more depth.
<HR>
<H2><A NAME="pub">Publishing Your Page</A></H2>
When you have finished your files, contact your Internet provider for information
on how to upload them. It varies from company to company, but many providers are
offering free space as part of their sign up offers.
<HR>
```

Like any good tutorial, this page assumes that it has only whetted your appetite and provides a section of further references. Following that, the work closes nicely with a short bio of the author, a link back to the Web site's home page in button and text, a copyright notice, a couple of "mailtos" for contacting author and webmaster and, finally, a signature in an address block. The

EXAMPLE 2—A TUTORIAL PAGE **285**

only thing that's missing is a timestamp so the reader knows how current the information is. Updated for HTML 3.2, the bio and copyright paragraphs would use paragraph containers with CLASS attributes to take advantage of styles.

```
<H2><A NAME="more">You want more!?</a></H2>
If you want more hints and tips, you can of course find these on the Web itself.
Here are a few places to start you off:
<P>
<A HREF="http://www.charm.net/~web/Vlib.html">The World Wide Web Virtual
Library</A> is a cornucopia of links to everything you need to know about making
World Wide Web pages. Explore thoroughly!
<P>
The <a href="http://www.charm.net/~web/Vlib/Providers/HTML.html">Virtual
Library's HTML index</A> is where you download The Beginner's Guide to HTML and
other information about HTML editing.
<P>
Some nice people at Rutgers University have a <A HREF="http://www-
ns.rutgers.edu/doc-images">collection of public domain graphics</A> to use in
your documents.
<P>
The <A HREF="http://gnn.com/gnn/netizens/construction.html">Home Page
Construction Kit</A> shows you how to create an HTML file and put the file on a
Web server.
<HR>
[content removed]
<HR>
Anna Smith - <A HREF="mailto:mjau@henry.demon.co.uk"> mjau@henry.demon.co.uk</A>
- learned typography at the London College of Printing, worked on magazine layout
in the days before DTP, was part of the editorial team at Micronet, and marketed
BT's Global Network Services. She is now a freelance Web designer.
<HR>
<A HREF="/~clifeuk/"><IMG ALIGN="MIDDLE" VSPACE="5" HSPACE="5"
SRC="/~clifeuk/graphics/cluklog3.gif" ALT="Computer Life UK logo"><I>[Back to
Computer Life UK Home Page]</I></a>
<HR>
Copyright Ziff-Davis UK Limited 1995. All rights reserved. This material may not
be reproduced or transmitted in any form in whole or in part without the written
consent of the publishers.<P>
<ADDRESS><A href="mailto:webmaster@ziff.com">webmaster@ziff.com</A></ADDRESS>
</BODY>
</HTML>
```

Figure 10.4 shows the tutorial as rendered by Netscape.

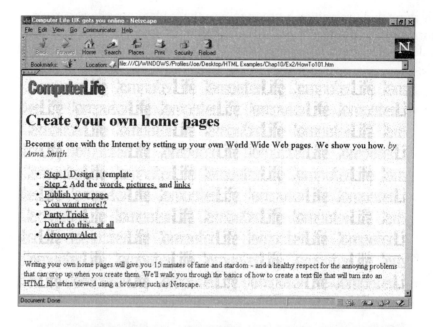

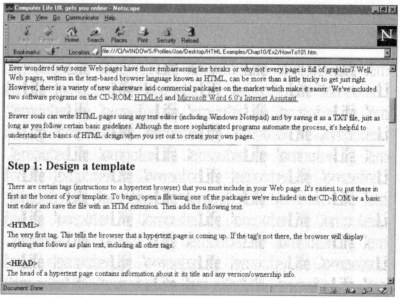

Figure 10.4: The tutorial as rendered by Netscape

EXAMPLE 2—A TUTORIAL PAGE **287**

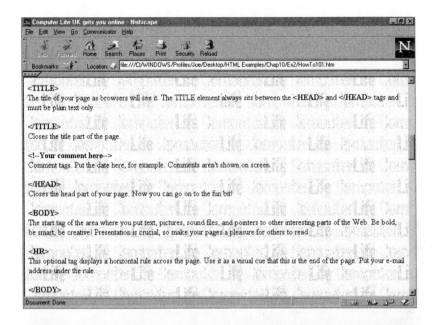

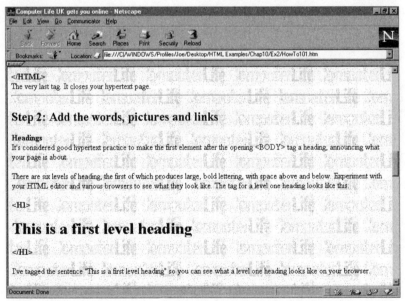

Figure 10.4: The tutorial as rendered by Netscape (Continued)

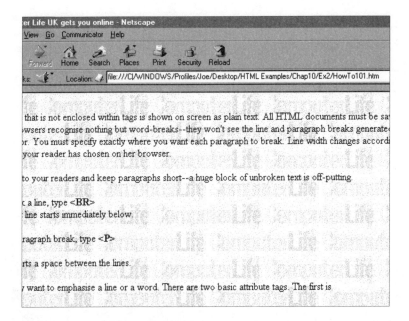

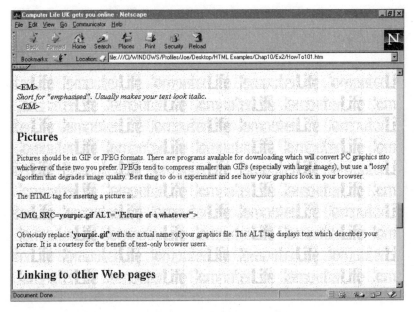

Figure 10.4: The tutorial as rendered by Netscape (Continued)

EXAMPLE 2—A TUTORIAL PAGE   **289**

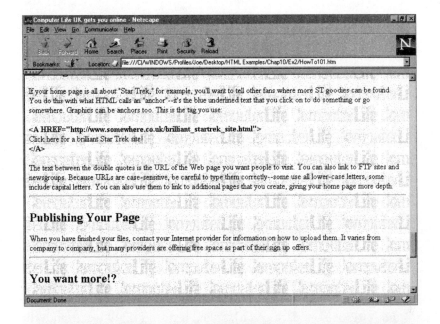

If your home page is all about "Star Trek," for example, you'll want to tell other fans where more ST goodies can be found. You do this with what HTML calls an "anchor"--it's the blue underlined text that you click on to do something or go somewhere. Graphics can be anchors too. This is the tag you use:

<A HREF="http://www.somewhere.co.uk/brilliant_startrek_site.html">
Click here for a brilliant Star Trek site!
</A>

The text between the double quotes is the URL of the Web page you want people to visit. You can also link to FTP sites and newsgroups. Because URLs are case-sensitive, be careful to type them correctly--some use all lower-case letters, some include capital letters. You can also use them to link to additional pages that you create, giving your home page more depth.

Publishing Your Page

When you have finished your files, contact your Internet provider for information on how to upload them. It varies from company to company, but many providers are offering free space as part of their sign up offers.

You want more!?

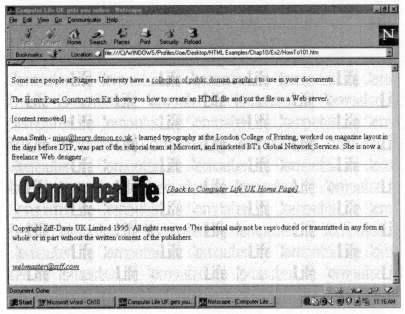

Some nice people at Rutgers University have a collection of public domain graphics to use in your documents.

The Home Page Construction Kit shows you how to create an HTML file and put the file on a Web server.

[content removed]

Anna Smith - mjau@henry.demon.co.uk - learned typography at the London College of Printing, worked on magazine layout in the days before DTP, was part of the editorial team at Micronet, and marketed BT's Global Network Services. She is now a freelance Web designer.

[Back to Computer Life UK Home Page]

Copyright Ziff-Davis UK Limited 1995. All rights reserved. This material may not be reproduced or transmitted in any form in whole or in part without the written consent of the publishers.

webmaster@ziff.com

Figure 10.4: The tutorial as rendered by Netscape (Continued)

EXAMPLE 3—A SMALL ORGANIZATION'S HOME PAGE

The New Jersey Macintosh User's Group (NJMUG) provides this World Wide Web site as a service to its members and the Macintosh user community at large. Most of the page is a collection of links to resources of interest to Macintosh users. The links are organized into a four-row-by-two-column table, each cell of the table containing an icon and text linked to a subpage in the Web site. I don't know if it was intentional, but there's not a single heading tag used in the entire document; nevertheless, this is a very nice presentation of information and references. The NJMUG home page was originally created by Steven Hatch. The site is now developed, hosted, and maintained by Jonathan Vafai and Mike Bielen, volunteers from The Turnaround Team, Inc. of Westfield, New Jersey. The URL of the page is www.njmug.org.

NJMUG's HTML code starts with a head section containing the page's title and an authorship link as well as some comments to identify the HTML file should it be viewed out of context. The <BODY> tag specifies colors for the background (#015050—a dark green), linked text (#FFEE00—a bright yellow) and visited links (#00FFFF—bright cyan). Although the background is fairly dark, it is still light enough that the text can be read on a grayscale display. Immediately following the <BODY> tag is a <CENTER> tag; the corresponding end tag, </CENTER>, is the last item of the HTML source before the closing </BODY> tag. Thus, the entire content of the page is aligned in the center of the reader's display window. Although this isn't strictly kosher HTML 3.2—a <DIV ALIGN="center"> is the preferred method—it is a very widespread practice and almost all browsers handle this code correctly.

The top of the page begins with an image, njmug_logo.gif, from a subdirectory called images. Following the logo is some text that includes a mailto link back to NJMUG's webmaster, rendered with citation tags (<CITE></CITE>). Because the enclosed text is not really a citation, it would have been better to use emphasis or italic style tags.

The <IMG> tag pointing to the NJMUG logo uses a bunch of HTML 3.2 attributes. The HEIGHT and WIDTH attributes reserve space for the image to speed up page formatting. The ALIGN attribute with the value "top" and the HSPACE attributes are not necessary here because the image stands alone. BORDER=0 turns off the frame around the image that would indicate it is an anchor for a link. This is good—the reader can determine that there is a link there by the way the mouse pointer changes to a hand when it's over the image. There's no ALT attribute in the image tag to describe the image for readers

EXAMPLE 3—A SMALL ORGANIZATION'S HOME PAGE   **291**

who don't automatically load images, although it's clear from other content (including the URL) that this is the NJMUG home page.

The four-by-two table that is the main part of the page is specified with a two-pixel border, which looks very nice. The table tag also specifies four pixels of padding separating the contents of each cell from the cell's walls. Each row of the table is properly enclosed in starting and ending table row tags, <TR></TR>, and, likewise, each data cell is enclosed in starting and ending table data tags, <TD></TD>.

Each data cell in the table is cleverly laid out to consist of an image and text emphasized with a <STRONG> attribute, both linked to a subpage. The author achieved a nice, clean look by turning off the anchor border that would surround the image. Normally, you would separate images such as these from the following text by inserting a blank space between the image tag and the text; in this case, however, that space would have been rendered with an underline because it is part of the anchor. Rather than duplicate the anchor tags for the image and the text, the author has added HSPACE=6 to force the spacing without the underline. Each data cell also specifies VALIGN=middle. This attribute could have been placed in the table rows tags, saving some typing, or, for that matter, eliminated entirely, as it is the default. Figure 10.5 shows the completed home page.

```
<HTML>
<HEAD>

<!-- OWNER_NAME="Jonathan Vafai" -->
<LINK rev=made href="mailto:jvafai@turnaround.com">
<!-- OWNER_INFO="The Turnaround Team, Inc., Westfield, NJ, 07090-1454" -->

<TITLE>NJ Macintosh Users Group Web</TITLE>

</HEAD>

<BODY  BGCOLOR="#015050" VLINK="#00ffff" link="FFEE00">

<center><IMG  WIDTH=300 HEIGHT=115 SRC="images/njmug_logo.gif" align=top hspace=6
border=0 >

<p><FONT size=+1><strong>A WWW service of the New Jersey Macintosh Users
Group.</strong></font>
<p><cite>Send any feedback to <A
HREF="mailto:webmaster@njmug.org">webmaster@njmug.org</a></cite>

<p>
```

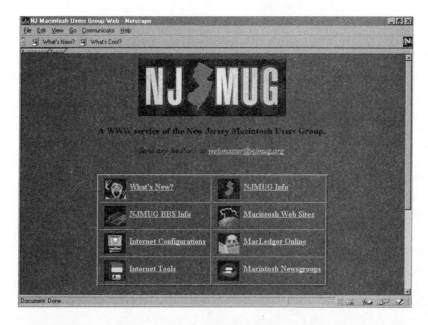

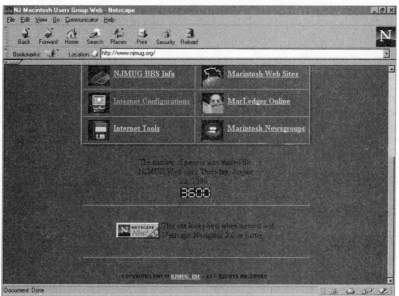

Figure 10.5: The home page of the N.J. Macintosh Users Group

Example 3—A Small Organization's Home Page   **293**

```
<BR>

<table border=2 cellpadding=4>
<TR><td width=50% valign=middle><A HREF="whats-new.html"><IMG ALIGN=middle
WIDTH=46 HEIGHT=42 SRC="images/help.gif" hspace=6 border=0><strong>What's
New?</strong></a></td>                              <td width=50% valign=middle><A
HREF="mug_info.html"><IMG ALIGN=middle WIDTH=46 HEIGHT=42 SRC="images/nj.gif"
hspace=6 border=0 ><strong>NJMUG Info</strong></A></td></TR>
<TR><td width=50% valign=middle><A HREF="njmug_bbs.html"><IMG ALIGN=middle
WIDTH=46 HEIGHT=42 SRC="images/phone.gif" hspace=6 border=0 ><strong>NJMUG BBS
Info</strong></A></td>                 <td width=50% valign=middle><A
HREF="sites.html"><IMG ALIGN=middle WIDTH=46 HEIGHT=42 SRC="images/net.gif"
hspace=6 border=0 ><strong>Macintosh Web Sites</strong></A></td></TR>
<TR><td width=50% valign=middle><A HREF="config.html"><IMG ALIGN=middle  WIDTH=46
HEIGHT=42 SRC="images/mac.gif" hspace=6 border=0 ><strong>Internet
Configurations</strong></A></td>   <td width=50% valign=middle><A
HREF="macledger/"><IMG ALIGN=middle WIDTH=46 HEIGHT=42 SRC="images/info.gif"
hspace=6 border=0 ><strong>MacLedger Online</strong></A></td></TR>
<TR><td width=50% valign=middle><A HREF="tools.html"><IMG ALIGN=middle WIDTH=46
HEIGHT=42 SRC="images/files.gif" hspace=6 border=0 ><strong>Internet
Tools</strong></A></td>                        <td width=50% valign=middle><A
HREF="usenet.html"><IMG ALIGN=middle WIDTH=46 HEIGHT=42 SRC="images/chat.gif"
hspace=6 border=0 ><strong>Macintosh Newsgroups</strong></A></td></TR>
</table>

<br clear=all>

<p>
```

In the next section, below the main directory, a visitor counter has been implemented. Each time a new visitor accesses this page the counter increments, so technically the counter actually counts page hits or accesses and not separate visitors. In the HMTL code, the counter is placed with a two-row-by-one-column table. This is a fairly common practice to keep text and images aligned and still be able to center the counter on the page. In the second row, an image tag calls the CGI-driven counter with the line:

```
<img src="http://207.92.234.100/cgi-shl/counter.exe?njmug">
```

Notice that this <IMG> tag is not within an anchor tag; it just sits on the page. Every time this page is loaded and this image appears, the counter program is called and the number goes up by one. There are many counter programs and images available on the Web; Appendix C lists a number of resources for them.

Following the counter is yet another table that contains a link for downloading Netscape Navigator. If you look carefully at the <A> code line, you'll see the term "mirror" as part of the path name. This indicates a directory of mirror sites—each of which contains the same files for downloading as the original site. Mirror sites are fairly common on the Web.

```
<center>
<TABLE width=240 border=0>
<TR><TD align=center>The number of people who visited the NJMUG Web since
Thursday, August 22, 1996: </TD></TR>
<TR><TD align=center><img src="http://207.92.234.100/cgi-
shl/counter.exe?njmug"></TD></TR></TABLE>
</center>

<HR size=4 width=60%>

<BR>

<TABLE border=0 cellpadding=2>
<TR><TD><A HREF="http://home.netscape.com/comprod/mirror/index.html"><IMG
border=0 SRC="images/NSnow8.gif" ALT="Download Netscape NOW!" ALIGN=MIDDLE
WIDTH="88" HEIGHT="31"></A></TD><TD>This site looks best when viewed
with<br>Netscape Navigator 2.0 or better.</TD></TR>
</table>

<BR>

<P>

<HR size=4 width=60%>

<BR>

<B><FONT SIZE=-2>COPYRIGHT 1995-97 <A HREF="mailto:webmaster@njmug.org">NJMUG,
INC</A> -- ALL RIGHTS RESERVED</B></FONT>

</center>

</BODY>
</HTML>
```

The page ends with a copyright statement in capital letters. Evidently, this did not look very good to the author, so he tweaked the typography by enclosing the line in font and bold style tags:

```
<B><FONT SIZE=-2> ... </B></FONT>
```

Example 4—A Large Organization's Home Page   **295**

The font tag reduces the size of the text a couple of notches. Note that this works even though the font and bold style tags overlap.

Example 4—A Large Organization's Home Page

After showing the previous examples of Web pages of individuals and small organizations, now is a good time to present an example of the home page of a large organization. On October 20, 1994, Vice President Al Gore announced the availability of The White House World Wide Web Server, an interactive citizens' handbook at www.whitehouse.gov. This page is the new White House home page at www.whitehouse.gov/wh/welcome.html.

This page continues a tradition of well-designed Web pages for the White House. The initial site was one of the first well-known sites to use imagemaps. As you'll see, there are still several built-in mechanisms to keep the page current and flexible. One of the more interesting things about this page is that—with a few exceptions—it is basically the same as the NJMUG page.

The very first thing you might notice about this page is that there is the link to a text alternative. This is a very democratic (with a small "d") option and one that should be applauded. Not only does it allow for a much speedier access to the content linked to this page, but it also allows nongraphic-oriented browsers complete access. This category includes browsers for the hearing impaired. (One of the ongoing concerns of the World Wide Web Consortium is to make allowances for speech-capable browsers.) Figure 10.6 shows the text-only version of this page.

```
<HTML>
<HEAD>
<TITLE>Welcome To The White House</TITLE>
</HEAD>

<BODY background="/WH/images/bg.gif" bgcolor="#FFFFFF" text="#000000"
link="#0000BB" alink="#00BB00" vlink="#BB0000">

<A href="/WH/Welcome-plain.html">[Text version]</A><P>
```

As you can see in Figure 10.7, the graphics at the top of the page are all contained in a table, as in the NJMUG page. One interesting difference: Notice the "Good Afternoon" over the image of the White House. Sometimes this page has a "Good Morning" or a "Good Evening" greeting. However, the HTML code names a generic "greeting.gif" to fill this spot, which indicates that the

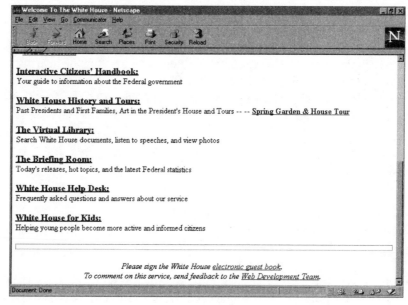

Figure 10.6: Text-only version of White House Web page

EXAMPLE 4—A LARGE ORGANIZATION'S HOME PAGE **297**

White House Web server is rotating files at specified times. For example, at 12 noon, a CGI program copies the "afternoon.gif" to the file "greeting.gif" overwriting the previously installed "morning.gif." It's a pretty clever method of demonstrating timeliness, but, of course, it does require some server-side programming.

The next series of images includes an oval cut-out picture of the White House. This sets up a visual metaphor that is carried out throughout the page in each of the navigational buttons below. Although you can't tell from the reproduction here, the flags on either side of the center image are GIF animations that appear to wave in the wind. There is no way to tell just from the HTML code whether a graphic is static or animated because each uses a .gif extension. This particular animation consists of eight separate images each 100 pixels wide by 55 pixels high. The rippling effect in each frame is achieved with a graphic manipulation package such as Adobe Photoshop.

```
<CENTER>
<TABLE cellpadding=0 cellspacing=0>
<TR>
<TD colspan=3 align=CENTER valign=CENTER><img border=0
src="/WH/images/greeting.gif" hspace=5 vspace=5><br></TD>
</TR>

<TR>
<TD align=CENTER valign=CENTER><img border=0 src="/WH/images/flag.gif" hspace=5
vspace=5 width=100 height=55 align=CENTER></TD>

<TD><img border=0 src="/WH/images/bevel.gif" hspace=5 vspace=5 align=CENTER
height=175 width=300 alt="White House"></TD>

<TD align=CENTER valign=CENTER><img border=0 src="/WH/images/flag.gif" hspace=5
vspace=5 width=100 height=55 align=CENTER></TD> </TR>
<TR>

<TD colspan=3 align=CENTER valign=CENTER><img border=0
src="/WH/images/welcome4.gif" hspace=5 vspace=5 width=275 height=92 alt="Welcome
to the White House"><br></TD>
</TABLE>
```

After the initial table of graphics comes a seemingly empty bit of code. Between two <P> tags is a preformatted text element with nothing in it. Well, almost nothing. Remember that usually anything the <PRE></PRE> pair encloses is reproduced verbatim in a monospaced font like Courier. Here nothing is noticeable until the "Show Paragraph Marks" command is turned on, and then a carriage return is revealed. The <PRE> tag is being used to provide

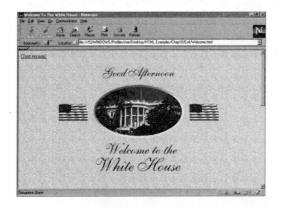

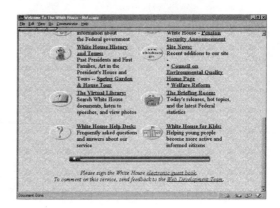

Figure 10.7: The White House Welcome page

Example 4—A Large Organization's Home Page **299**

a "hard return" or line break. This is perfectly acceptable, although it's not clear why the far simpler <BR> tag was not used.

In the five-row-by-four-column table structure that follows, each of the <TD> tags sets the VALIGN attribute to the top. Because no table border is visible, the "top" is a good choice—however, it doesn't really matter in this case, just as long as the same choice is made for all the images and text blocks. This assures that everything is lined up properly and gives an orderly appearance without a noticeable structure (such as a border) visible.

```
<p>
<pre>

</pre>
<p>
<table width=600>
<TR>
<TD valign=TOP width=75><FONT size=+1><A href="/WH/EOP/html/principals.html"><img
border=0 src="/WH/images/pin_pres_vp.gif" align=LEFT height=50 width=75 hspace=5
vspace=5></A><br></TD>

<TD valign=TOP width=225><A href="/WH/EOP/html/principals.html"><B>The President
&amp; Vice President:</B></A><br> </FONT>Their accomplishments, their
<BR>families, and how to send them electronic mail <br clear=ALL><p>
</TD>

<TD valign=TOP width=75><FONT size=+1><A href="/WH/Services"><img border=0
src="/WH/images/pin_citizen2.gif" align=LEFT height=50 width=75 hspace=5
vspace=5></TD>

<TD valign=TOP width=225><A href="/WH/Services"><B>Commonly Requested Federal
Services:</B></a><br>Direct access to Federal Services</TD>
<br clear=ALL>
</tr>
<tr>
<TD valign=TOP><FONT size=+1><A href="/WH/html/handbook.html"><img border=0
src="/WH/images/pin_citizen2.gif" align=LEFT height=50 width=75 hspace=5
vspace=5></A><br></TD>

<TD valign=TOP><A href="/WH/html/handbook.html"><B>Interactive Citizens'
Handbook:</B></A></FONT> Your guide to information about <BR>the Federal
government<br clear=ALL><p>
</TD>

<TD valign=TOP><FONT size=+1><A HREF="/WH/New"><img border=0
src="/WH/images/pin_calendar.gif" align=LEFT height=50 width=75 hspace=5
```

```
vspace=5></A><br> </TD>

<TD valign=TOP><A HREF="/WH/New"><B>What's New:</B></A><br></FONT> What's
happening at the White House - <a href="/WH/New/html/pbgc.html"><b>Pension
Security Announcement</b></a> <br clear=ALL><p> </TD>
</TR>

<TR>
<TD valign=TOP><FONT size=+1><A href="/WH/glimpse/top.html"><img border=0
src="/WH/images/pin_history.gif" align=LEFT height=50 width=75 hspace=5
vspace=5></A><br></TD>

<TD valign=TOP><A href="/WH/glimpse/top.html"><B>White House History and
Tours:</B></A><br></FONT>Past Presidents and First Families, Art in the
President's House and Tours -- <a href="/WH/Tours/gardentour.html"><b>Spring
Garden & House Tour</b></a><br clear=ALL><p> </TD>

<TD valign=TOP><FONT size=+1><A href="/WH/Site_News"><img border=0
src="/WH/images/pin_www1.gif" align=LEFT height=50 width=75 hspace=5
vspace=5></A><br> </TD>

<TD valign=TOP><A href="/WH/Site_News"><B>Site News:</B></A><br></FONT>Recent
additions to our site - <br><b>*</b> <a href="/CEQ"><b>Council on Environmental
Quality Home Page</b></a><br><b>*</b> <a href="/WH/Welfare/"><b>Welfare
Reform</b></a></TD>
</TR>

<TR>
<TD valign=TOP><FONT size=+1><A href="/WH/html/library.html"><img border=0
src="/WH/images/pin_library.gif" align=LEFT height=50 width=75 hspace=5
vspace=5></A><br></TD>

<TD valign=TOP><A href="/WH/html/library.html"><B>The Virtual
Library:</B></A><br></FONT>Search White House documents, listen to speeches, and
view photos<br clear=ALL><p></TD>

<TD valign=TOP><FONT size=+1><A href="/WH/html/briefroom.html"><img border=0
src="/WH/images/pin_briefing.gif" align=LEFT height=50 width=75 hspace=5
vspace=5></A><br></TD>

<TD valign=TOP><A href="/WH/html/briefroom.html"><B>The Briefing
Room:</B></A><br></FONT>Today's releases, hot topics, and the latest Federal
statistics<br clear=ALL><p></TD>
</TR>

<TR>
<TD valign=TOP><FONT size=+1><A href="/WH/html/helpdsk.html"><img border=0
```

Example 4—A Large Organization's Home Page **301**

```
src="/WH/images/pin_info2.gif" align=LEFT height=50 width=75 hspace=5
vspace=5></A><br></TD>

<TD valign=TOP><A href="/WH/html/helpdsk.html"><B>White House Help
Desk:</B></A><br></FONT>Frequently asked questions and answers about our
service<br clear=ALL><p></TD>

<TD valign=TOP><FONT size=+1><A href="/WH/kids/html/kidshome.html"><img border=0
src="/WH/images/pin_kids2.gif" align=LEFT height=50 width=75 hspace=5
vspace=5></A><br></TD>

<TD valign=TOP><A href="/WH/kids/html/kidshome.html"><B>White House for
Kids:</B></A><br></FONT>Helping young people become more active and informed
citizens<br clear=ALL><p></TD>
</TR>
</TABLE>
</CENTER>
```

There is one exceptional link within the preceding table. The Virtual Library is actually a multimedia storehouse of governmental information. Everything is linked to a searchable database where you can find documents by keyword and/or date. Most documents are in a straightforward ASCII text format, although some forms are in PDF format that you can browse using an Adobe Acrobat plug-in. The official photo archive is displayed using thumbnail GIFs; clicking on them downloads the larger JPEG file. There are even audio archives of the President's Saturday Radio Address in both a downloadable AU file format and Real Audio's streaming audio format.

```
<p><CENTER>
<img src="/WH/images/footer.gif" alt="[flag footer graphic]" width=468
height=25><p>

<p><I>Please sign the White House<A target="_top"
HREF="/WH/html/Guest_Book.html">electronic guest book</A>.</I><br><I>To comment
on this service, send feedback to the <A target="_top" HREF="/cgi-
bin/Correspondence/Mail_Developers">Web Development Team</A>.</I> </CENTER>

</BODY>
</HTML>
```

A long, thin graphic is used as a visually expressive horizontal rule near the bottom of the page. This image—"footer.gif" in the preceding code—is a good example of a very common bit of Web clip art. Appendix C lists sources for more clip art.

The final element appears at first glance to be a simple mailto, asking for comments and feedback. But, if selected, this response form will replace the current page. This is indicated by the TARGET="_top" attribute. You may remember this value being used in the section on frames. Whenever "_top" is set as the target, the page called takes the place of what's on screen.

EXAMPLE 5—A PAGE OF INTERNET RESOURCES

The Web is amazingly self-documenting. Every aspect of Web production can be found on the Web itself. One of the more coherent examples of a page of Internet Resources is the one at www.december.com/web/text/ by John December, entitled Internet Web Text. This page is very good HTML. Unlike some of the other examples in this chapter, it needed very little reformatting to make the code more readable.

As shown in Figure 10.8, this Web page is a really good example of a column layout done with tables. The page puts the Web site navigational categories ("About," "Orient," "Guides," and so on) on the left and the main body of the information on the right. What seems to be a fairly simple two-column table at first glance is actually a somewhat complex three-column-by-two-row table with two additional embedded tables. The code that follows has been commented to point out where the various tables, rows, and cells begin and end. Let's go through the HTML step by step.

At the very top of the page is the page title and authorship information. The <LINK> tag here directs anyone who needs more information on this revision ("Rev") to a mailto form for John December. The original version of this page also contains a CGI routine that calls a rotating advertisement; the reference (an anchor tag) was omitted because it needs connection to the server to reproduce it.

```
<HTML><!-- @version STD-HEAD style 01 Oct 1996 -->
<HEAD>
   <TITLE>Internet Web Text: Index</TITLE>
   <LINK Rev="made" Href="mailto:john@december.com">
</HEAD>

<BODY BGcolor="#FFFFFF" ALink="#00FF7F">
```

The outermost table is shown next. If you look ahead to the end of the code, you'll see that it goes all the way to the end; the ending </TABLE> tag doesn't appear until just before the </BODY> tag. The first cell, in the first

EXAMPLE 5—A PAGE OF INTERNET RESOURCES   **303**

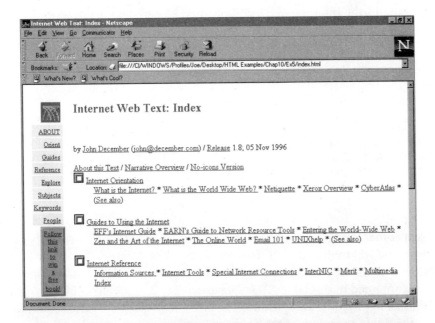

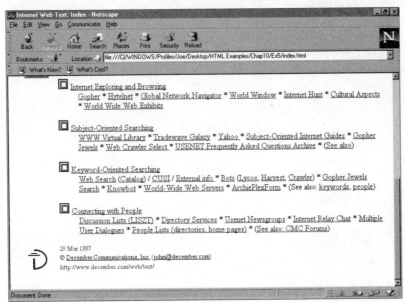

Figure 10.8: John December's Internet Web Text

row, contains the Internet Web Text Logo that appears in the upper-left corner of the page.

```
<!-- Start of the outer table -->
<TABLE Border="0" Cellpadding="1" Cellspacing="5">

<!-- This starts the first row -->
<TR>
<!-- Start of first cell -->
<TD VAlign="top" Align="right">
<FONT Size="-1" Color="#8E2323">
<P><P><A Href="http://www.december.com/web/text/"><IMG Border="0" Width="40"
Height="40" Alt=" " Src="http://www.december.com/web/text/images/icon.gif"></A>
<P>
<P>
```

Next comes the first embedded table. The important thing to remember is that you are still in the first cell. The double paragraph tags just shown are intended to give a little separation between the logo and the navigational keywords contained in this table. The table uses a BGCOLOR attribute to establish a light yellow background. The NOWRAP attribute is turned on to force the cell to the width of the data and prevent it from wrapping.

```
<!-- First table inside the first cell -->
<TABLE Border="0" Cellpadding="2" Cellspacing="0">
<TR><TD Nowrap Align="right" BGColor="#FFFFCC"><FONT Size="-1"><A
Href="http://www.december.com/web/text/about.html">ABOUT</A></FONT></TD></TR>
<TR><TD Nowrap Align="right" BGColor="#FFFFCC"><FONT Size="-1"><A
Href="http://www.december.com/web/text/nar-
orient.html">Orient</A></FONT></TD></TR>
<TR><TD Nowrap Align="right" BGColor="#FFFFCC"><FONT Size="-1"><A
Href="http://www.december.com/web/text/nar-
guides.html">Guides</A></FONT></TD></TR>
<TR><TD Nowrap Align="right" BGColor="#FFFFCC"><FONT Size="-1"><A
Href="http://www.december.com/web/text/nar-
reference.html">Reference</A></FONT></TD></TR>
<TR><TD Nowrap Align="right" BGColor="#FFFFCC"><FONT Size="-1"><A
Href="http://www.december.com/web/text/nar-
explore.html">Explore</A></FONT></TD></TR>
<TR><TD Nowrap Align="right" BGColor="#FFFFCC"><FONT Size="-1"><A
Href="http://www.december.com/web/text/nar-
subject.html">Subjects</A></FONT></TD></TR>
<TR><TD Nowrap Align="right" BGColor="#FFFFCC"><FONT Size="-1"><A
Href="http://www.december.com/web/text/nar-
keyword.html">Keywords</A></FONT></TD></TR>
<TR><TD Nowrap Align="right" BGColor="#FFFFCC"><FONT Size="-1"><A
```

EXAMPLE 5—A PAGE OF INTERNET RESOURCES **305**

```
Href="http://www.december.com/web/text/nar-
people.html">People</A></FONT></TD></TR>
</TABLE>
<!-- End of the first table inside cell -->
<P>
```

Immediately after the first embedded table comes a second table. This is a one-cell table with an expanded border that gives the text a button-like appearance. This is the last item in the first cell.

```
<!-- Start of the second table inside cell -->
<P><TABLE Border="4" Cellpadding="2" Cellspacing="0" Width="5"><TR><TD
Align="center" BGColor="#00FF7F"><FONT Size="-1"><A
Href="http://www.december.com/works/giveaway.html">Follow this link to win a free
book!</A></FONT></TD></TR></TABLE>
<!-- End of the second table inside cell -->

</FONT>
</TD>
<!-- End of the first cell -->
```

The next three lines of HTML code definitely qualify as a webmaster trick-of-the-trade. After I mentioned that the layout on this page used a three-column-by-two-row design, you may have looked at Figure 10.8 and said, "Where's the third column?" The thin brown (onscreen) line separating the left navigation column from the right main text column *is* the missing column! As you can see by the HTML that follows, it is only 1 pixel wide and it spans the two rows (so it goes all the way to the bottom of the page). The table data <TD> tag is empty except for the line break, <BR>, which is all it needs to fill out the column with color. Although you could also do this with Internet Explorer's advanced table attributes, this example will work with any browser that supports tables.

```
<!-- Start of the 2nd cell in the first row -->
<TD Rowspan="2" BGColor="#8E2323" Width="1"><BR></TD>
<!-- End of the 2nd cell in the first row -->
```

Next, the third cell in the first row is set up. This cell also spans both rows in the outer table, like the "column-line" we just examined. This is the main part of the page, and begins with a link to a narrative overview. This entire part of the page is structured as a series of definition lists with <DL></DL> tags enclosing definition term <DT> and definition description <DD> tags. Each definition term (except the first) is composed of two anchors, the first enclosing a small square icon image and the second enclosing a text label. Both point to a single-page version of the information contained in the definition description paired with the definition term. The icon points to a graphic version of the page, the label to a narrative version. The page ends with a short copyright notice using the character entity © for the copyright symbol (©). Most browsers will now recognize © for this symbol.

Remember that one of the results of using the <DL> and <DT> tags is the indentation of the terms; you can see this in Figure 10.8. Within each of the <DT> tags, John has separated the items with an asterisk. This list of categories could have also been accomplished by using the bulleted list feature of an unordered list, although this method is far more compact.

```
<!-- Start of the 3rd cell in the first row -->
<TD Rowspan="2" VAlign="top">
<H2><FONT Color="#8E2323">Internet Web Text: Index</FONT></H2>
<P>
<!-- BEGIN CONTENT -->

<P>
by <A Href="http://www.december.com/john/">John December</A>
    (<A Href="mailto:john@december.com">john@december.com</A>) /
<A Href="releases.html">Release</A> 1.8; 05 Nov 1996


<DL>
<DT>
<A Href="about.html">About this Text</a> /
<A Href="narrative.html">Narrative Overview</a> /
<A Href="no-icons.html">No-icons Version</a>
<P>

<DT><A Href="orient.html"><img src="images/page.gif" ALT="Orientation List"></A>
    <A Href="nar-orient.html">Internet Orientation</A>
    <DD>
    <A Href="inetwhat.html">What is the Internet? </a>
    * <A Href="webwhat.html">What is the World Wide Web? </a>
    * <A Href="ftp://ftp.merit.edu/documents/fyi/fyi28.txt"> Netiquette</a>
    * <A
Href="http://pubweb.parc.xerox.com/hypertext/wwwvideo/wwwvideo.html">Xerox
Overview</A>
    * <A Href="cyberatlas.html">CyberAtlas</a>
    * (<A Href="http://www.december.com/cmc/info/internet-introduction.html">See
also</a>)
</DL>
<DL>
<DT><A Href="guides.html"><img src="images/page.gif" ALT="Guides List"></A>
    <A Href="nar-guides.html">Guides to Using the Internet</A>
```

Example 5—A Page of Internet Resources **307**

```
    <DD>
    <A HREF="http://www.eff.org/papers/eegtti/eegttitop.html">EFF's Internet
Guide</a>  *
    <A HREF="http://www.earn.net/gnrt/notice.html#contents">EARN's Guide to
Network Resource Tools</a> *
    <A HREF="http://www.eit.com:80/web/www.guide/"> Entering the World-Wide
Web</a>  *
    <A HREF="http://sundance.cso.uiuc.edu/Publications/Other/Zen/zen-
1.0_toc.html">Zen and the Art of the Internet</a>  *
    <A HREF="http://login.eunet.no/~presno/index.html">The Online World</a>  *
    <A
HREF="ftp://uiarchive.cso.uiuc.edu/pub/etext/gutenberg/etext93/email025.txt">Email
 101</a>  *
    <A HREF="http://www.nova.edu/Inter-Links/UNIXhelp/TOP_.html">UNIXhelp</A>
     *
    (<A Href="http://www.december.com/cmc/info/internet-navigating-
guides.html">See also</a>)

</DL>
<DL>
<DT><A Href="reference.html"><img src="images/page.gif" ALT="Reference List"></A>
    <A Href="nar-reference.html">Internet Reference</A>
    <DD>
    <A HREF="http://www.december.com/cmc/info/">
    Information Sources </a>  *
    <A HREF="http://www.december.com/net/tools/">
     Internet Tools</a>  *
    <A HREF="http://www.spectracom.com/islist/">
     Special Internet Connections</a>  *
    <A Href="http://www.internic.net">
     InterNIC</a>  *
    <A Href="ftp://nic.merit.edu">
     Merit</a>  *
    <A Href="http://viswiz.gmd.de/MultimediaInfo/">
     Multimedia Index</a>
</DL>
<DL>
<DT><A Href="explore.html"><img src="images/page.gif" ALT="Explore List"></A>
    <A Href="nar-explore.html">Internet Exploring and Browsing</A>
    <DD>
    <A Href="gopher://gopher.micro.umn.edu:70/1">
    Gopher</a>  *
    <A Href="http://library.usask.ca/hytelnet/">
     Hytelnet</a>  *
    <A Href="http://nearnet.gnn.com/gnn/GNNhome.html">
     Global Network Navigator</a>  *
    <A Href="telnet://library.wustl.edu">
```

```
     World Window</a>  *
    <A Href="http://www.hunt.org/">
     Internet Hunt</a>  *
    <A Href="http://www.december.com/cmc/info/culture.html">
     Cultural Aspects</a>  *
    <A Href="http://sunsite.unc.edu/expo/ticket_office.html">
     World Wide Web Exhibits</a>
</DL>
<DL>


<DT><A Href="subject.html"><img src="images/page.gif" ALT="Subjects List"></A>
    <A Href="nar-subject.html">Subject-Oriented Searching</A>
    <DD>
    <A Href="http://www.w3.org/hypertext/DataSources/bySubject/Overview.html">
     WWW Virtual Library</a>  *
    <A Href="http://www.einet.net/galaxy.html">
     Tradewave Galaxy</a>  *
    <A Href="http://www.yahoo.com/">
     Yahoo </a>  *
    <A Href="http://www.clearinghouse.net/">
     Subject-Oriented Internet Guides</a>  *
    <A Href="http://galaxy.einet.net/GJ/index.html">
     Gopher Jewels</a>  *
    <A Href="http://www.webcrawler.com/select/">
     Web Crawler Select </a>  *
    <A Href="http://www.cis.ohio-state.edu/hypertext/faq/usenet/">
     USENET Frequently Asked Questions Archive</a>
     *
    (<A Href="http://www.december.com/cmc/info/internet-searching-
subjects.html">See also</a>)
</DL>
<DL>


<DT><A Href="keyword.html"><img src="images/page.gif" ALT="Keywords List"></A>
    <A Href="nar-keyword.html">Keyword-Oriented Searching</A>
    <DD>
    <A Href="http://cuiwww.unige.ch/meta-index.html">
     Web Search</a>
    (<A Href="http://cuiwww.unige.ch/w3catalog">Catalog</a>)
     /
    <A Href="http://web.nexor.co.uk/public/cusi/cusi.html">CUSI</a>
     /
    <A Href="http://www_is.cs.utwente.nl:8080/cgi-bin/local/nph-
susil.pl">External info </a>
      *
    <A Href="http://www.botspot.com/">Bots</a>
    (<A Href="http://lycos.cs.cmu.edu/">Lycos</a>,
```

Example 5—A Page of Internet Resources **309**

```
    <A Href="http://www.town.hall.org/brokers/www-home-
pages/query.html">Harvest</a>,
      <A Href="http://webcrawler.com/">Crawler</a>)
        *
    <A Href="http://galaxy.einet.net/gopher/gopher.html">
    Gopher Jewels Search</a> *
    <A Href="telnet://info.cnri.reston.va.us:185">
    Knowbot</a> *
    <A Href="http://www.w3.org/hypertext/DataSources/WWW/Servers.html">
    World-Wide Web Servers</a> *
    <A Href="http://web.nexor.co.uk/archie.html">ArchiePlexForm</a>
      *
    (See also: <A Href="http://www.december.com/cmc/info/internet-searching-
keyword.html">keywords</a>,
    <A Href="http://www.december.com/cmc/info/internet-searching-
people.html">people</a>)

</DL>
<DL>
<DT><A Href="people.html"><img src="images/page.gif" ALT="People List"></A>
    <A Href="nar-people.html">Connecting with People</A>
    <DD>
    <A Href="http://www.liszt.com/">
    Discussion Lists (LISZT)</a> *
    <A Href="gopher://gopher.nd.edu/11/Non-
Notre%20Dame%20Information%20Sources/Phone%20Books--Other%20Institutions">
      Directory Services</a> *
    <A Href="http://www.liszt.com/cgi-bin/news.cgi">
    Usenet Newsgroups</a> *
    <A Href="http://www.kei.com/irc.html">
    Internet Relay Chat</a> *
    <A Href="http://www.cis.upenn.edu/~lwl/mudinfo.html">
    Multiple User Dialogues</a> *
    <A Href="http://www.december.com/cmc/info/culture-people-lists.html">
    People Lists (directories, home pages)</a> *
    (<A Href="http://www.december.com/net/tools/cmc.html">See also: CMC
Forums</a>)
</DL>

<P>
<FONT Size="-1" Color="#8E2323">
29 Mar 1997
<!-- END CONTENT -->
<BR>&#169; <A Href="http://www.december.com/">December Communications, Inc.</A>
(<A Href="mailto:john@december.com">john@december.com</A>)
<BR>http://www.december.com/web/text/
</FONT>
```

```
</TD></TR>
<!-- End of the third cell and the first row -->
<P>
```

That's the end of the major section of the page as well as the third and final cell of the first row. Next comes a single cell on the second row whose only occupant is John's "D" logo. By placing it in its own cell and having the other two columns span this row with the ROWSPAN=2 attribute in each of the previous columns, John assures that the logo will appear at the bottom. This cell is really the final element on the page and all the closing tags—</TD>, </TR>, </TABLE>, </BODY>, and </HTML>—follow immediately after.

```
<!-- Start of the second row, only cell -->
<TR>
<TD VAlign="bottom" Align="right">
<FONT Size="-1" Color="#8E2323"><P>

<P><A Href="http://www.december.com/"><IMG Border="0" Width="40" Height="40"
Alt=" " Src="http://www.december.com/images/d.gif"></A>
</FONT>
</TD></TR>
<!-- End of the second row -->

</TABLE>
<!-- End of the outer table -->

</BODY>
</HTML>
```

In addition to being an excellent example of HTML coding, this page is a terrific reference point. Each of the links is a great jumping off place for these important technical issues.

Example 6—Inside an Extranet

The final example takes a look at an entire Web site and the HTML coding required to maintain its organization. The site belongs to The Earth School, a progressive public school in New York City. In many ways, the Earth School site (www.idest.com/earthschool/) is structured very much like an *extranet*— an intranet-like structure where the balance is more on the external access. Much of the purpose of the Earth School site is to communicate with a wide range of personnel—teachers, staff, parents, and children. The posting of the organization's philosophies and policies plays a major role in the site, as does the consistent updating of vital information such as meetings, school holidays,

EXAMPLE 6—INSIDE AN EXTRANET **311**

and events. But because the personnel involved here are widely distributed both in place and in the time of access (before, during, and after school), the site must be available externally and internally. We'll cut a swath through the Earth School Web site looking at how the code connects to all the various sections.

The site was largely developed by Kate Hogan, a founder of the Earth School and the current teacher for the combined 5th and 6th grades. Given the ecological focus of the school, it is only natural that Kate has given the home page, shown in Figure 10.9, a nice rotating globe on a lush green background (BGCOLOR="#1E6746") as its central image. The globe is an animated GIF file and uses the LOWSRC attribute set to the first frame of the animation to act as a placeholder while the animation is loading. After the opening statement, three navigational buttons—Mission, Staff, and Arts—are centered on the page. Additional links are given in a bulleted list set up with the <UL> tag. Near the end of the page is a link to a page of staff e-mail addresses—a handy way to centralize communications.

```
<!DOCTYPE HTML PUBLIC "-//W3C//DTD HTML 3.2//EN">
<HTML>
<HEAD>
    <TITLE>Home at The Earth School</TITLE>
</HEAD>
<BODY TEXT="#000000" BGCOLOR="#1E6746" LINK="#E5B417" VLINK="#FF00FF"
ALINK="#FF0000">

<H3 ALIGN=CENTER>Welcome<BR>
to<BR>
<IMG SRC="newlogo1.gif" HEIGHT=48 WIDTH=368 ALIGN=BOTTOM></H3>

<H3 ALIGN=CENTER><IMG SRC="EARTH3_112K.GIF" LOWSRC="earthlow.gif" HEIGHT=100
WIDTH=100></H3>

<H3 ALIGN=CENTER><IMG SRC="newlogo2a.gif" HEIGHT=45 WIDTH=122 ALIGN=BOTTOM></H3>

<CENTER><P>The Earth School is a public school in Community School District One
in New York City. It is an ecological institute which maintains a core curriculum
that fosters environmental awareness and earth stewardship. It focuses its
studies on the natural world and the local community. Founded by teachers, it
opened its doors in September 1992. 
<HR SIZE="5"><A HREF="es.htm"><IMG SRC="Mission.gif" BORDER=0 NATURALSIZEFLAG="3"
HEIGHT=34 WIDTH=86></A><A HREF="staff.htm"><IMG SRC="Staff.gif" BORDER=0
NATURALSIZEFLAG="3" HEIGHT=35 WIDTH=81></A><A HREF="earthlings.htm"><IMG
SRC="Arts.gif" BORDER=0 NATURALSIZEFLAG="3" HEIGHT=34 WIDTH=83></A></P></CENTER>
```

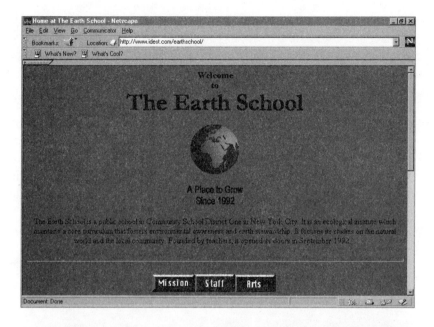

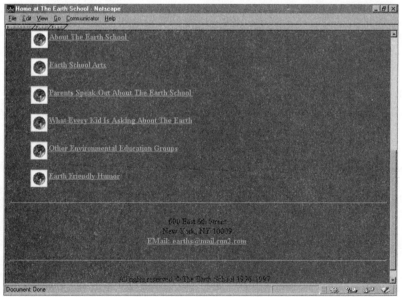

Figure 10.9: The Earth School home page

EXAMPLE 6—INSIDE AN EXTRANET **313**

```
<UL>
<LI><A HREF="es.htm"><IMG SRC="bb1.gif" NATURALSIZEFLAG="0" HEIGHT=14 WIDTH=13
ALIGN="middle"></A><B><A HREF="es.htm">About The Earth School </A></B><BR>
</LI>

<LI><A HREF="earthlings.htm"><IMG SRC="bb1.gif" NATURALSIZEFLAG="0" HEIGHT=14
WIDTH=13 ALIGN="middle"></A><B><A HREF="earthlings.htm">Earth School
Arts</A></B><BR>
</LI>

<LI><A HREF="families.htm"><IMG SRC="bb1.gif" NATURALSIZEFLAG="0" HEIGHT=14
WIDTH=13 ALIGN="middle"></A><B><A HREF="families.htm">Parents Speak Out About The
Earth School </A></B><BR>
</LI>

<LI><A HREF="aae.htm"><IMG SRC="bb1.gif" NATURALSIZEFLAG="0" HEIGHT=14 WIDTH=13
ALIGN="middle"</A><B><A HREF="aae.htm">What Every Kid Is Asking About The
Earth</A></B> <BR>
</LI>

<LI><A HREF="eeg.htm"><IMG SRC="bb1.gif" NATURALSIZEFLAG="0" HEIGHT=14 WIDTH=13
ALIGN="middle"></A><B><A HREF="eeg.htm">Other
Environmental Education Groups</A></B><BR>
</LI>

<LI><A HREF="eh.htm"><IMG SRC="bb1.gif" NATURALSIZEFLAG="0" HEIGHT=14 WIDTH=13
ALIGN="middle"></A><B><A HREF="eh.htm">Earth
Friendly Humor</A></B></LI>
</UL>

<P>
<HR ALIGN=LEFT></P>

<CENTER><P>600 East 6th Street<BR>
New York, NY 10009<BR>
<B><A HREF="sea.htm">EMail: earths@mail.con2.com<BR>

<HR></A></B>All rights reserved.&copy; The Earth School 1996-1997 
</P></CENTER>

</BODY>
</HTML>
```

Throughout this example, I will show the relationships between the pages in the site. Today, when you are writing HTML, you almost never create just a single page; it is important to see the how the links are structured on a given site. One of the better Web site management tools is FrontPage 97 by Microsoft. The FrontPage Editor is a very robust, up-to-the-minute WYSIWYG editor capable of handling Java, ActiveX, JavaScript, and standard HTML. The other half of the program is called FrontPage Explorer and, as you can see in Figure 10.10, it does an excellent job illustrating the Web structure. The icon labeled "Home at The Earth School" is the page depicted a moment ago. All the icons to the right represent each of the links on the page. There are other valuable views within FrontPage Explorer, but this discussion concentrates on the Web structure view.

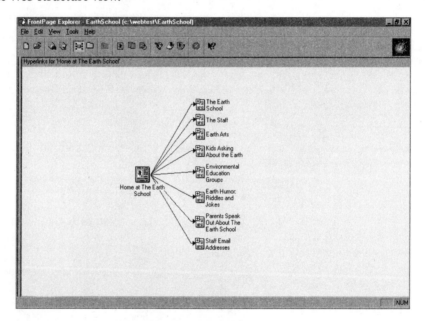

Figure 10.10: Earth School Links from the home page.

Now let's follow the link to the Staff page. As you can see in Figure 10.11, this is a very simple page that follows a basic formula. The various staff members are listed under their grades or duties, which are fashioned as links. This page does double-duty as a directory and navigation center. The sole graphic on the page is a link back to the home page with a small inline earth image. Using the image in place of words is effective, especially when the ALIGN attribute in the IMG tag is set to "middle".

```
<!DOCTYPE HTML PUBLIC "-//IETF//DTD HTML//EN">
<html>
```

EXAMPLE 6—INSIDE AN EXTRANET   **315**

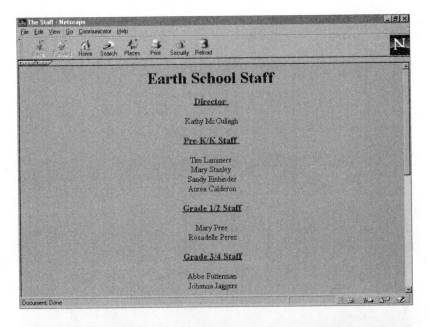

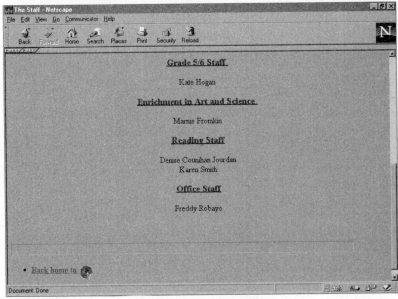

Figure 10.11: The Staff page of the Earth School site

```
<head>
<title>The Staff</title>
</head>

<body bgcolor="#C59C9A">

<h1 align="center">Earth School Staff</h1>

<h3 align="center"><a href="director.htm">Director </a></h3>

<p align="center">Kathy McCullagh</p>

<h3 align="center"><a href="Pre-KK.htm">Pre-K/K Staff </a></h3>

<p align="center">Tim Lammers <br>
Mary Stanley <br>
Sandy Einbinder<br>
Aurea Calderon</p>

<h3 align="center"><a href="Grade12.htm">Grade 1/2 Staff</a></h3>

<p align="center">Mary Pree <br>
Rosadelle Perez</p>

<h3 align="center"><a href="Grade34.htm">Grade 3/4 Staff</a></h3>

<p align="center">Abbe Futterman <br>
Johanna Jaggers</p>

<h3 align="center"><a href="Grade56.htm">Grade 5/6 Staff </a></h3>

<p align="center">Kate Hogan</p>

<h3 align="center"><a href="enrich.htm">Enrichment in Art and
Science </a></h3>

<p align="center">Marnie Fromkin</p>

<h3 align="center"><a href="reading.htm">Reading Staff</a></h3>

<p align="center">Denise Counihan Jourdan<br>
Karen Smith</p>

<h3 align="center"><a href="office.htm">Office Staff</a></h3>

<p align="center">Freddy Robayo</p>
```

EXAMPLE 6—INSIDE AN EXTRANET **317**

```
<p> </p>

<hr size="21" align="left" width="91%">

<ul>
    <li><a href="index.htm"><b>Back home to </b></a><a

        href="index.htm"><img src="earthbuttongifs/image9.gif"
        align="middle" border="0" width="32" height="32"
        naturalsizeflag="3"></a></li>
</ul>
</body>
</html>
```

As you can see from Figure 10.12, the links from the staff page are quite extensive and the Web site is beginning to grow. Notice how FrontPage includes all the links, including the one back to the Earth School's home page. Next we'll follow the link from the staff page to Kate Hogan's class page, the 5/6 grades.

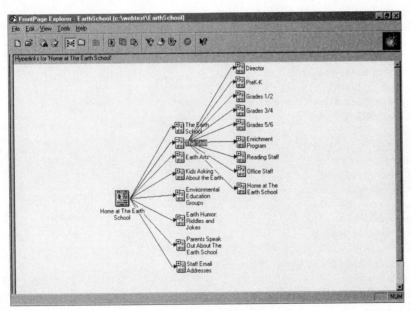

Figure 10.12: The links from the home page to the staff page

The 5th/6th grade page (Figure 10.13) opens with an digital self-portrait of the teacher, Kate Hogan. Kate is very interested in digital photography and her images from school events are easily included as JPEG files on the Web site. Further down the page, there is a numbered list that is coded with the <OL> tag. In the first line of the listing, an image tag is inserted. This serves to break up the block of text. By aligning the image to the right with the ALIGN attribute, a wrapped text effect is achieved. You could also use a <BR CLEAR="all"> tag after the text in combination with ALIGN="right" to cause all the text to wrap away from the picture.

The mailto reference at the bottom of the page could have been handled better. There really is no need to repeat the e-mail address when linking to a mailto because clicking on the link will bring up the e-mail form. A better solution would be to incorporate the mailto link in a more natural way, such as:

```
<P ALIGN="center">: <A HREF="mailto:earths@mail.con2.com">Email for the
Serendipity Class</A></P>
```

Here is the full code for the Grade 5/6 page of the Earth School Web site.

```
<!DOCTYPE HTML PUBLIC "-//IETF//DTD HTML//EN">
<html>

<head>
<meta http-equiv="Content-Type"
content="text/html; charset=iso-8859-1">
<meta name="GENERATOR" content="Microsoft FrontPage 2.0">
<title>Grades 5/6</title>
</head>

<body bgcolor="#8A5552">

<p align="center"><img src="Kate.gif" width="158" height="117"
naturalsizeflag="3"><br>
Kate Hogan<br>
Teacher and Co-Founder </p>

<h4 align="center">Fifth and Sixth Grade <br>
Grade 5/6<br>
&quot;The Serendipity Class&quot;<br>
Goals, Expectations, Curriculum <br>
<br>
Social/Personal </h4>

<ol>
    <li>Each class member honors and appreciates the personal,
        cultural and academic differences of all other members.</li>
```

EXAMPLE 6—INSIDE AN EXTRANET   **319**

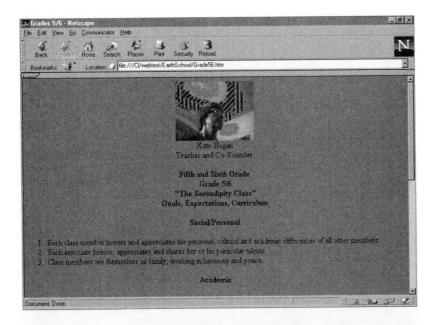

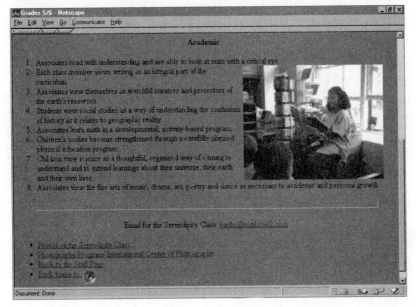

Figure 10.13: The 5ᵗʰ/6ᵗʰ Grade page of the Earth School site

```
    <li>Each associate honors, appreciates and shares her or his
        particular talents. </li>
    <li>Class members see themselves as family, working in
        harmony and peace. </li>
</ol>

<h4 align="center">Academic </h4>

<ol>
    <li>Associates read with understanding and are able to look
        at texts with a critical eye.<img src="BelenReading.gif"
        align="right" hspace="5" width="300" height="226"></li>
    <li>Each class member views writing as an integral part of
        the curriculum.</li>
    <li>Associates view themselves as watchful curators and
        protectors of the earth's resources.</li>
    <li>Students view social studies as a way of understanding
        the continuum of history as it relates to geographic
        reality.</li>
    <li>Associates learn math in a developmental, activity-based
        program.</li>
    <li>Children's bodies become strengthened through a carefully
        planned physical education program.</li>
    <li>Children view science as a thoughtful, organized way of
        coming to understand and to extend learnings about their
        universe, their earth and their own lives. </li>
    <li>Associates view the fine arts of music, drama, art,
        poetry and dance as necessary to academic and personal
        growth</li>
</ol>

<hr size="13" width="91%">

<p align="center">Email for the Serendipity Class: <a

href="mailto:earths@mail.con2.com">earths@mail.con2.com</a><br>
</p>

<ul>
    <li><a href="56Photo.htm">Photos of the Serendipity Class</a><br>
        </li>
    <li><a href="ICP.htm">Photography Program/ International
        Center of Photography</a><br>
        </li>
    <li><a href="staff.htm">Back to the Staff Page</a> <br>
        </li>
    <li><a href="index.htm">Back home to </a><a href="index.htm"><img
```

EXAMPLE 6—INSIDE AN EXTRANET   **321**

```
        src="earthbuttongifs/IMAGE9.GIF" align="middle"
        border="0" width="32" height="32" naturalsizeflag="3"></a></li>
</ul>
</body>
</html>
```

One of the nicer features of FrontPage is that it depicts all the links—
whether they are to other pages on the Web site, other external Web sites, or, as
in Figure 10.14, mailto addresses.

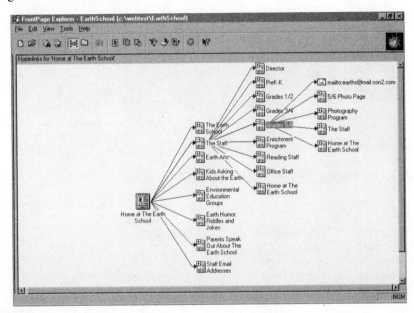

Figure 10.14: Three levels deep into the Earth School site

Our final stop on the Earth School Web site is the page covering the photography program. As shown in Figure 10.15, this clean layout uses a combination of text sizes and graphic images to introduce the page's concept and then
tell a brief story. The HTML code includes a two-column table with a +4 font
size on the left, which balances the images, and phrases on the right. The right
column stacks the images and captions one above the other, alternating the
image placement.

```
<!DOCTYPE HTML PUBLIC "-//IETF//DTD HTML//EN">
<html>
```

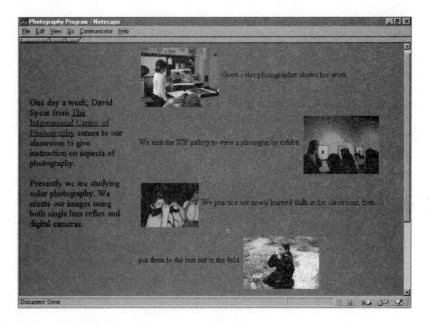

Figure 10.15: The photography program at The Earth School

```
<head>
<meta http-equiv="Content-Type"
content="text/html; charset=iso-8859-1">
<meta name="GENERATOR" content="Microsoft FrontPage 2.0">
<title>Photography Program</title>
</head>

<body bgcolor="#D56926">
<div align="right">

<table border="0" cellpadding="10">
    <tr>
        <td width="25%"><font size="4">One day a week, David
        Spear from </font><a href="http://www.icp.org"><font

        size="4">The International Center of Photography</font></a><font

        size="4"> comes to our classroom to give instruction on
        aspects of photography. </font><p><font size="4">Presently
        we are studying color photography. We create our images
        using both single lens reflex and digital cameras.</font></p>
        </td>
```

Example 6—Inside an Extranet **323**

```
      <td><img src="Nina.gif" align="middle" hspace="5"
      width="156" height="117" naturalsizeflag="0">Guest color
      photographer shows her work.<br>
      <br>
      We visit the ICP gallery to view a photography exhibit.<img

      src="Cynthia.gif" align="middle" hspace="5" width="152"
      height="115" naturalsizeflag="0"><br>
      <br>
      <img src="Abaddon.gif" align="middle" hspace="5"
      width="116" height="87" naturalsizeflag="0">We practice
      our newly learned skills in the classroom, then.....<br>
      <br>
      put them to the test out in the field.<img src="Kat.gif"
      align="middle" hspace="5" width="154" height="104"
      naturalsizeflag="0"></td>
    </tr>
</table>
</div>

<p><br>
<br>
<br>
</p>

<hr size="13" align="left">

<ul>
    <li><a href="Grade56.htm">Back to the 5/6 Page</a> </li>
</ul>

<p><br>
<br>
</p>
</body>
</html>
```

Figure 10.16 traces our path through the Earth School Web site from the home page to the photography program. Notice that the external link to www.ICP.com is shown as well as all the internal links.

As a parting note, let me put in my vote for an HTML programmer's favorite browser function. Actually, it's a tie between View Source and Save As. View Source is great for gleaning a quick answer to the ever-possible question, "How did they do that?" The Save As command makes standing on the shoulders of giants truly possible. When you come across a really impressive site,

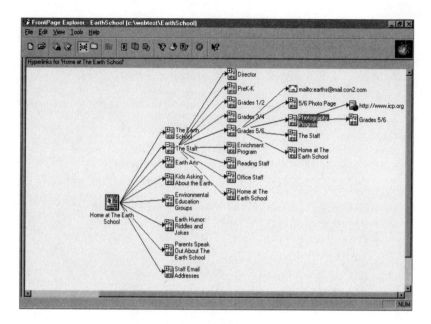

Figure 10.16: Links from the home page to the photography program

download the code and take a close look. Then take the lessons you've learned and build your next site. You'll find yourself learning at an amazing rate—and producing world-class Web sites.

Appendix A:
HTML Quick Reference

The following listing of HTML markup elements is taken from the HTML 3.2 specification and the release notes from both Netscape Navigator 3.0 and Microsoft Internet Explorer 3.0. It should be considered neither definitive nor 100 percent complete; rather, it's a compact guide to the most useful and commonly found features of Hypertext Markup Language.

Markup Tags

The presentation of each markup element includes the syntax of the tag, a short description, and the attributes that can be specified with the tag. The syntax description takes one of two forms, for example:

<IMG>	Indicates an empty tag.
<H1>...</H1>	Indicates a container or nonempty tag. The ellipsis (...) stands for some portion (possibly none) of the document's content.

Attributes take one of two forms: Either *attribute="value"*, where *value* is some text enclosed in quotes, or, just simply, *attribute*, without a value. In the table that follows, value may take one of the following forms:

url	The value is a Uniform Resource Locator.
name	The value is a name supplied by the user.
number	The value is a number supplied by the user.

percent	The value is a percentage (*number*%).
pixels	The value is a whole number of pixels.
nchars	The value is a whole number of character positions.
text	The value is a text supplied by the user.
color	The value is an rgb color value (#rrggbb) or color name.
server	The value is server-dependent text.
x,y	The value is a coordinate measured in pixels.
[A | B | ...]	The value is one from a fixed set of values, A, B, ...

COMMON ATTRIBUTES

Attribute	Definition
ALIGN	Specifies the alignment of content with respect to the reader's display window. Possible values are "left", "center", "right", and "justify".
CLASS	Provides a name token that classifies the element and can be addressed in style sheets. The value is an SGML name.
ID	Provides a name for the location of the element on the page that can be referenced by anchors and other HTML elements. The value is an SGML name.
LANG	Designates the language conventions to be used with respect to quotation marks, ligatures, and scan direction.

DOCUMENT STRUCTURE

The basic document structure tags are required for an HTML document. Although some browsers may accept code without one or more of these tags, there is no guarantee that future browser releases will continue to be so forgiving.

Tag	Description	Attributes
<!DOCTYPE...>	Document type	

Tag	Description	Attributes
\<BODY>...\</BODY>	Designates the content of an HTML document	BGCOLOR=color BACKGROUND=url TEXT=color LINK=color ALINK=color VLINK=color
\<HEAD>...\</HEAD>	Defines the head of the document, the part containing information about the page	
\<HTML>...\</HTML>	Defines the beginning and the end of an HTML document	

STYLE MARKUP

Style markup is permitted within all other HTML markup. You should avoid structural markup within style markup. In the following descriptions of HTML markup, a code indicates the source: (N) means the feature is a Netscape extension, (IE) means the feature is an Internet Explorer extension, and (D) means the feature is depreciated and has fallen from general use. Otherwise, the feature is from the HTML 3.2 specification.

Tag	Description	Attributes
\<B>...\</B>	Bold style	
\<BASEFONT>	Basefont	SIZE=number [1-7]
\<BIG>...\</BIG>	Big; display text with a larger font	
\<BLINK>...\</BLINK>	Blinking text (N)	
\<CITE>...\</CITE>	Citation style; for titles of other works	
\<CODE>...\</CODE>	Coding style; for samples of computer programs	

Tag	Description	Attributes
<DFN>...</DFN>	The defining instance of a term	
<EM>...</EM>	Emphasis	
<FONT>...</FONT>	Specifies font attributes	SIZE=±number COLOR=color FACE=name (IE only)
<I>...</I>	Italics style	
<KBD>...</KBD>	Keyboard style for text to be keyed exactly as given (D)	
<SAMP>...</SAMP>	Sample style; used for examples	
<SMALL>...</SMALL>	Small style; display text using a smaller font	
<STRIKE>...</STRIKE>	Strikethrough style	
<STRONG>...</STRONG>	Strong emphasis style	
_{...}	Subscript	
^{...}	Superscript	
<TT>...</TT>	Typewriter style	
<U>...</U>	Underline	
<VAR>...</VAR>	Variable style; for names to be supplied by reader	

STRUCTURAL MARKUP

With only a few exceptions, you should avoid structural markup inside of other structural markup. The exceptions are the <CENTER>, <DIV>, <DD>, <DT>, <FIGURE>, <FORM>, <TH>, and <TD> tags, which you can use within any other markup.

Page Markup

Tag	Description	Attributes
<BASE>	Base; provides a reference to resolve relative addressing	HREF=url TARGET=text (IE,N)
<ISINDEX>	Indicates that a searchable index for the document is available on the server	
<LINK>	Provides information relating the current document to other documents or entities	HREF=url TITLE=text REL=server REV=server
<META>	Sends an http command to the server	HTTP-EQUIV=server CONTENT=number; url
<STYLE>... </STYLE>	Allows inclusion of style sheet information	TITLE=text TYPE=text
<TITLE>... </TITLE>	Document title; must be in document head	

Hypertext Links

Tag	Description	Attributes
<A>...</A>	Anchor; marks the start (HREF) or end (NAME) of a link	HREF=url NAME=name TARGET=name (IE,N)
<MAP>... </MAP>	Provides links for client-side imagemaps	NAME=name
<AREA>	Defines an area within an imagemap	ALT=name COORDS=x,y,x,y HREF=url NOHREF SHAPE=[rect I rectangle I circ I circle I poly I polygon] TARGET=name (IE,N)

Inline Images and Sound

Tag	Description	Attributes
<BGSOUND>	Sound; plays a sound or music file (WAV or MIDI format) (IE)	LOOP=nchars SRC=url
<IMG>	Image; used to place an inline image into the page	SRC=url ALT=text ISMAP ALIGN=[left | right | top | texttop | middle | absmiddle | baseline | bottom | absbottom] BORDER=pixels HEIGHT=pixels WIDTH=pixels HSPACE=pixels VSPACE=pixels USEMAP VRML=url (IE,N)

Block Elements

Tag	Description	Attributes
<ADDRESS>...</ADDRESS>	Address style; used for addresses, signatures, authorship info, and so on	
<BLOCKQUOTE>...</BLOCKQUOTE>	For material quoted from an external source	
 	Line break; starts a new line	
<CENTER>...</CENTER>	Center page content	
<DIV>...</DIV>	Division; for classifying a subsection of the document	

Tag	Description	Attributes
<H1>...</H1>	Level 1 heading	
<H2>...</H2>	Level 2 heading	
<H3>...</H3>	Level 3 heading	
<H4>...</H4>	Level 4 heading	
<H5>...</H5>	Level 5 heading	
<H6>...</H6>	Level 6 heading	
<HR>	Horizontal rule; draws a line across the page	SIZE=pixels WIDTH=percent NOSHADE
<PRE>...</PRE>	Preformatted style	WIDTH=nchars
<P>...</P>	Paragraph break	

List Elements

Tag	Description	Attributes
<DIR>...</DIR>	Directory list; used for lists typically containing short items such as filenames; uses <LI> (D)	
<DL>...</DL>	Definition list; used for glossaries; uses <DT> and <DD>	
<DD>...</DD>	Definition description; part of a definition list item	
<DT>...</DT>	Definition term; part of a definition list item	
<LI>...</LI>	List item	
<MENU>...</MENU>	Menu list; uses <LI> (D)	
<OL>...</OL>	Ordered list; uses <LI>	START=number TYPE=name
<UL>...</UL>	Unordered list; uses <LI>	TYPE=[disc | circle | square]

Table Elements

Tag	Description	Attributes
<CAPTION>...</CAPTION>	Defines a caption to a table	ALIGN=[TOP | BOTTOM]
<TABLE>...</TABLE>	Defines a table	ALIGN=[left | right] BACKGROUND=url (IE) BGCOLOR=color (IE,N) BORDER=pixels BORDERCOLOR=color (IE) BORDERCOLORDARK=color (IE) BORDERCOLORLIGHT=color (IE) CELLSPACING=pixels CELLPADDING=pixels FRAME=[void | above | below | hsides | lhs | rhs | vsides | box] (IE) HEIGHT=pixels | percent (IE) RULES=[none | basic | rows |
<TBODY>...</TBODY>	Table body section (IE)	
<TD>...</TD>	Table data cell	ROWSPAN=number COLSPAN=number ALIGN=[LEFT | CENTER | RIGHT] VALIGN=[TOP | MIDDLE | BOTTOM]
<TFOOT>...</TFOOT>	Table footer section (IE)	
<TH>...</TH>	Table header cell; contents bold and centered	ROWSPAN=number COLSPAN=number ALIGN=[LEFT | CENTER | RIGHT] VALIGN=[TOP | MIDDLE | BOTTOM]

Tag	Description	Attributes
<THEAD>...</THEAD>	Table head section (IE)	
<TR>...</TR>	Table row	ALIGN=[LEFT | CENTER | RIGHT] VALIGN=[TOP | MIDDLE | BOTTOM]

Form Elements

Tag	Description	Attributes
<FORM>...</FORM>	Input form; for defining an area on the page to contain objects for input from the reader	ACTION=url METHOD=[GET | POST] ENCTYPE=name
<INPUT>	Defines an input object in a form	ALIGN=[Left | Right | Top | Texttop | Middle | Absmiddle | Baseline | Bottom | Absbottom] CHECKED HEIGHT=pixels MAXLENGTH=nchars NAME=name SIZE=nchars SRC=url TYPE=[TEXT | CHECKBOX | RADIO | SUBMIT | RESET | HIDDEN | IMAGE] VALUE=text WIDTH=pixels
<OPTION>...</OPTION>	Defines an item for a SELECT input object	SELECTED
<SELECT>...</SELECT>	Selection input object, pop-up menu	NAME=name SIZE=number MULTIPLE

Tag	Description	Attributes
<TEXTAREA>... </TEXTAREA>	Multiline input object	NAME=name ROWS=number COLS=nchars

FRAMES

Although frames are not a HTML 3.2 standard feature, they are in widespread use. This reference is provided as a guide to current usage. Please refer to Chapter 8 for more information.

Tag	Description	Attributes
<FRAME>... </FRAME>	Single frame definition	FRAMEBORDER=[yes | no] FRAMESPACING=pixels (IE) MARGINWIDTH=pixels MARGINHEIGHT=pixels NORESIZE NAME=[name | _blank | _self | _parent | _top] SCROLLING=[yes | no | auto] SRC=url
<FRAMESET>... </FRAMESET>	Main division for a frame	ROWS=[pixels | percent | * | nchars*] COLS==[pixels | percent | * | nchars*]
<NOFRAMES>... </NOFRAMES>	Displays alternative content for browsers not frame-enabled	

CHARACTER ENTITIES

To correctly render characters that do not appear on the standard keyboard (Latin 1 Characters) and characters used to note HTML tags (markup entities), HTML uses a system known as character entities. Unlike markup tag and attribute names, character entities are case sensitive.

MARKUP ENTITIES

Definition	How It Appears	Entity
less than	<	&lt;
greater than	>	&gt;
ampersand	&	&amp;
quote	"	&quot;
copyright	©	&copy;
registered	®	&reg;
nonbreaking space		

LATIN 1 CHARACTERS

Definition	How It Appears	Entity
Uppercase AE diphthong (ligature)	Æ	&AElig;
Uppercase A, acute accent	Á	&Aacute;
Uppercase A, circumflex accent	Â	&Acirc;
Uppercase A, grave accent	À	&Agrave;
Uppercase A, ring	Å	&Aring;
Uppercase A, tilde	Ã	&Atilde;
Uppercase A, dieresis or umlaut mark	Ä	&Atilde;
Uppercase C, cedilla	Ç	&Ccedil;
Uppercase E, acute accent	É	&Eacute;
Uppercase E, circumflex accent	Ê	&Ecirc;
Uppercase E, grave accent	È	&Egrave;
Uppercase E, dieresis or umlaut mark	Ë	&Euml;
Uppercase I, acute accent	Í	&Iacute;
Uppercase I, circumflex accent	Î	&Icirc;
Uppercase I, grave accent	Ì	&Igrave;

Definition	How It Appears	Entity
Uppercase I, dieresis or umlaut mark	Ï	&Iuml;
Uppercase N, tilde	Ñ	&Ntilde;
Uppercase O, acute accent	Ó	&Oacute;
Uppercase O, circumflex accent	Ô	&Ocirc;
Uppercase O, grave accent	Ò	&Ograve;
Uppercase O, slash	Ø	&Oslash;
Uppercase O, tilde	Õ	&Otilde;
Uppercase O, dieresis or umlaut mark	Ö	&Ouml;
Uppercase U, acute accent	Ú	&Uacute;
Uppercase U, circumflex accent	Û	&Ucirc;
Uppercase U, grave accent	Ù	&Ugrave;
Uppercase U, dieresis or umlaut mark	Ü	&Uuml;
Uppercase Y, acute accent	Y	&Yacute;
Lowercase a, acute accent	á	&aacute;
Lowercase a, circumflex accent	â	&acirc;
Lowercase ae diphthong (ligature)	æ	&aelig;
Lowercase a, grave accent	à	&agrave;
Lowercase a, ring	å	&aring;
Lowercase a, tilde	ã	&atilde;
Lowercase a, dieresis or umlaut mark	ä	&auml;
Lowercase c, cedilla	ç	&ccedil;
Lowercase e, acute accent	é	&eacute;
Lowercase e, circumflex accent	ê	&ecirc;
Lowercase e, grave accent	è	&egrave;

Definition	How It Appears	Entity
Lowercase e, dieresis or umlaut mark	ë	&euml;
Lowercase i, acute accent	í	&iacute;
Lowercase i, circumflex accent	î	&icirc;
Lowercase i, grave accent	ì	&igrave;
Lowercase i, dieresis or umlaut mark	ï	&iuml;
Lowercase n, tilde	ñ	&ntilde;
Lowercase o, acute accent	ó	&oacute;
Lowercase o, circumflex accent	ô	&ocirc;
Lowercase o, grave accent	ò	&ograve;
Lowercase o, slash	ø	&oslash;
Lowercase o, tilde	õ	&otilde;
Lowercase o, dieresis or umlaut mark	ö	&ouml;
Lowercase sharp s, German, (commonly substituted for the sz ligature)	ß	&szlig;
Lowercase u, acute accent	ú	&uacute;
Lowercase u, circumflex accent	û	&ucirc;
Lowercase u, grave accent	ù	&ugrave;
Lowercase u, dieresis or umlaut mark	ü	&uuml;
Lowercase y, acute accent	y	&yacute;
Lowercase y, dieresis or umlaut mark	ÿ	&yuml;

NUMBERED CHARACTER ENTITIES

Decimal Code	Character	Description
&#00; - &#08;		Unused
&#09;		Horizontal tab
&#10;		Line feed
&#13;		Carriage return
&#11; through 		Unused
&#32;		Space
&#33;	!	Exclamation point
&#34;	"	Quotation mark
&#35;	#	Number sign
&#36;	$	Dollar sign
&#37;	%	Percent sign
&#38;	&	Ampersand
&#39;	'	Apostrophe
&#40;	(	Left parenthesis
&#41;	)	Right parenthesis
&#42;	*	Asterisk
&#43;	+	Plus sign
&#44;	,	Comma
&#14; through &#31;		Unused
&#45;	-	Hyphen
&#46;	.	Period (fullstop)
&#47;	/	Solidus
0 through 9	0 through 9	Decimal digits
&#58;	:	Colon

Decimal Code	Character	Description
&#59;	;	Semicolon
&#60;	<	Less than
&#61;	=	Equal sign
&#62;	>	Greater than
&#63;	?	Question mark
&#64;	@	Commercial at sign
A through Z	A through Z	Uppercase letters
&#91;	[	Left square bracket
&#92;	\	Reverse solidus (backslash)
&#93;	]	Right square bracket
&#94;	^	Caret
&#95;	_	Horizontal bar
&#96;	`	Grave accent
a through z	a through z	Lowercase letters
&#123;	{	Left curly brace
|	|	Vertical bar
&#125;	}	Right curly brace
&#126;	~	Tilde
&#127; through Ÿ		Unused
	†	Nonbreaking space
&#161;	¡	Inverted exclamation point
&#162;	¢	Cent sign
&#163;	£	Pound sterling
&#164;	¤	General currency sign
&#165;	¥	Yen sign

Decimal Code	Character	Description
&#166;	¦	Broken vertical bar
&#167;	§	Section sign
&#168;	¨	Umlaut
&#169;	©	Copyright
&#170;	ª	Feminine ordinal
&#171;	«	Left angle quote
&#172;	¬	Not sign
&#173;	—	Soft hyphen
&#174;	®	Registered trademark
&#175;	¯	Macron accent
&#176;	°	Degree sign
&#177;	±	Plus or minus
&#178;	2	Superscript two
&#179;	3	Superscript three
&#180;	´	Acute accent
&#181;	µ	Micro sign
&#182;	¶	Paragraph sign
&#183;	·	Middle dot
&#184;	¸	Cedilla
&#185;	1	Superscript one
&#186;	º	Masculine ordinal
&#187;	»	Right angle quote
&#188;	¼	Fraction one-fourth
&#189;	½	Fraction one-half
&#190;	¾	Fraction three-fourths
&#191;	¿	Inverted question mark
&#192;	À	Capital A, grave accent

Decimal Code	Character	Description
&#193;	Á	Capital A, acute accent
&#194;	Â	Capital A, circumflex accent
&#195;	Ã	Capital A, tilde
&#196;	Ä	Capital A, dieresis or umlaut mark
&#197;	Å	Capital A, ring
&#198;	Æ	Capital AE diphthong (ligature)
&#199;	Ç	Capital C, cedilla
&#200;	È	Capital E, grave accent
&#201;	É	Capital E, acute accent
&#202;	Ê	Capital E, circumflex accent
&#203;	Ë	Capital E, dieresis or umlaut mark
&#204;	Ì	Capital I, grave accent
&#205;	Í	Capital I, acute accent
&#206;	Î	Capital I, circumflex accent
&#207;	Ï	Capital I, dieresis or umlaut mark
&#208;	‹	Capital Eth, Icelandic
&#209;	Ñ	Capital N, tilde
&#210;	Ò	Capital O, grave accent
&#211;	Ó	Capital O, acute accent
&#212;	Ô	Capital O, circumflex accent
&#213;	Õ	Capital O, tilde
&#214;	Ö	Capital O, dieresis or umlaut mark
&#215;	x	Multiply sign
&#216;	Ø	Capital O, slash
&#217;	Ù	Capital U, grave accent
&#218;	Ú	Capital U, acute accent
&#219;	Û	Capital U, circumflex accent

Decimal Code	Character	Description
&#220;	Ü	Capital U, dieresis or umlaut mark
&#221;	Ý	Capital Y, acute accent
&#222;	fi	Capital THORN, Icelandic
&#223;	ß	Small sharp s, German (sz ligature)
&#224;	à	Small a, grave accent
&#225;	á	Small a, acute accent
&#226;	â	Small a, circumflex accent
&#227;	ã	Small a, tilde
&#228;	ä	Small a, dieresis or umlaut mark
&#229;	å	Small a, ring
&#230;	æ	Small ae dipthong (ligature)
&#231;	ç	Small c, cedilla
&#232;	è	Small e, grave accent
&#233;	é	Small e, acute accent
&#234;	ê	Small e, circumflex accent
&#235;	ë	Small e, dieresis or umlaut mark
&#236;	ì	Small i, grave accent
&#237;	í	Small i, acute accent
&#238;	î	Small i, circumflex accent
&#239;	ï	Small i, dieresis or umlaut mark
&#240;	›	Small eth, Icelandic
&#241;	ñ	Small n, tilde
&#242;	ò	Small o, grave accent
&#243;	ó	Small o, acute accent
&#244;	ô	Small o, circumflex accent
&#245;	õ	Small o, tilde
&#246;	ö	Small o, dieresis or umlaut mark

Decimal Code	Character	Description
&#247;	÷	Division sign
&#248;	ø	Small o, slash
&#249;	ù	Small u, grave accent
&#250;	ú	Small u, acute accent
&#251;	û	Small u, circumflex accent
&#252;	ü	Small u, dieresis or umlaut mark
&#253;	ý	Small y, acute accent
&#254;	fl	Small thorn, Icelandic
&#255;	ÿ	Small y, dieresis or umlaut mark

Appendix B:
Cascading Style Sheet
Reference

This reference guide is based on the Cascading Style Sheet Level 1 (CSS1) recommendation issued by the World Wide Web Consortium. Currently, the browser implementation is limited, but anticipated to increase. For more details see Chapter 8.

Selectors

Cascading Style Sheets use the *selector* to indicate which part of an HTML document can be altered by the following declaration. The different kinds of selectors are listed here.

Type	Description	Example
Tag	Any HTML tags	H1,EM,BLOCKQUOTE
Class	Document specific, defined in HTML tag attribute CLASS	<P CLASS=contract>
Pseudo-Class	Used to relate styles to different element types, based on user actions	A:link (unvisited links) A:visited (visited links) A:active (active links)
Pseudo-Element	Used to relate styles to different element parts, contextually based	P:first-letter (first letter of a paragraph) P:first-line (first line of a paragraph

Properties

Cascading Style Sheet *properties* define what part of the selector is being altered. The following table lists the CSS1 properties, their possible values, and whether or not they can be inherited. Where applicable, the default is in **bold** type. Values appearing in angle brackets (< and >) represent CSS1-specific values, which appear the first time in square brackets.

Font Properties

Properties	Values	Inherited
font-family	Any font, any generic font [serif | sans-serif | cursive | fantasy | monospace]	No
font-style	**normal** | italic | oblique	Yes
font-variant	**normal** | small-caps	Yes
font-weight	**normal** | bold | bolder | lighter | 100 | 200 | 300 | 400 | 500 | 600 | 700 | 800 | 900	Yes
font-size	<absolute-size> [xx-small | x-small | small | medium | large | x-large | xx-large]| <relative-size> [larger | smaller] | | <length> | <percentage>	Yes

Color and Background Properties

Properties	Values	Inherited
color	name=[one of 16 values] hexadecimal=#rrggbb decimal=rgb(r,g,b) percent=rgb(r%,g%,b%)	Yes
background-color	**transparent** | <color>	No
background-image	<url> | none	No
background-repeat	repeat | repeat-x | repeat-y | no-repeat	No
background-attachment	scroll | fixed	No

Properties	Values	Inherited
background-position	[<percentage> I <length>]I [top I center I bottom] II [left I center I right]	No

Text Properties

Properties	Values	Inherited
word-spacing	**normal** I <length>	Yes
letter-spacing	**normal** I <length>	Yes
text-decoration	**none** I [underline I overline I line-through I blink]	No
vertical-align	**baseline** I sub I super I top I text-top I middle I bottom I text-bottom I <percentage>	No
text-transform	**none** I capitalize I uppercase I lowercase	Yes
text-align	left I right I center I justify	Yes
text-indent	<length> I <percentage>	Yes
line-height	**normal** I <number> I <length> I <percentage>	Yes

Box Properties

Properties	Values	Inherited
margin-top	<length> I <percentage> I auto	No
margin-bottom	<length> I <percentage> I auto	No
margin-right	<length> I <percentage> I auto	No
margin-left	<length> I <percentage> I auto	No
padding-top	<length> I <percentage>	No
padding-bottom	<length> I <percentage>	No
padding-right	<length> I <percentage>	No

Properties	Values	Inherited
padding-left	<length>	<percentage>	No
border-top-width	thin	medium	thick	<length>	No
border-right-width	thin	medium	thick	<length>	No
border-left-width	thin	medium	thick	<length>	No
border-bottom-width	thin	medium	thick	<length>	No
border-width	[thin	medium	thick	<length>]	No
border-color	<color> (up to four values denoting top, right, bottom, left, respectively)	No
border-style	[none	dotted	dashed	solid	double	groove	ridge	inset	outset] (up to four values denoting top, right, bottom, left, respectively)	No
width	<length>	auto	No
height	<length>	auto	No
float	left	right	**none**	No
clear	none	left	right	both	No

List Properties

Properties	Values	Inherited
list-style-type	**disc**	circle	square	decimal	lower-roman	upper-roman	lower-alpha	upper-alpha	none	Yes
list-style-image	<url>	none	Yes
list-style-position	inside	outside	Yes

Appendix C: Resources

O ne of the most thoroughly documented areas of knowledge within the World Wide Web is the Web itself. The first part of this appendix contains an extensive, but by no means exhaustive, listing of URLs that you can use to tap into the Web-based knowledge bank. The second section will guide you to some of the many Web development tools available. Finally, the third part gives you the Internet addresses for newsgroups devoted to Web development.

As always, keep in mind that the Web is a very dynamic organism and all the URLs listed below are subject to change.

Web-Based Information

This section lists Web addresses for some of the useful information resources on the Internet, the World Wide Web, HTML, and Web development. You can also use this book's Web site as a "launching pad" for accessing any of these URLs; all of the links are live online. Start your journey at www.mcp.com/zd-press/features/5299/.

General Guides to Cyberspace

The Clearinghouse for Subject-Oriented Internet Resource Guides
    http://www.clearinghouse.net/

The Virtual Library: Subject Catalogue
    http://www.w3.org/pub/DataSources/bySubject/Overview.html

A Guide to Cyberspace
  http://www.hcc.hawaii.edu/guide/www.guide.html

Internet Resources Meta-Index
  http://www.ncsa.uiuc.edu/SDG/Software/Mosaic/MetaIndex.html

InterNIC Directory Services
  http://www.internic.net/

The Awesome List
  http://www.clark.net/pub/journalism/awesome.html

Nuttin' but Links
  http://pages.prodigy.com/bombadil/home.htm

Oneworld Directory
  http://oneworld.wa.com/

The Learned InfoNet
  http://info.learned.co.uk/

Charm Net Home Page
  http://www.charm.net/

Planet Earth Home Page
  http://www.nosc.mil/planet_earth/www.html

The World Wide Web

World Wide Web Home Page
  http://www.w3.org/

World Wide Web Servers
  http://www.w3.org/hypertext/DataSources/WWW/
  Geographical.html

Entering the World-Wide Web: A Guide to Cyberspace
  http://www.eit.com/web/www.guide/

Technical Aspects of the World-Wide Web
  http://www.w3.org/pub/WWW/Technical.html

WWW Search Services

WWW Search Engines
http://pubweb.nexor.co.uk/public/cusi/cusi.html

Lycos Search Engine
http://www.lycos.com/

Excite
http://www.excite.com/

AltaVista
http://www.altavista.com/

Yahoo
http://www.yahoo.com/

The WORLD WIDE WEB WORM
http://wwww.cs.colorado.edu/wwww

HTML

Introduction to HTML
http://www.cwru.edu/help/introHTML/toc.html

A Beginner's Guide to HTML
http://www.ncsa.uiuc.edu/General/Internet/WWW/
HTMLPrimer.html

HyperText Markup Language
http://www.w3.org/pub/WWW/MarkUp/MarkUp.html

Style Guide for Online Hypertext
http://www.w3.org/hypertext/WWW/Provider/Style/Overview.html

HTML Design Guide
http://ncdesign.kyushu-id.ac.jp/

MacMillan HTML Workshop
http://www.mcp.com/general/workshop

HTML Design Notebook
http://www.w3.org/hypertext/WWW/People/Connolly/drafts/
html-design.html

Netscape's Extensions to HTML
http://webreference.com/html3andns/

Web Development

The WWW Developer's Virtual Library
http://WWW.Stars.com/

Archive of HTML Translators
ftp://src.doc.ic.ac.uk/computing/information-systems/www/tools/
translators/

HTML Tools Library
http://www.awa.com/nct/software/webtools.html

The Common Gateway Interface: FORMS
http://hoohoo.ncsa.uiuc.edu/cgi/forms.html

HTML & CGI Unleashed
http://www.december.com/works/hcu.html

Introduction to Webscaping Documentation
http://www.utoronto.ca/webdocs/HTMLdocs/NewHTML/intro.html

Netscape's How to Create Web Services
http://home.netscape.com/home/how-to-create-web-services.html

Netscape Developer's DevEdge Online
http://developer.netscape.com/home.html

Microsoft Developer's Sitebuilder
http://www.microsoft.com/sitebuilder/home-text.asp

WWW Software Products
http://www.w3.org/pub/WWW/Status.html

CERN's Tools for WWW Providers
http://www.w3.org/hypertext/WWW/Tools/

Filters
http://www.w3.org/pub/WWW/Tools/Filters.html

Internet Tools Summary
http://www.december.com/net/tools/index.html

The Server Guide
    http://www.w3.org/hypertext/WWW/Daemon/User/Guide.html

The Common Gateway Interface
    http://hoohoo.ncsa.uiuc.edu/cgi/overview.html

Mosaic 2.0 Fill-Out Form Support
    http://www.ncsa.uiuc.edu/SDG/Software/Mosaic/Docs/fill-out-forms/overview.html

Check Your HTML with WEBlint
    http://www.unipress.com/cgi-bin/WWWeblint

Tools

Not only can you seek out information on the Web, you can also find a wide variety of software tools. Many of the URLs listed here will lead you to downloadable demos or shareware programs that you can use. If you don't find what you're looking for at one site, feel free to follow any available links—surfing the Net is a great way to chance upon new tools.

General Sources

Shareware.Com
    http://www.shareware.com

Strouds
    http://www.strouds.com

TuCows—Internet software for most systems
    http://www.tucows.com/

Browsers

Amaya (CSS1 Browser)
    http://www.w3.org/pub/WWW/Amaya/

Microsoft Internet Explorer
    http://home.microsoft.com/ie/

NCSA Mosaic
    http://www.ncsa.uiuc.edu/SDG/Software/mosaic-w/

Netscape Navigator
http://home.netscape.com/

Plug-Ins

Plug-In Plaza
http://browserwatch.iworld.com/plug-in.html

Plug-In Gallery
http://www2.gol.com/users/oyamada/

Plug-In Today
http://www.hitznet.com/isocket/

Unplugged!
http://www.neca.com/~vmis/plugins.html

Netscape Inline Plug-Ins
http://www.netscape.com/comprod/products/
navigator/version_2.0/plugins/index.html

HTML Editors—Windows

4W Publisher
http://www.4w.com/4wpublisher/

Aardvark Pro
http://www.fbs.aust.com/aardvark.html

Almost Reality's HTML+ Editor
http://www.lm.com/~pdixon/html.html

ANT_HTML
http://mcia.com/ant/

AOLPress
http://www.aolpress.com/press/index.html

Arachnid HTML
http://rhwww.richuish.ac.uk/resource.htm

Aspire
http://www.aspire-x.com/

Atrax, The Web Publisher
http://www.winwareinc.com/atrax.html

Backstage
http://www.iband.com/sotware/backstage/designer/index.html

CGI*Star
http://www.webgenie.com/software/cgistar.html

CMed
http://www.iap.net.au/~cmathes/

CU_HTML.DOT
http://www.cuhk.hk/csc/cu_html/cu_html.htm

DiDa
http://home.netvigator.com/~godfreyk/dida/

Dummy
http://www.sausage.com/dummy.htm

E-Publish Internet
http://www.stattech.com.au/

Easy HTML
http://ox.ncsa.uiuc.edu/easyhtml/easy.html

EdWin
http://www.vantek.net/pages/msutton/edwin.htm

Einstein HTML
http://www.algonet.se/~perji/index.htm

Emissary
http://www.attachmate.com/

FrontPage
http://www.microsoft.com/msoffice/frontpage/default.htm

Gomer
http://www.clever.net/gomer/

GT_HTML
http://www.gatech.edu/word_html/

Hippie
>   http://pages.prodigy.com/Hippie/

Home Page
>   http://www.claris.com/products/clarispage/enquirer/Docs/
>   download.html

HomeSite
>   http://www.dexnet.com/homesite.html

HotDog
>   http://www.sausage.com/

HotDog Professional
>   http://www.sausage.com/

HoTMetaL
>   http://www.sq.com/products/hotmetal/hm-ftp.htm

HoTMetaL PRO
>   http://www.sq.com/products/hotmetal/hmp-org.htm

HTML Assistant Pro
>   http://www.brooknorth.com/

HTML Author
>   http://www.salford.ac.uk/iti/

HTML Builder
>   http://www.flfsoft.com/HTMLBuilder.html

HTML Easy!
>   http://www.trytel.com/~milkylin/htmleasy.html

HTML Editor
>   http://www.owens.cc.oh.us/Computer_Services/Html_Editor/

HTML Handler
>   http://www.happypuppy.com/digitale/hthand.html

HTML HyperEdit
>   http://www.curtin.edu.au/curtin/dept/cc/packages/
>   htmledit/home.html

HTML Notepad
http://www.cranial.com/software/htmlnote/

HTML Pad
http://www.odyssee.net/~gie/htmlpad

HTML Writer
http://lal.cs.byu.edu/people/nosack/

HTMLed
http://www.ist.ca/htmled/

HTMLed Pro
http://www.ist.ca/htmledpro/

HWA/HTML
http://nz.com/olson/

Hype-It 1000
http://cykic.com/

Hypertext Master
http://www.soton.ac.uk/~mjt495/anarchy/htmled31.html

Internet Assistant
http://www.microsoft.com/MSOffice/Word/ia/default.htm

Internet Creator
http://www.forman.com/

Internet Homepage Generator
http://www.wimsey.com/~fmcleod/

Live Markup
http://www.mediatec.com/mediatech/

Multilingual Publisher
http://www.accentsoft.com/product/pubeng.htm

Ned's Speedy HTML Markup Maker
http://www.eskimo.com/~nedg/spdy.html

Personal Web Weaver for HTML
http://www.livelink.com/llwebwev.html

Quick and Easy HTML
http://members.aol.com/qipsoft

Spider
http://www.incontext.ca/articles/webware/control1.html

SwagMan
http://www.iinet.net.au/~bwh/swagman.html

Symposia
http://www.grif.fr/prod/sympro.html

Visual HTMLBoard
http://www.adaptive-computer.com

W3e
http://www.nce.ufrj.br/~cracky/w3e.html

Web Media Publisher
http://www.wbmedia.com/software.html

Web Publisher
http://www.wing.net/skisoft/index.html

Web Weaver
http://www.tiac.net/users/mmm/webweav.html

WEB Wizard: The Duke of URL
http://www.halcyon.com/webwizard/welcome.htm

WebAuthor
http://www.qdeck.com/qdeck/products/WebAuthr/

WebWord
http://jumper.mcc.ac.uk/~careyb/webword/webword.html

Webber
http://www.csdcorp.com/webber.htm

WebEd
http://www.ozemail.com.au/~kread/webed.html

Kenn Nesbitt's WebEdit
http://www.nesbitt.com/

WebElite
> http://www.safety.net/webelite/

WebMania!
> http://www.q-d.com/wm.htm

WebMaster
> http://www.ozemail.com.au/~vtech/webmastr.html

WebMaster Gold
> http://www.ozemail.com.au/~vtech/webmastr.html

WebRite
> http://www.earthlink.net/~jalerta/frame1.html

WebSite Maker
> http://www.thisoftware.com/

WebText
> http://www.pacificrim.net/~proactiv/webtext/

WebThing
> http://www.arachnoid.com/lutusp/webthing.htm

WSKA HTML W3rite
> http://www.wska.com/

HTML Editors—Macintosh

Alpha
> http://www.cs.umd.edu/~keleher/alpha.html

ANT_HTML
> http://mcia.com/ant/

AOLPress
> http://www.aolpress.com/press/index.html

Arachnid
> http://www.uiowa.edu/~sec-look/sec-look.html

Backstage
> http://www.iband.com/sotware/backstage/designer/index.html

BBEdit
> http://www.barebones.com/bbedit.html

BBEdit HTML extensions
> http://www.barebones.com/html.html

Easy HTML
> http://ox.ncsa.uiuc.edu/easyhtml/easy.html

FrontPage
> http://www.microsoft.com/msoffice/frontpage/default.htm

GNNpress
> http://www.tools.gnn.com/press/index.html

golive
> http://www.golive.com/

GT_HTML
> http://www.gatech.edu/word_html/

Home Page
> http://www.claris.com/products/clarispage/enquirer/Docs/
> download.html

HoTMetaL
> http://www.sq.com/products/hotmetal/hm-ftp.htm

HoTMetaL PRO
> http://www.sq.com/products/hotmetal/hmp-org.htm

HTML Editor
> http://dragon.acadiau.ca/~giles/HTML_Editor/Documentation.html

HTML Grinder
> http://www.nets.com/site/matterform/grinder/htmlgrinder.html

HTML-Hypereditor
> http://www.lu.se/info/Editor/HTML-HyperEditor.html

HTML Pro
> http://www.ls.umu.se/~r2d2/

HTML SuperText
http://www.potsdam.edu/HTML_SuperText/About_HTML_S.html

HTML Web Weaver
http://www.miracleinc.com/SharewareAndFreeware/WWLite/index.html

HTML.edit
http://www.metrics.nttc.edu/tools/htmledit/HTMLEdit.html

Jon's HTML Editor
http://www.uwtc.washington.edu/JonWiederspan/HTMLEditor.html

Myrmidon
http://www.terrymorse.com/

PageSpinner
http://www.algonet.se/~optima/pagespinner.html

Simple HTML Editor (S H E)
http://www.lib.ncsu.edu/staff/morgan/simple.html

Tapestry
http://www.concept1.com/

Web Warrior
http://www.bact.wisc.edu/webwarriortop/

Webtor
http://informatik.th-darmstadt.de/~neuss/webtor/webtor.html

WordPerfect
http://wp.novell.com/

World Wide Web Weaver
http://www.miracleinc.com/Commercial/W4/index.html

HTML Editors—Unix

Applix HTML Author
http://www.applix.com/appware/oa/HTML.html

ASHE (A Simple HTML Editor)
http://www.cs.rpi.edu/~puninj/TALK/head.html

City University HTML Editor
http://web.cs.city.ac.uk/homes/njw/htmltext/htmltext.html

Cybersistant
http://smgi.com/wsi/cybersis.html

Easy HTML
http://ox.ncsa.uiuc.edu/easyhtml/easy.html

GNNpress
http://www.tools.gnn.com/press/index.html

HoTMetaL
http://www.sq.com/products/hotmetal/hm-ftp.htm

HoTMetaL PRO
http://www.sq.com/products/hotmetal/hmp-org.htm

Phoenix
http://www.bsd.uchicago.edu/ftp/pub/phoenix/README.html

Symposia
http://www.grif.fr/prod/sympro.html

tkHTML
http://www.ssc.com/~roland/tkHTML/tkHTML.html

Webcrafter
http://www.webville.com/

WebMagic
http://www.sgi.com/Products/WebFORCE/WebMagic/index.html

WebWeave
http://www.waste.org/~oxymoron/webweave

Graphic Tools

3D RenderLib DEMO
ftp://gatekeeper.dec.com/pub/micro/msdos/win3/demo/

ACDC
http://vvv.com/acd/

Adobe Systems—Premiere, Acrobat, Pagemaker
http://www.adobe.com/

Autocad
http://www.autocad.com

AVI format, Video for Windows
ftp://ftp.microsoft.com/developr/drg/Multimedia/

AVI-MPEG conversion
ftp://x2ftp.oulu.fi/pub/msdos/programming/convert/

Capture It
ftp://gatekeeper.dec.com/pub/micro/msdos/win3/desktop/

CGIRend
http://pc.inrird.com/cgirend.html

CU-SeeMe
ftp://gated.cornell.edu/pub/video/

Cyberview 3D Document Generator
http://www.geom.umn.edu/apps/cyberview3d/about.html

GIF Construction Set
http://www.mindworkshop.com/

Gnuplot
http://www.cs.dartmouth.edu/gnuplot_info.html

Graphic Display System
ftp://ftp.netcom.com/pub/ph/photodex

Graphics and Desktop Publishing
http://www.mcp.com/softlib/graphics-dtp/

Graphics Workshop
ftp://gatekeeper.dec.com/pub/micro/msdos/win3/desktop/

Image Alchemy
ftp://ftp.switch.ch/mirror/simtel/msdos/graphics/

Image'n Bits
ftp://gatekeeper.dec.com/pub/micro/msdos/win3/desktop/

ImageMagick
    http://www.wizards.dupont.com/cristy/ImageMagick.html

Imaging Machine
    http://www.vrl.com:80/Imaging/

Imagizer
    http://www.minet.com/minet/www/imagizer.html

Improces
    ftp://ftp.switch.ch/mirror/simtel/msdos/graphics/

Interactive Graphics Generation
    http://www.engg.ksu.edu:8872/

Lview
    ftp://gatekeeper.dec.com/pub/micro/msdos/win3/desktop/

Lview Pro
    www.xmission.com/~dtubbs/lviewp1a.zip

MapMaker DEMO
    ftp://gatekeeper.dec.com/pub/micro/msdos/win3/demo/

Media Blastoff
    ftp://oak.oakland.edu/SimTel/msdos/windows3/

Media Center
    http://www.jasc.com/

Morphing
    ftp://oak.oakland.edu/SimTel/msdos/graphics/

MOVIE animation utility (movie40.zip)
    ftp://gatekeeper.dec.com/pub/micro/msdos/win3/demo/

NeoPaint (neopnt30.zip, 670K)
    ftp://x2ftp.oulu.fi/pub/msdos/programming/utils/

netpbm (netpbm-1mar1994.tar.gz)
    ftp://ftp.x.org/R5contrib/

NView Viewer(nview140.zip)
    http://www.tu-chemnitz.de/~nomssi/readme.html

OCR info
ftp://x2ftp.oulu.fi/pub/msdos/programming/news/ocr_code.txt

OCR etc (DIMUND Document Image Understanding Information Server)
http://documents.cfar.umd.edu/

PageDraw
http://jasper.ora.com/CTAN/tex-archive/graphics/pagedraw/

Paint Shop Pro
http://www.jasc.com/

Photoworks
http://www.solutionsrc.com/PHOTOWORKS/pw7.htm

Picavu
http://vvv.com/acd/

Picture Man (pman155.zip)
ftp://gatekeeper.dec.com/pub/micro/msdos/win3/desktop/

PNG (Portable Network Graphics) Specification
http://sunsite.unc.edu/boutell/png.html

PowerPoint DEMO
ftp://gatekeeper.dec.com/pub/micro/msdos/win3/demo/

Professional Capture Systems (PCS)
http://icicle.winternet.com:80/~jasc/

QPEG (qpeg15b.zip)
ftp://ftp.tu-clausthal.de/pub/msdos/graphics/view/

QuickTime Cross-platform
http://www.astro.nwu.edu/lentz/mac/qt/home-qt.html

QuickTime to MPEG (qt2mpeg.zip)
ftp://x2ftp.oulu.fi/pub/msdos/programming/convert/

Quicktime for Windows (qtw200.zip)
ftp://aql.gatech.edu/pub/utils/pc/

QuickTime Guide by NCSA
   http://www.ncsa.uiuc.edu/SDG/Software/MacMosaic/
   QuickTimeGuide.html

Quicktime to MPEG converter
   ftp://suniams1.statistik.tu-muenchen.de/incoming/qt2mpeg

Ray Tracing
   http://www.cm.cf.ac.uk:80/Ray.Tracing/

Ray Tracing—Photon4D RayTracer
   http://www.essi.fr/~diard/photon4d.html

Ray Tracing
   ftp://oak.oakland.edu/SimTel/msdos/graphics/

Robochart
   http://www.csn.net:80/digins/

SmartCap
   ftp://ftp.intel.com/pub/IAL/Indeo_video

SmartSketch (sketch.zip)
   ftp://gatekeeper.dec.com/pub/micro/msdos/win3/demo/

Snapgrafx (snapgrfx.zip)
   ftp://gatekeeper.dec.com/pub/micro/msdos/win3/desktop/

Sparkle
   gopher://gopher.archive.merit.edu:7055/40/mac/graphics/

Sterograms
   ftp://ftp.univie.ac.at/pc/dos/graphics/

Tek Illustrator
   http://www.tiac.net/users/tommy/etsw001.htm

TeX and graphics
   http://jasper.ora.com/homepage.cgi

Text to ASCII graphics
   http://www.usis.com/cgi-bin/figlet

TIFF file programs
ftp://gatekeeper.dec.com/contrib/src/crl/xv-2.21/src/tiff/

TIFF file viewers, specs, toolkit
ftp://ftp.switch.ch/mirror/simtel/msdos/tiff/

Top Draw (topdr10a.zip, topdr10b.zip)
ftp://gatekeeper.dec.com/pub/micro/msdos/win3/desktop/

Video for Windows Runtime (VFW11A.ZIP)
ftp://ftp.microsoft.com/developr/drg/Multimedia

Vidvue (vidvue.zip)
ftp://ftp.intel.com/pub/IAL/tools_utils_demos/

WinDraw working model (windraw.zip)
ftp://gatekeeper.dec.com/pub/micro/msdos/win3/demo/

WinGIF (wingif14.zip)
ftp://gatekeeper.dec.com/pub/micro/msdos/win3/desktop/

WinJPEG (winjp276.zip)
ftp://gatekeeper.dec.com/pub/micro/msdos/win3/desktop/

wmorph10.zip
ftp://ftp.univie.ac.at/pc/dos/graphics/

xpaint (xpaint-2.1.1.tar.Z)
ftp://ftp.switch.ch/mirror/X11/R5-contrib/

xv (xv-3.00a.tar.Z)
ftp://ftp.cis.upenn.edu/pub/xv/">

WWW Viewers and Utilities
http://edhs1.gsfc.nasa.gov/Info/Software.html

Graphic Collections

A+ Art
http://aplusart.simplenet.com/aplusart/index.html

Balls, Lines & Icons
http://www.ultimate.org/images/graphics/

Backgrounds, Textures, Buttons, Bars, Rules
http://www.wanderers.com/rose/backgrou.html

The Ball Boutique Free Graphics
http://www.octagamm.com/boutique/mainball.htm

Barry's Clip Art Server
http://www.barrysclipart.com/

BenBer Does Icons
http://www.benber.com

The Bit Map Vault: session
http://www.cs.uwm.edu:2010/cgi-bin/start_session

BizCafe's Free Graphics!
http://www.bizcafe.com/freegrfx.html

Bogus' Icon Service
ftp://bluehouse.go.kr/pub/WWW/icons/Icons_kor.html

Brent's HTML Resource Page
http://users.aol.com/brentleim/htmlres.htm

Button Factory—Intro
http://www.clever.net/gld/buttonup/buttonup.htm

BUTTON WORLD
http://www.demon.co.uk/Tangent/buttonworld/buttons.html

Buttons Picture Page
http://www.phoenix.net/~ace/test/btnpic.html

Celine's Original .GIFs
http://www.geocities.com/SoHo/9377/

cool cat icons
http://www.asahi-net.or.jp/~ld8j-ktmk/

Customized License Plate
http://members.aol.com/suryana/index.html

Daryl's Image, Ball, Line & Background Archive
http://www-engr.uvic.ca/~dstorey/Icons/

Directory of /pub/clipart
http://www.geocities.com/SiliconValley/Heights/6355/

Directory of /WWW/images
ftp://ftp.brunel.ac.uk/WWW/images/

Eric's Hot Icons
http://holly.colostate.edu/~embarnes/icons/

Fairy Suryana's 3-D Library
http://members.aol.com/Fairy73/3D/index.html

Four11 Graphics Library
http://wp.com/g/graphicsindex.html

FOUR BEES—Free Web Graphics
http://web2.airmail.net/lrivera/

Free-Art
http://www.mcs.net/~wallach/freeart/buttons.html

Free Buttons—Set 1
http://www.tgn.net/~pambytes/button1.html

Free Clip Art from New World Creations
http://www.conknet.com/~r_cloe/

Terry Goulds Home Page Graphics
http://www.vol.it/mirror/Graphics/list1.html

Graphic Element Samples
http://www.duke.edu/images/gifs/Index.html

Icon Browser
http://www.cli.di.unipi.it/iconbrowser/icons.html

The Icon Depot
http://www.geocities.com/SiliconValley/6603/

The Icon Island
http://home.earthlink.net/~lazybutt/

ICON LIB la bibliothèque d'icones
http://www.emse.fr/ICONLIB/

IconBAZAAR
http://www.iconbazaar.com/

Icons
http://moon.inf.uji.es/icons/

Icons, Buttons, Backgrounds, and Logos
http://nansen.jhuapl.edu:80/iconlib/

The Purple Page
http://www.preferred.com/~morgan/purple/

Jelane's Free Web Graphics
http://www.erinet.com/jelane/families/

Jim's Image Library
http://erau.db.erau.edu:80/~blandine/image_lib.html

net/~rodt/intro.html

JZ Presents: Pardon My Icons
http://www.zeldman.com/icon.html

Kamtec—Image Archive
http://www.netlink.co.uk/users/kamtec/images/

kira's icon library
http://www59.metronet.com/kicons/

Lines For Use In Mosaic
http://www.eecs.wsu.edu/~rkinion/lines/lines.html

m/ggmyg/toc.html

Net-User
http://www.net-user.com/graphics/

The Online Bonsai Icon Collection
http://www.hav.com/~hav/tobicus.html

Paul's Graphic's Corner
http://www.ccc.nottingham.ac.uk/~pczpra/General/Graphics.html

Pictures Library
http://www.infotehna.si/guest/bob/pictures/index.html

Pixelsight Home
http://www.pixelsight.com/

PLANET EARTH HOME PAGE—IMAGES, ICONS AND FLAGS
http://www.nosc.mil/planet_earth/images.html

Police Graphics Library
http://www.murlin.com/~webfx/cops/library.html

Psyched Up Graphics
http://www.econ.cbs.dk/people/nagemal/psyched/index.html

Realm Graphics
http://www.ender-design.com/rg/

The Rocket Shop
http://www.rocketshop.holowww.com/

The Sharp End / Graphics
http://www.redpnt.com/redpnt/sharpend/graphics.html

Syed's Bullets, Buttons and Other Gizmos
http://www.sconnect.net/Simple Connectivity Inc.

Tim's HTML Assistant
http://web-designer.com/~towheed/sswg/gizmos.html

HTML Validators

Weblint
http://www.cre.canon.co.uk/~neilb/weblint/

WebTechs HTML Validation Service
http://www.webtechs.com/html-val-svc/

A Kinder, Gentler Validator
http://ugweb.cs.ualberta.ca/~gerald/validate/

HTML Validation Service
http://www.harbinger.net/html-val-svc/

htmlchek

> http://uts.cc.utexas.edu/~churchh/htmlchek.html

MOMspider

> http://www.ics.uci.edu/WebSoft/MOMspider/

Missinglink

> http://www.rsol.com/ml/

Lightweight Unified Validation Interface

> http://www.ccur.com/external/misc/luvi.html

Webxref

> http://www.sara.nl/cgi-bin/rick_acc_webxref

Checkweb

> http://www.stuff.com/~bcutter/home/programs/checkweb.html

lvrfy

> http://www.cs.dartmouth.edu/~crow/lvrfy.html

Verify Web Links

> http://wsk.eit.com/wsk/dist/doc/admin/webtest/verify_links.html

htmlchk

> ftp://ftp.cre.canon.co.uk/pub/perl/www/htmlchk.pl

WWW Link Checker

> http://www.ugrad.cs.ubc.ca/spider/q7f192/branch/checker.html

Doctor HTML

> http://imagiware.com/RxHTML.cgi

Newsgroups

For ongoing, truly in-depth information, it is best to join one or more of the available newsgroups. By subscribing to one of the newsgroups listed next, not only can you read the continuing discussion threads, but you can also post specific questions, and when you're ready, share some of your own hard-earned knowledge.

Authoring-Related Groups

news:comp.infosystems.www.authoring.cgi

news:comp.infosystems.www.authoring.html

news:comp.infosystems.www.authoring.images

news:comp.infosystems.www.authoring.misc

Browser Software Groups

news:comp.infosystems.www.browsers.mac

news:comp.infosystems.www.browsers.ms-windows

news:comp.infosystems.www.browsers.x

news:comp.infosystems.www.browsers.misc

Web Server Groups

news:comp.infosystems.www.servers.mac

news:comp.infosystems.www.servers.ms-windows

news:comp.infosystems.www.servers.unix

news:comp.infosystems.www.servers.misc

Other Discussion

news:comp.infosystems.www.advocacy

news:comp.infosystems.www.misc

Index

Note: Page numbers in italic denote references to figures.

Symbols

#!/bin/sh (UNIX shell script identifier), 143
(PERL hash mark), 144
(pound sign), 23, 104–106
$mailprog variable, 144, 146
$ (PERL dollar sign), 144
$recipient variable, 144, 146
% (percent character), 79, 135, 143
&, 24, 242
& (ampersand), 8, 23, 24, 143, 242
©, 24
>, 24, 26, 75, 242
<, 24, 26, 242
 , 24, 255, 256
", 24
®, 24
* (asterisk), in password fields, 139
+ (plus sign), 143
; (semicolon), 8, 23, 160, 188
< and > (angle brackets), 8
<!— (comment start), 27–28, 78

< (left-angle bracket or less-than sign), 24, 75, 242
—> (comment end), 27–28, 78
> (right-angle bracket or greater-than sign), 24, 75, 242
"" (curly quotes), 243
"" (double quote mark), 24
"" (straight ASCII quotes), 243
™ (trademark symbol), 25
~ (tilde), 23–24
\ (backward slash), 78
© (copyright symbol), 24
® (registered mark), 24
? (question mark), 142–143
/@ (PERL slash@ sign), 144
@referers array, 146
// (double slash), 46
// (JavaScript double slash), 46
" " (nonbreaking space), 24
. (one dot for current directory), 78
/ (slash), 25, 75, 78, 79
/// (triple slash), 78–79
.. (two dots for parent directory), 78

A

<A> (anchor) tag
  HREF (Hypertext Reference) attribute, 44, 85
  and links, 43–44
  NAME attribute, 44
  SHAPE attribute, 120–121
  and tails, *77*
  TARGET attribute, 183–184, *184*
  and URL syntax, 45
ABOVE <LAYER> tag attribute, 196
absolute and relative
  addressing, 45–46, 148
  measurements, 249
ACTION <FORM> tag attribute, 134, 144, *136*, *145*
ActiveX Control Pad tool, 157
ActiveX controls
  and HTML, 14, 15, 156–158, *157*
  versus Java, 156
  and <OBJECT> tag, 156–157
  and OLE (Object Linking and Embedding), 156
  using VBScript with, 158–159
  Web address, 159

X

<XMP> tag, 40, 77

Y

Yahoo, 30, 69

Z